BUILDINGS FOR BLUESTOCKINGS

BUILDINGS *for* BLUESTOCKINGS

The Architecture and Social History of Women's Colleges in Late Victorian England

by
Margaret Birney Vickery

Newark **University of Delaware Press**
London **Associated University Presses**

DELAWARE

Associated University Presses
440 Forsgate Drive
Cranbury
NJ 08512
United States of America

Associated University Presses
16 Barter Street
London
WC1A 2AH
United Kingdom

Associated University Presses
P.O. Box 338, Port Credit
Mississauga
Ontario
Canada
L5G 4L8

ISBN 0-87413-697-0

The paper used in this publication meets the requirements of the American National Standard for Permanence of Paper for Printed Library Materials z39.48-1984.

LIBRARY OF CONGRESS CATALOGING-IN-PUBLICATION DATA

Vickery, Margaret Birney, 1963–
Buildings for bluestockings : the architecture and social history of women's colleges in late Victorian England / Margaret Birney Vickery.
p. cm.
Includes bibliographical references and index.
ISBN 0-87413-697-0 (alk. paper)
1. Women's colleges – England – Buildings. 2. Architecture, Victorian – England. 3. Architecture, Modern – 19th century – England. 4. Women's colleges – Social aspects – England – History – 19th century. I. Title.

NA6605.G7 V53 2000
727'.3'0820942–dc21

99-047386
CIP

PRINTED IN SLOVENIA BY GORENJSKI TISK

CONTENTS

LIST OF ILLUSTRATIONS

Color illustrations (after page 128)

ACKNOWLEDGMENTS

AS THIS PROJECT HAS PROGRESSED I HAVE HAD HELP AND SUPPORT FROM MANY QUARTERS, which has made this work a real pleasure. Thanks go to the archivists at all the colleges for all their organized archives and helpful access to vital research materials. I am extremely grateful to my colleagues in Britain, most notably Dr. Geoffrey Tyack, Alan Crawford and Andrew Saint, for reading my work, offering useful advice, and encouraging me and my ideas. The staff at the Victorian Society in London, especially Kit Wedd for her editorial skills and Tamar Jeffers for her long-standing friendship, merit special thanks. Dr. Paul V. Turner was a wonderful advisor during my Ph.D. research and has continued to advise and counsel generously during this phase of my work. For help with the illustrations I want to thank the helpful staff at the Camera Place and Dana Doyle and Glen Gollrad. Unless otherwise stated, all photographs are by the author.

Finally, I owe a great deal to the Lucases for their friendship during my English sojourn and to my family, especially my parents, Jane and Scott Birney, whose support has been unfailing, in this and all things. I dedicate this to my husband, Peter Vickery, with many thanks for late night editing and much love.

INTRODUCTION

"A woman who is not Feminine is a Monster in Creation"
Elizabeth Missing Sewell, 1865 [1]

IN 1847 ALFRED LORD TENNYSON IMAGINED A COLLEGE FOR WOMEN IN HIS EPIC POEM, *The Princess.* This work glamorized the idea of a secluded compound of "Six hundred maidens clad in purest white,"[2] who had devoted themselves to higher education, while pointedly highlighting the unnaturalness of women who put knowledge before family and marriage. The poet tells the story of a Princess who, under the influence of a bitter widow and an idealistic friend, determines to establish a college for women. Consequently she breaks her lifelong engagement with a young Prince from a neighboring kingdom. The plot thickens when the Prince and his two friends infiltrate the college dressed as women, and attempt to retrieve the Prince's betrothed. At times throughout the poem, Tennyson seems to credit women with the potential for equal intellect, but he is then quick to remind the reader that in this women's college, women's minds may develop, but their true loving and maternal natures are lost.

For much of the story, the Princess remains firm in her convictions and when she discovers the Prince, she coldly rejects his favors. Tennyson depicts her devotion to this feminist cause as a cold and icy veneer, which the noble and chivalric Prince must shatter. The poem ends when the Princess, moved by pity and remorse as the Prince lies close to death, renounces her "foolish" ways and learns to love him. When he awakens from his illness and the couple kiss, the Princess is practically reborn:

> *Her falser self slipt from her like a robe,*
> *And left her woman, lovelier in her mood*
> *Than in her mould that other, when she came*
> *From barren deeps to conquer all with love* [3]

She admits defeat and gives up her education, while the Prince benevolently forgives her rebellious spirit, excusing it as that of an untrained girl, reassuring her that she shall be better guided when they are wed. The Prince promises that she shall learn all that will be necessary to blossom and grow as a woman, wife and mother, within her own separate but equal sphere.

With the defeat of the Princess's educational scheme, and Tennyson's patronizing suggestion that such independent women were merely misguided, this poem was not a model for the women's colleges which evolved in the second half of the nineteenth century in Britain. But Tennyson's descriptive warning that a college for women would destroy the feminine character and upset what he, and most of society, considered the natural order of things, did condition the ways in which the women's colleges developed.

This book examines the architecture of six of the earliest, purpose-built, residential colleges for women founded in the latter half of the nineteenth century in England. These are Girton and Newnham at Cambridge, Lady Margaret Hall and

1. Elizabeth Missing Sewell, *Principles of Education drawn from Nature and Revelation and Applied to Female Education in the Upper Classes*, 2 vols. (London: Longman, Green, Longman, Roberts & Green, 1865), 2:291.
2. Alfred Lord Tennyson, *The Princess: A Medley* (1847; reprint, London: Macmillan, 1899), 39.
3. Ibid., 126.

Somerville at Oxford, and Westfield and Royal Holloway, both eventually associated with the University of London. The focus of this study is how the floorplans of these nineteenth century building-types encoded widely held beliefs about women's role in society, and how the architectural styles which clothed these colleges facilitated their evolution. As built, these colleges are a unique blend of domestic and collegiate traditions, and an examination of their origins, design and layout provides the focus for an inquiry into Victorian ideals regarding women and education.

The women's colleges were not built to mirror their male Oxbridge predecessors. Instead they relied on a domestic model both architectural and social. The architectural facade of domestic normalcy enabled women to make progress toward equal education without attracting the controversy which haunted the suffragettes. The women's colleges were not the only Victorian institutions to rely on the domestic example. Lunatic asylums, hospitals, boys' public schools and even prisons to some extent, borrowed the ideas of segregation, privacy and domestic order for their architectural and social structures. The architects and founders of all these building-types shared a common ideology: that architecture was an important means to control and improve society.

The women who attended and supported the women's colleges were generally from the middle and upper-middle classes, the daughters of clergymen or professionals such as doctors and lawyers. Some attended college simply for the pleasure of learning. Those with limited financial means often needed an education in order to support themselves as governesses or teachers. While all were to some extent rebelling against the restricted options offered to women in the nineteenth century, most were not openly seeking radical social alternatives. As the study of their architectural environment and lifestyles makes clear, the early students did not abandon convention but clung to it as a means of protecting their cause.

Other institutions for women such as convents, teachers' training colleges and the American women's colleges, are discussed in this study only where they played an influential role in the development of a particular college. Because of their religious purpose, convents did not serve as an obvious model for the women's colleges, though their buildings were also domestic in character. Teachers' training colleges were primarily a working class phenomenon, and for the most part students lodged in boarding houses. Women's colleges in America shared similar concerns for women's health and safety, but had little impact on the development of most of the colleges discussed.

Feminist issues such as social equality, political rights and the role of women in the rapidly changing Victorian society are naturally investigated here. As my research shows, some reformers of women's education were quite radical in their views, but many were conservatives who were threatened by profound changes to society's organization. These conservatives were involved in women's education because they believed it could train women to be better wives, mothers, and if necessary, governesses. The debate was not waged along gender lines, with women for reform and men against it. The architecture of these colleges reflects some of these conflicts and ambiguities by conforming with certain expected notions of a residence for women and, in part due to the very nature of such an institution, by breaking free of other accepted norms. Thus the architecture of these six colleges for women sheds light on some of the complex social networks which conditioned the lives of women in the nineteenth century.

Until recently, little work has been done in architectural history to chart the crucial interaction between architecture and social history, particularly in the context of women's lives. Originally, feminist architectural historians focused on a re-examination of the canon to include the work of women architects and interior designers. During the 1980s and 1990s there has been growing interest in the relationship between women and the built environment, and architectural historians and archeologists have been researching the ways in which cultural attitudes towards gender are built into the structures in which we live and work. As a study of a gender-specific building type, this book focuses on the vital and wide-reaching connections between architecture and ideological theories about women and their physical and educational abilities.

BUILDINGS FOR BLUESTOCKINGS

1 THE "LITTLE BAND OF PIONEERS"

Girton College

I am anxious that the building should be as beautiful as we can make it. As we cannot have traditions and associations we shall want to get dignity in every other way that is open to us.
Emily Davies, 1867 [1]

GIRTON COLLEGE, CAMBRIDGE, WAS THE FIRST PURPOSE-BUILT COLLEGE FOR women in England. It was begun under the leadership of Emily Davies, who hoped to see women's education rise to the same standard as men's. Her ambition, which was unusual for the time, should be understood within the context of general trends in women's education in the nineteenth century. As Victorian culture grew increasingly specialized and hierarchical, women's roles in the home began to change. Households required more servants to carry out specialized domestic tasks. Middle-class women were assigned the smooth running of the household and required to learn the "accomplishments," which included needlework, watercolors, some rudimentary skills in the French language and piano playing. For the majority of women this resulted in often uninspiring lives, which, together with their lack of political and marital rights, left them trapped in domestic situations over which they had little control.[2]

Victorian society assumed that middle-class women would marry and raise families, and they were not to work unless it was for a philanthropic cause. When financial difficulties forced a woman to seek work as a governess, her status in society immediately plummeted and she hovered in an undefined sphere—a lady without the proper ladylike lifestyle. The trials of the governess were poignantly described by Charlotte Brontë in her two novels, *Jane Eyre*, of 1847, and *Villette*, written in 1853. In her writings, Brontë called for sympathy and respect for women forced to work outside the home and for greater educational opportunities for women.

By the middle of the century, reformers in women's education had two paradigms with which to work. There was the woman caught at home whose general boredom could lead to nervous complaints and ill-health, and the governess whose isolation and lack of a respectable position in society often had tragic consequences. The governess received help from the Christian Socialists, a group of men led by Charles Kingsley, Thomas Hughes and the Reverend F. D. Maurice, which was devoted to reforming and improving society without actually changing its structures. It was from this group that the idea of "Muscular Christianity," linked with a code of chivalry that had been reinterpreted for contemporary needs, emerged. "Muscular Christianity" embodied the concept of a strong, rugged, yet morally pure man who took care of the weak or helpless and did battle with the impure and evil. Maurice and Kingsley's ideals led them to found the Working Men's College, which was begun as a night school in 1848 in Great Ormond's Yard, London, and evolved into

1. Emily Davies to Barbara Bodichon, B5, 29 January 1867, Girton College Archives.
2. For more information on this see Theresa M. McBride, *The Domestic Revolution: The Modernization of Household Service in England and France 1820–1920* (London: Croom Helm, 1976), and L. Davidoff and C. Hall, *Family Fortunes: Men and Women of the English Middle Class 1780–1850* (London: Hutchinson, 1987).

the Working Men's College in Red Lion Square, where such notables as William Morris, Dante Gabriel Rossetti and Edward Burne-Jones taught on occasion. This project was an attempt to take education from the hands of the elite and disseminate it among the less fortunate.

Another project in which Kingsley and Maurice became involved in 1848 was Queen's College, Harley Street, London. Queen's College for women was just beside the Governesses' Benevolent Institution, or GBI. This had been founded in 1843 in an attempt to help poor, destitute and unemployed governesses. It offered accommodation for those between work, helped to place governesses in new positions, and raised money for stipends for retired governesses. Largely as a result of the work of the GBI, the need for a more coherent system of standards and education for governesses was recognized. Queen's College filled that need and offered courses in English, Theology, Latin and Mathematics, amongst others. The college held its own exams and offered certificates to graduates. Charles Kingsley lectured there and Maurice was more involved, becoming principal in 1851.

A similar venture was begun in 1849 in nearby Bedford Square. A wealthy widow named Elizabeth Reid had devoted her time and money to a variety of philanthropic projects for many years. She founded a college for women, not in competition with Queen's, but in order to offer further opportunities to women. Bedford College was to be religious but non-sectarian (Mrs. Reid was herself a Unitarian), and was to provide proper moral and spiritual training in addition to offering a wider and more thorough overall education than was usually available to women. Neither Queen's nor Bedford was residential at first, although Bedford took in boarders later in the century, and eventually moved into its own purpose-built buildings in 1913.

The founders of both colleges saw a need for improved education for women, not so that they could become more like men, or even equal to them, but in order to bring out more fully their womanly qualities and better prepare them for their duties as wives, mothers, moral guardians and if necessary, governesses. This aim will recur often throughout this study of women's colleges. What might be called the chivalric mission of certain educators was never an attempt to place women in competition with men or to expand their career options. These educators were an important facet of the movement for higher education for women because they carefully avoided any suggestions of change and were appalled by the more strident voices of feminists. Both the men and women involved in this sort of education saw it in a positivist light, believing that steps taken to improve women's lives were part of a greater move towards a progressive and morally more pure society. Their approach, while it may have frustrated feminists at the time and can be gratingly patronizing to the twentieth-century reader, was instrumental in winning the support of many skeptics and had the advantage of seldom alienating supporters as its methods and prose were always familiar and non-threatening. Although Emily Davies was more ambitious for her college for women, she did not ignore the example set by these educators, but often publicly couched her ideas in their familiar terminology.

Less accommodating was a group of women who called themselves the "Ladies of Langham Place" because of the rooms they took in a building on that street in

London (see appendix). This small, tightly knit circle first met in 1857, under the leadership of Barbara Leigh Smith Bodichon and Bessie Parkes. In that same year the group began publishing the *English Women's Journal*. Throughout its years of publication this was an informative voice for the women's movement and for other social campaigns. The women involved actively called for greater political and marital rights for women, for equal education for women and girls, for revised laws regarding prostitution and for greater employment opportunities for women. In all their causes, they called for real changes to be made in women's lives.

Emily Davies became a staunch supporter of women's rights and education, largely as a result of the fierce battle for admission that she helped her close friend Elizabeth Garrett (later Anderson) wage against the University of London (see appendix). In the early 1860s, Davies' platform was the Social Science Association, in which her brother, the Reverend Llewelyn Davies, was active. Earlier in 1859, while visiting her brother in London, Davies had met Barbara Bodichon who was to prove a faithful friend and ally, and who played an important role in the founding of Girton College. Because of her radical views, Bodichon's contribution to Girton, though constant, was limited to private correspondence and behind-the-scenes support. The friendship between Bodichon and Davies was long and supportive, in spite of, or perhaps because of, the very different natures of the two women.

There were other instruments of educational change in the 1860s which helped pave the way for the founding of Girton College. Davies was a member of the Kensington Society, which was made up of women who concerned themselves with female education. Its members included Miss Frances Mary Buss, principal of North London Collegiate School, a day school for girls, and Miss Dorothea Beale, principal of the highly respected, Cheltenham Ladies College in the west of England. Also involved was Frances Power Cobbe (see appendix). In the early 1860s Davies participated in the campaign for equal education for the sexes, fighting to open the Local Examinations to girls as well as boys. Increasingly, she saw the need for examinations to be offered to girls and women as a means of raising and standardizing the quality of their education. As was to be her wont, Davies wanted the same examinations for girls as those offered to boys in order to equalize the standard of education for both sexes, and to give the girls qualifications that were as respectable as the boys'. This idea grew to include training girls for the Higher Local Examinations. These Local and Higher Local Examinations were standardized by universities such as Oxford and Cambridge and administered in various parts of the country to boys in order to measure their level of knowledge and competency to enter university. Because of their growing expertise in the field of female education, Davies, Buss and Beale all testified in 1865 before the Schools Inquiry Commission, headed by Lord Bryce. This Commission took the bold step of including girls' education in their report, thereby calling attention to the overall neglect of female education. Exempted from the report's criticisms was the work of Miss Buss and Miss Beale in girls' secondary schools.

In 1862, Frances Power Cobbe gave a paper to the Social Science Association in London, calling for university degrees for women, but her pleas were largely unheard or ridiculed. In 1865, Elizabeth Missing Sewell, an influential, very conservative author of books on women's domestic role, had discussed a college for governesses which would be residential and run by ladies, but she made no attempt herself to realize such an institution. As Davies' ideas grew, she published *The Higher Education of Women* in 1866, which expressed her ambition to offer standard tests to girls. Her book was read and appreciated by many of the leaders of educational reform. F. P. Cobbe responded enthusiastically, and praised her "quick bits of sarcasm."[3] She went on to encourage Davies, saying:

I think the book can't fail to do good, for you have met the enemy at every point, and your quotations are quite an armoury . . . The tone of calm good sense is precisely one to be assumed in the question. Half our mischief comes from screaming *American advocates.*[4]

The question of "tone" became an issue that was to concern Davies and all other pioneers in women's higher education. The threat of a growing race of masculine bluestockings and society's subsequent dissolution overshadowed these women's actions and conditioned their ambitions. Davies was acutely aware that the tide of public opinion could turn against her at the first sign of an overly aggressive, or masculine, stance. It was vital for her to adopt a "tone of calm good sense" so as not to alienate anyone with even the slightest interest in her work.

By 1867 Davies had determined to found a college for women which would offer the same education and examinations as men received in the universities. She was in contact with the leading figures of her day, anxious to garner support from influential quarters. George Grote, Vice Chancellor of London University and eminent professor of Greek history, agreed with her that women's education was in a sorry state, although he was reluctant to endorse the details of her proposed remedy, and Matthew Arnold responded positively as well. These were important allies. More controversial, however, was the modest support from George Eliot, or Mrs. Lewes, as Davies preferred to call her. Although her encouragement was appreciated, George Eliot's domestic arrangement caused Davies some concern. Eliot's notoriety was regarded as a potential threat to the more circumspect, middle-class supporters whom Davies desperately needed to make the college socially acceptable. Somewhat ironically, George Eliot herself was quite cautious in her support of the scheme. She was concerned that the differences between men and women should not be diminished in any way or that women should lose their gentle, affectionate and maternal natures through too much intellectual education.[5]

Another novelist, whose fame was enormous but whose reputation was spotless, was Charlotte Yonge. In December 1867, Anna Richardson, an old friend, wrote to Davies encouraging her to seek Miss Yonge's support for the scheme because: "'Her name is so well known and so well liked by vast numbers of young ladies, and her own claims to solid culture so real.'"[6] When asked, however, Miss Yonge was not encouraging. In July 1868, she responded to Davies:

I have decided objections to bringing large numbers of girls together, and I think that home education under the inspection or encouragement of sensible fathers . . . is far more valuable, both intellectually and morally than any external education. . . . All the most superior women I have known have thus been formed, by home influences, and I think that girls in large numbers always hurt one another in manners and tone if nothing else.[7]

3. Emily Davies, "Family Chronicle," unpublished manuscript, 1866–68, Girton College Archives, Girton College, Cambridge, 479.
4. Ibid.
5. Ibid., 637.
6. Ibid., 564.
7. Ibid., 622.

Elizabeth Sewell, who had previously called for a college for governesses run under the supervision of ladies, was also unenthusiastic about Davies' scheme.

The task before Davies was not a simple one. While many supported improvements in women's education, they were unconvinced of the need for women to compete in male examinations, and most objected to women residing away from home at a period in their lives when, it was generally believed, they should be at home finding husbands or looking after their families. In 1868, Davies wrote an article, "Some Account of A Proposed College for Women," which was published in the *Contemporary Review.* In this, she presented her case for women's higher education, quoting Mr. Fearon, the Assistant Commissioner for London District under the Schools Inquiry Commission, who reported on the poor standard of girls' education. She discussed the lethargic and apathetic lives of women who had no purpose in life and whose chances of marriage were slight. Education, she argued, would provide an added stimulus to women's lives and improve the moral tone of home life by exposing young women to serious thought and education, rather than the frivolous trivia which so often filled their minds.

In her article, Davies cautioned that such a college was in no way intended to replace the home in a woman's life. Rather, she presented the education it would offer as a supplement to the domestic duties of each woman, and a means of improving homelife and subsequently, society. She stressed that the female students would be under the care of a lady, and that all elements of social propriety would be observed. Davies knew that the general bias of public opinion would be against her, and thus took care to cushion the radical nature of her proposal in terms that would not threaten the public and could, indeed, win supporters. By stressing the domestic aspects of a college for women, its beneficial effects on the students' health and morality, and its seclusion from the outside, male realm, she could allay fears that college and higher education would spoil women for their natural domestic sphere. She promised that her college would not mean the ruin of society and that girls would not become selfish and goal oriented, or abandon marriage and family life for a masculine career. Davies had the difficult task of setting before the public a radical and ambitious scheme couched in terms that would not challenge the status quo, and yet which dramatically pointed to the need for change and offered an alternative.

Davies drew attention to the fact that women's lives were no longer spent in useful domestic tasks, and that most households had servants responsible for the practical running of the household. The college of which she wrote:

> *will not be specifically directed towards changing the occupations of women, but rather towards securing that whatever they do shall be done well. Whether as mistresses of households, mothers, teachers, or as labourers in art, science, literature, and notably in the field of philanthropy, so largely occupied by women, their work suffers from the want of previous training.*[8]

Significantly, Davies stressed the domesticity of her planned college for women, by reassuring her readers that the discipline and organization of the college would mirror that of the homes which the students had left. The mistress and resident lecturers would take a maternal role in governing the young women, and make sure

8. Davies, "Some Account of a Proposed New College for Women," *Contemporary Review,* 9 (December 1868): 550.

that proper ladylike behavior was encouraged. Already at this early stage, domesticity was conjured up as a reassurance and guard against abnormal or undisciplined behavior. Furthermore, Davies couched many of her arguments in Christian terms, citing passages from the Gospels to strengthen her points, and presented her ideas in terms familiar to the average, middle or upper-middle class reader.

Between 1866 and 1868, Davies was beginning to visualize the material reality of her college. As early as 1868, she wrote to Anna Richardson about the ideal location of such a college for women. The site was vitally important both for academic and social reasons. At the start, Davies was not certain whether her college would become affiliated with Cambridge or the University of London. Already, the Local Examinations were being offered to girls in Cambridge, and the movement was afoot in Cambridge to organize the Higher Local Examinations for women over the age of eighteen. However, London University, being younger and not as bound to tradition, also appeared sympathetic.

Davies wanted her college located conveniently between London and Cambridge for two reasons. Firstly, lecturers from both universities could offer courses for the women at the beginning, and therefore Davies could get a better idea which university showed the most promise. The problem posed by siting the college in Cambridge was one much discussed. In a letter to Anna Richardson of 4 February 1868, Davies reflected upon the potential discipline problems which would come from siting the college in or near such a male bastion. She warned that the supervision would have to be very strict so as to prevent the college from falling victim to the destructive forces of "gossip and scandal."[9] She cited the example of Oxford, where "unmarried ladies are obliged to be excessively cautious in their demeanor,"[10] and were not free to go about as they pleased.

In her article in the *Contemporary Review*, she also argued against siting the college too close to London because of the distractions of society which it offered. She assured parents that their daughters would have ample time for social delights after their period of serious study or during their holidays. Furthermore she argued in favor of a site in the country which offered fresh air and healthy living, away from the stresses of society and the dangers of an all male university town. The location ultimately chosen to begin this experiment was the small town of Hitchin, Hertfordshire, which Davies described as "the only place which combines the essential conditions of *rurality*, healthiness and accessibility."[11]

The same article also discussed the requirements of a women's college and the economical and practical reasons which made it necessary to build a house in which to begin. Davies pointed out:

> *It is certain that no ordinary dwelling-house would answer the purposes of the College without extensive and costly alterations, and the result of some inquiry has been that no house at all, in any degree likely to be suitable, has offered itself. This is not surprising. As precisely the same conditions which are required for the College, namely, a healthy site, abundance of water, easy accessibility, &c., are also desired by people who want country residences, houses presenting these advantages are pretty sure to have occupants.*[12]

This presents a crucial outline of Davies' prospectus for the buildings of the college

9. Davies, "Family Chronicle," 577.
10. Ibid.
11. Ibid., 598.
12. Davies, "Some Account," 556.

1. Balliol College, Oxford (by Alfred Waterhouse, 1867–68).

as presented to the public. Two points are significant to this study. The first is that she quite clearly proposes a *house* in which to begin her college, and that this house should share with the average domicile all the necessary healthy attributes. Secondly, she was fully aware that by advertising the domestic nature of her college, she might win over skeptics who feared for the moral and physical health of the young women away from home. The domestic house was regarded by the Victorians as a safe bastion of moral purity and safety. John Ruskin sang its praises, calling it "the place of Peace"[13] a haven from the trials and evils of the outside world. Thus Davies, by setting her scheme in a domestic context, sought to quiet fears of an ambitious or threatening novelty, the women's college.

But that she was ambitious for the college is clear. By June 1868, a year before any tuition was actually begun or students were found, Davies had requested the main committee to approve Alfred Waterhouse as the architect of the college. Waterhouse had several personal connections with the early college. His brother-in-law, Thomas Hodgkin, was involved with the finances of the college. As a Quaker, Waterhouse was connected to the other Quakers on the committee such as Russell Gurney, MP, and his wife, as well as Lady Goldsmid.[14]

In her letters, Davies explained her preference for Waterhouse as the architect because of his Manchester Assize Courts of 1859, now demolished. She thought this building was beautiful "with gardens and grounds and everything that is good for body and soul and spirit."[15] This was his first major commission and was a grand essay in the High Gothic of the 1850s and 1860s. Moreover, Davies noted, Waterhouse had recently finished rebuilding the Master's Lodge, and added a small range of rooms for Balliol College, Oxford (1867–68), and was thus familiar with collegiate architecture.[16]

Davies was clearly driven by contradictory impulses. While she wanted to assure the public of the college's domestic security, she visualized an institution for women

13. John Ruskin, *Sesame and Lilies* (1865; reprint, London: George Allen and Sons, 1908), 109.
14. Colin Cunningham and Prudence Waterhouse, *Alfred Waterhouse 1830–1905: Biography of a Practice* (Oxford: Clarendon Press, 1992), 70.
15. Davies to Anna Richardson, 25 October, 1866, quoted in Barbara Stephen, *Emily Davies and Girton College* (London: Constable, 1927), 149.
16. Davies to Barbara Bodichon, B5, 29 January 1867, Girton College Archives.

2. Benslow House, Hitchin. *Reproduced courtesy of the Mistrss and Fellows, Girton College, Cambridge.*

on a grand and dignified scale, built by an important architect of institutional and public buildings. Her interest in Waterhouse's work at Balliol suggests that the traditional collegiate example was important to her. Yet she wrote of building a house and admitted that the domestic elements of planning were necessary to her college. The history of Girton and its architecture is that of a struggle to reconcile these two basically contradictory desires, and the result is a compromise between ambition and social decorum.

Davies was not averse to beginning on a small scale, provided the venture was to begin soon. She was always pragmatic, if impatient, and her committee, while eager, often pointed out the need for patience or financial temperance. But Davies' ambition could not be reined in for long. For instance, in 1869, after the first term had begun at Hitchin, Davies wrote to Bodichon of her wish to build a beautiful house, even if it were only to serve their purposes for a decade or so, likening it to a flower which may only blossom a short while but which produces the seed from which future flowers grow. However, she insists, "I want *now*, not to build on a very large scale, but to begin as soon as possible."[17]

Davies' ambition had to be curbed for practical and fiduciary reasons. In 1869, the committee decided to take on the lease of Benslow House in Hitchin in which to begin the first experiment in residential, collegiate living for women. Benslow House was situated atop chalk cliffs above Hitchin, and had a large, lovely old garden. Davies wrote to Bodichon:

I don't think we shall be able to make very much of the house at Hitchin, but having a foundation of plainness and solidity, we may by touches of prettiness and originality here and there, save it from being ugly or depressingly commonplace.[18]

17. Davies to Bodichon, B38, 13 December 1869, Girton College Archives.
18. Davies to Bodichon, B32, 21 August 1869, Girton College Archives.

Though the appearance of the house was not exactly to her liking, Davies was excited to have her scheme realized, if in a more modest form than she had anticipated. She wrote warmly of the first five students whose letters promised good behavior and enthusiasm. Each student was given a room of her own, which was used as both a bedroom and sitting room. There was a common room, or drawing room, which was also used as a lecture room, and the dining room was in the basement. It was by no means luxurious, but it served its purpose. Davies wrote to Bodichon in February 1869 to request her help with decorating, believing that she was best suited to make the house "pretty and picturesque."[19] The first five students arrived in October of that year and were greeted eagerly by Davies. In spite of her public reassurances that the college would be conducted much like a household, in certain respects Davies sought to base some of the routine on the male example. For instance, she arranged the dining room with the table of five students facing the "High Table", as in the traditional college hall. However, the young women rebelled against this, seeing such academic formality as absurd when imposed on so few in such a small place.[20]

The students proved more spirited than Davies had expected, and there was much to be done to adjust to college life on the part of both Davies and the five young women. Yet the venture began to flourish, and by the summer of 1870, discussion was begun on how to best house additional students who wanted to attend in the autumn. It was the opinion of the committee that it was still too soon to purchase a site and begin building a house of their own, and no existing house in Hitchin was suitably large and convenient. In the Victorian tradition of expediency and practicality embodied in the Crystal Palace, a series of iron rooms was erected behind Benslow House to accommodate the overflow. Although not particularly attractive or comfortable, especially when the rain bounced on the iron roofs with thunderous energy, or leaked into the students' rooms, they were described by one of the early students as: "two nice little clean bare rooms with polished deal as high as my shoulder and a wooden ceiling."[21] It is interesting to note that in this first, temporary structure built for what was to be Girton College, each student was allocated two rooms, a bedroom and a sitting room. This was in imitation of the men's colleges and set a precedent that Girton was to follow throughout its building history.

As noted, from the very start of the scheme, there had been debate as to the optimum location for the college. Hitchin had been chosen because it was conveniently situated halfway between London and Cambridge on the railway line, and lecturers came from both universities to teach the students. It was also far removed from the distractions of both cities and did not raise the difficulty of supervising the women in either place. Thus Hitchin seemed safe and convenient. Yet even at the beginning, there were voices of dissent on the committee from those not happy with the distance from Cambridge and the subsequent difficulties of commuting faced by the lecturers.

For instance, in December 1869, just three months after the college had begun, Sedley Taylor, an executive committee member and an economist at Trinity College, Cambridge, wrote to Bodichon expressing his concern over the cost of travel and time involved for the lecturers in coming to teach such a small number of students. He suggested that this inconvenience would be removed if the venture were to be relocated in Cambridge.[22] In his next letter, he told her of the lecture scheme about

19. Davies to Bodichon, B20, 20 February 1869, Girton College Archives.
20. Barbara Stephen, *Girton College* (Cambridge: Cambridge University Press, 1933), 28.
21. Constance Louisa Maynard, Diaries, 1872–75, 19 October 1872, Queen Mary and Westfield College Archives, CLM/MSS/D:5.
22. M. S. Taylor to Bodichon, B402, 2 December 1869, Girton College Archives.

to begin in Cambridge for women, led by Henry Sidgwick and a distinguished team of lecturers,[23] perhaps with the idea of merging the two. This second scheme was to evolve into Newnham College, and its very existence caused Davies considerable chagrin. Upon the resignation of Mr. Stuart, a mathematics lecturer, in January 1870, Mr. Taylor wrote again urging a move to Cambridge.[24]

His urgings yielded results in attitude if not in action. By November, the committee had resolved to look for a site near Cambridge and Emily Davies' grandiose vision of a college for women had been tempered by practicality. As she wrote to Bodichon:

Evidently our plan of preparing a 'fair and civil building' as Disraeli would call it, . . . cannot be carried out. The little band of pioneers must accrete a modest building round them. Is there not some animal that develops a shell? If not there ought to be. I am in favour of building on a very small scale, within a walk of the Lecturers, in time to migrate when this lease expires.[25]

Davies and the committee were still distrustful of the masculine society of Cambridge, and a location was sought at a distance of two or three miles outside the town. A plot of sixteen acres near the village of Girton was chosen, a little over two miles from the center of Cambridge.

Although Davies had to compromise on scale and location, she was allowed to keep her favorite architect, Alfred Waterhouse, and by the end of 1871 he was working up plans for the building. Although we cannot know precisely what was requested of Mr. Waterhouse by the committee, the letters of Davies to Bodichon reveal some of the issues toyed with at the start of planning. For instance, in a letter from January 1872, Davies was discussing the issue of the plans for the building. Rather dispiritedly, she wrote:

Mr. Tomkinson [a friend of Davies and committee member] *has invented one* [plan] *on the 'well' system, without attics, and will try and see Mr. Waterhouse before we meet on Wednesday and find out what difference it would make in the cost. It involves having eight pairs of rooms with a North-East aspect! If it would save* much, *I suppose we must reconcile ourselves to that and other drawbacks.*[26]

This "well system" refers to the traditional staircase system of the Oxbridge colleges, which had been in use for centuries. In men's colleges several staircases within a residential range lead up two or three storeys onto several sets of private suites of greater or lesser elegance depending on the status of the undergraduate. Each suite was an independent unit with one large room and two or three smaller ones. In the one Oxbridge college in which the corridor system was used, Keble College, at Oxford, designed by William Butterfield and opened in 1870, the results were found to be "unsatisfactory and destructive of collegiate character."[27] Keble's corridors were later partitioned to restrict the "bear-fighting, cricket and football"[28] for which the male undergraduates had used them.

The traditional independent stairwells afforded relatively free and unmonitored access and exit for the men, allowing them to come and go until late evening when the

23. Taylor to Bodichon, B403, 11 December 1869, Girton College Archives.
24. Taylor to Bodichon, B405, 4 January 1870, Girton College Archives.
25. Davies Bodichon, B44, 2 November 1870, Girton College Archives.
26. Davies to Bodichon, B57, 21 January 1872, Girton College Archives.
27. Basil Champneys, "The Planning of Collegiate Buildings," *Journal of the Royal Institute of British Architects* 10, 3rd series (1903): 207.
28. Edward Warren, "Collegiate Architecture," *Journal of the Royal Institute of British Architects* 19 (19 February 1912): 292.

3. Perse and Legge Buildings, floorplan, Gonville and Caius College, Cambridge, 1617–19 (demolished).

A–G: chambers
s: studies

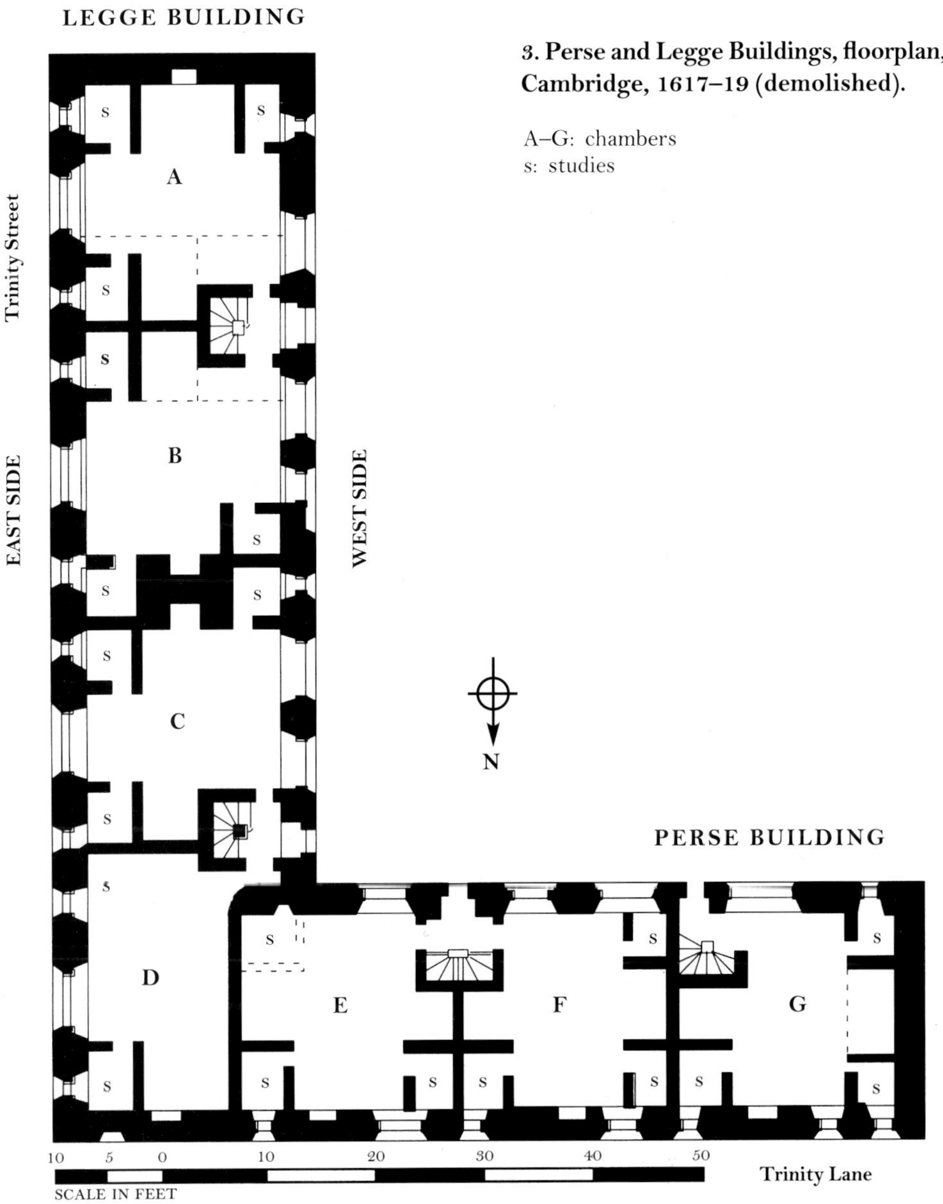

gates of the college were locked. But according to an account of an undergraduate's day at Oxford in 1888, when locked out the men had a small "gate bill"[29] to pay which did not curtail their activities. Similarly, when within the college, undergraduates had a degree of personal freedom to visit friends, play at billiards, drink wine and port and to keep their own schedule in a manner that would not have been acceptable to those involved with the women's colleges.

Thus the fact that traditional stairwells were considered by the committee founding a college is understandable. The fact that they were considered and rejected by a committee founding a college for women raises questions vital to the study of the women's colleges in England. Although Davies does not go into detail about the

29. An Undergraduate, "A Day in His Life at Oxford," *Murray's Magazine* 3 (1888): 666.

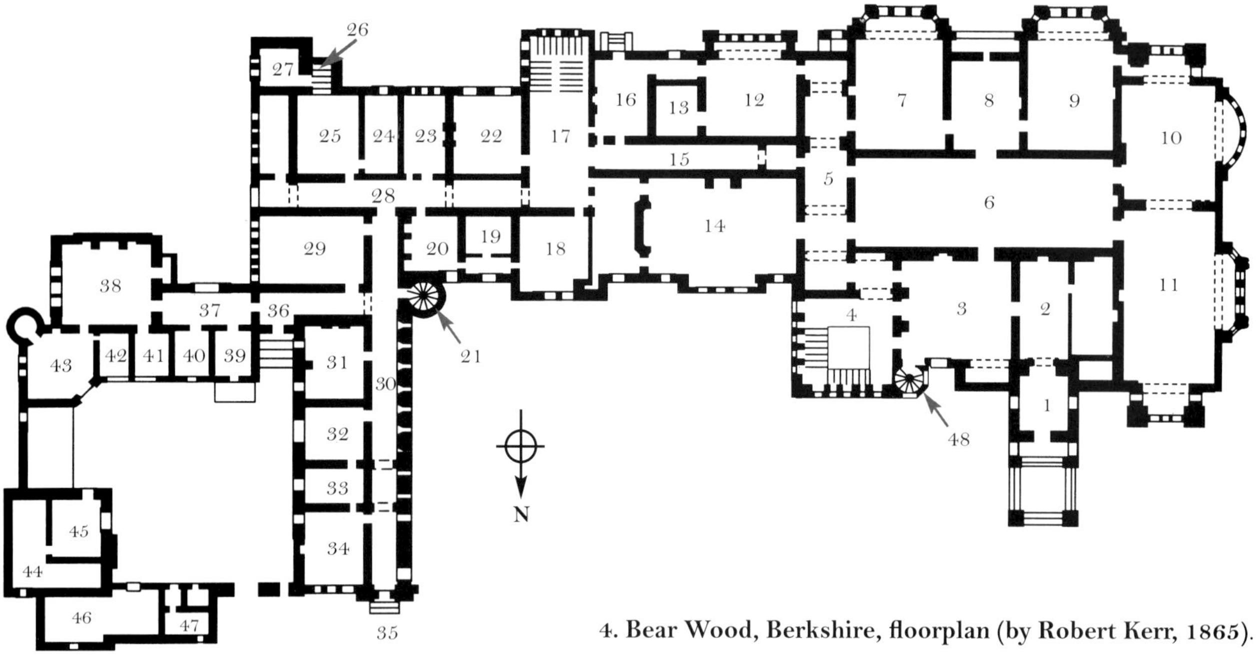

4. Bear Wood, Berkshire, floorplan (by Robert Kerr, 1865).

1. porch
2. entry
3. entrance hall
4. Principal stair
5. transverse corridor
6. picture gallery
7. gentleman's room (or library)
8. garden entrance
9. library
10. morning room
11. drawing room
12. billiard room
13. deed room
14. dining room
15. butler's corridor
16. entrance or waiting room
17. back stairs
18. butler's pantry
19. plate safe
20. butler's bedroom
21. women's stairs
22. odd room
23. gun room
24. footman's room
25. brushing room
26. men's room
27. cleaning room
28. men's corridor
29. servants' hall
30. housekeeper's corridor
31. women's work room
32. still room
33. store room
34. housekeepers' room
35. luggage entrance
36. kitchen entrance
37. kitchen lobby
38. kitchen
39. larder
40. pantry
41. pantry
42. fuel closet
43. scullery
44. coal
45. engine house
46. coal house
47. dust bin
48. bachelors' stair

"other drawbacks" of the scheme, it is clearly not just the north-east aspect that disturbs her. By the 1860s the Victorian house had become an elaborate maze of corridors, staircases and rooms which were organized so as to separate the sexes and classes from each other. With servants and men and women segregated through architectural means, it was believed that behavior could be monitored and controlled. Robert Kerr's book, *The Gentleman's House* of 1865, described in great detail the necessary arrangements of the house, which included elaborate corridor systems assigned to specific members of the household, such as bachelors' stairs leading up to bachelors' rooms with a private entry from the outside, morning rooms and drawing rooms for the women, and libraries and smoking rooms for the men. Men and women, therefore, met only in pre-assigned spaces, such as the dining room. The servants were even more segregated from each other and their employers, having gender-specific stairways so as to avoid chance meetings in the relative seclusion of a stairwell, as well as separate corridors to reach their respective rooms.

Such organization, together with other elements of planning which Kerr insisted

5. St. Mary's Convent, Wantage, Oxfordshire (by G. E. Street, 1854).

upon such as privacy, aspect and a healthy setting, was believed to exert a powerful influence over the inhabitants, and therefore, to be beneficial to society as a whole. These elements of the domestic house were employed in the planning of asylums, hospitals, boys' public schools and even prisons for the beneficial effects they were considered to have on the inmates.[30] Thus for Davies, a house had several crucial advantages which would help her cause. As she pointed out in her article of 1868, a house was conducive to the discipline of a familial household. It encouraged community, with a drawing room, a prayer room, and corridors which provided easy access to the mother, governess, or in the case of Girton, the mistress. It provided protection from the elements, enabling women to stay indoors in inclement weather. It was safe, as the only access through the front and back doors could be checked by parents, the butler, or again in Girton's case, the mistress. Whoever had the keys could determine who could enter and leave, and when.

In contrast, the staircase system at the men's colleges promised no such security. The idea of community was diminished by the nature of separate stairways and suites of rooms. With no connecting corridor, each student would be isolated in her stairwell from the mistress and those students who did not share her stairway. If a common-room, and prayer room were provided, the women would have to venture outside, no matter what the weather, in order to join the others. Indeed, she would be subjected to the elements for every meal, lecture or tea party. Furthermore, each student would require her own key to her stairway and no comprehensive supervision or discipline could be established by the mistress.

Community, health and supervision were vital ingredients in the publicity of the college and to forfeit them would have endangered or quite probably foiled the scheme altogether. In 1872 the building at Girton was one of the few places intended solely for women ever built in England, with the exception of convents. While the Catholic associations ruled out this building type as a prevalent model, there are similarities.

30. For more information on the planning of asylums see Andrew Scull, "A Convenient Place To Get Rid of Inconvenient People: The Victorian Lunatic Asylum," in *Buildings and Society*, ed. Anthony D. King (London: Routledge & Kegan Paul, 1980), or Elaine Showalter, "Victorian Women and Insanity," in *Madhouses, Mad-Doctors and Madmen: the Social History of Psychology in the Victorian Era*, ed. Andrew Skull (London: Athlone Press, 1981). For information on the planning of hospitals see Adrian Forty, "The Modern Hospital in England and France: the Social and Medical Uses of Architecture," in *Buildings and Society*, ed. Anthony D. King. For information on prisons see Robin Evans, *The Fabrication of Virtue: English Prison Architecture 1750–1840* (Cambridge: Cambridge University Press, 1982), and Michel Foucault, *Discipline and Punish*, trans. Alan Sheridan (London: Penguin Books, 1977).

For example, G. E. Street's convent for the nuns of St. Mary's in Wantage of 1855–56, is basically a domestic house. It was small, built in the local stone, with pretty dormer windows, and a corridor running through connecting all the rooms with each other. While such a precedent was probably not consciously conjured up by the committee at Girton, it is likely that Waterhouse would have known of Street's work.

Whether or not the conventual precedent had any bearing on the committee's decision is less important than the other considerations which did. The issue of education for girls and women equal to that for boys and men raised an outcry in society. Much of the argument against such an idea was couched in terms of the health of women and their delicate and susceptible constitutions. Widely publicized and supported by physicians such as Dr. Henry Maudsley, was the "theory of appropriateness"[31] which posited that the education and lifestyles of women must be tailored to their special nature. This theory argued that when a woman received the same education as a man,

her physical degeneracy and that of her offspring result; and it certainly tends to lower those refining and elevating influences which society cannot afford to lose, and which women hold in trust for both sexes at all ages.[32]

While Davies argued that much of this accepted weakness in women was due to the languorous and frivolous lives they led, she and her committee had little actual proof to counter the fears of the doctors and parents who prescribed caution or who rejected women's claims to education outright. In addition to her battery of arguments claiming the beneficial effects of knowledge on the moral development of women, it was equally crucial that Davies show that physical health was not neglected, that the women were kept from overwork, and that their lodgings were healthy. The "well system" could not promise to protect women's health, and thus it is hardly surprising that such a plan was not realized.

Further evidence exists that the domestic house served as a key model for the building at Girton. A letter to Bodichon suggests that Davies and the committee used the plans of Benslow House as a guide for Waterhouse to use in terms of size and type of room. Davies wrote:

I have been studying the plans and comparing them with that of the present house at Hitchin which I have here. This plan gives the measurements of all the rooms, and as they have been lived in, we can judge exactly how they work.[33]

The plans of Benslow House are now in the Girton College Archives. The ground floor shows a large central drawing room with a bay window, a moderately-sized dining room, a smaller drawing room, a breakfast room and central and back stairs. The "Chamber floor" has seven bedrooms and a water closet. The measurements of each room are marked. It is a small and compact house with all rooms opening on to a central passageway. How much Waterhouse used these plans in designing Girton it is difficult to know. That Davies relied on them as a paradigm is significant, as it provided a standard on which Davies and the committee based many of their requirements.

31. H. Cowell, "Sex in Mind and Education: A Commentary," *Blackwood's Magazine* 115 (June, 1874): 748.
32. Ibid., 749.
33. Davies to Bodichon, B70, November 1872, Girton College Archives.

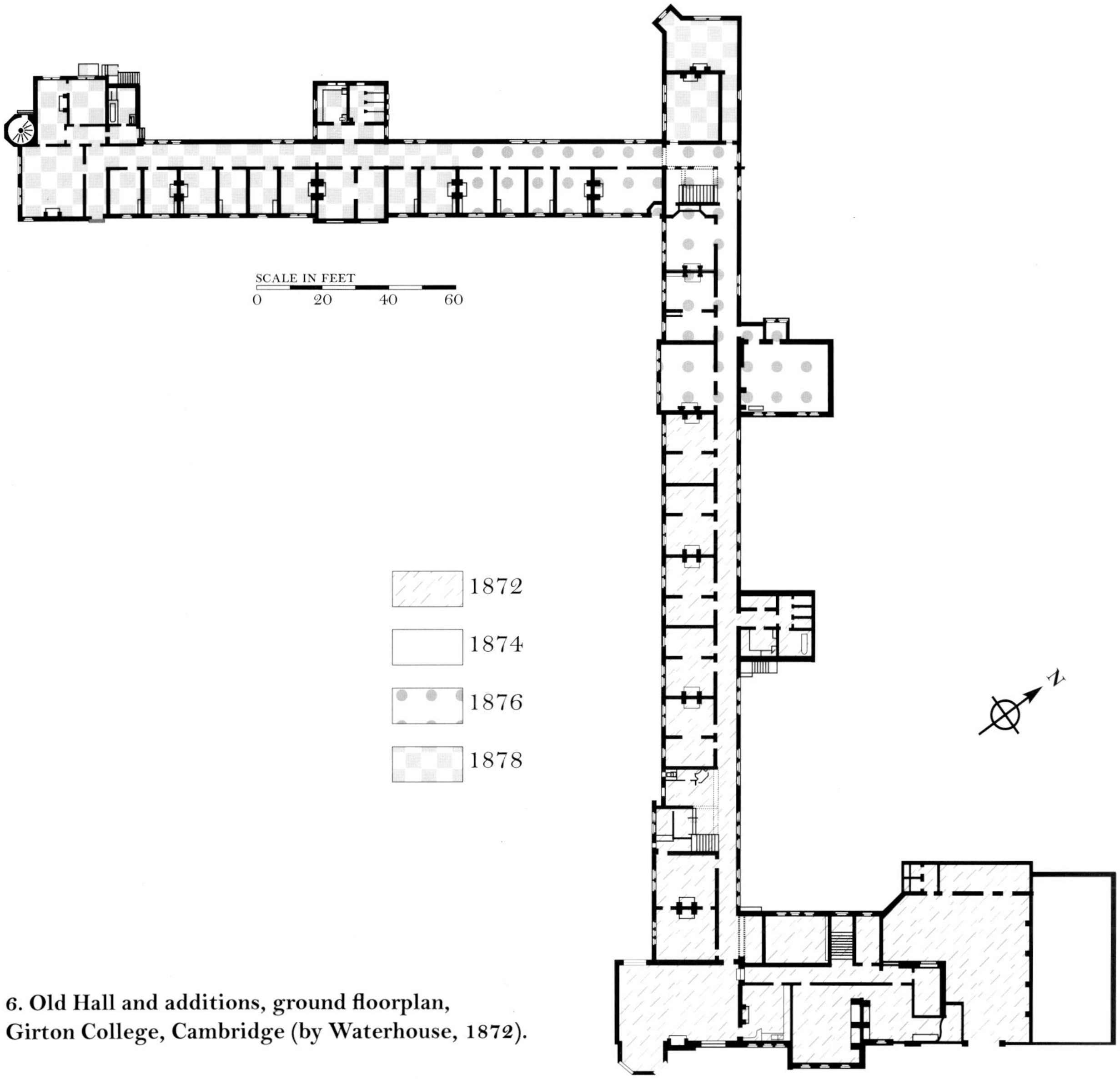

6. Old Hall and additions, ground floorplan, Girton College, Cambridge (by Waterhouse, 1872).

The new plans were finalized and agreed to by 1872 when work began. The plans in Girton's archives show the original hall, but projected additions were outlined. The first part built, what is called Old Hall, had rooms for twenty one students, the mistress, and a resident lecturer, as well as three lecture rooms and a prayer room. As Davies had promised in the *Contemporary Review*, each student was given two adjoining rooms, a bedroom and sitting room, a concession to the Oxbridge tradition. Entry to the ground floor is on the right of the southern facade and brings the visitor into a cheerful foyer with a cozy fireplace and small waiting room just to the left, and the main stair to the right. Branching off to either side is the corridor which runs along the north side of the building giving a southern aspect to all the rooms. To the left, it extends down past five sets of rooms. To the right of the entry were two lecture rooms, and immediately beyond those, the dining room. On the north side of the corridor is a small gyp room, three earth closets and a bath. Including such areas for private hygiene was an important departure from the men's colleges in which men had to leave their lodgings for such purposes. Here, as in the domestic house, these conveniences were included within the same walls.

The kitchen wing stretches away towards the north, with a back stair for the servants' wing, typical of the patterns of segregation in the Victorian house. The first floor continues the series of students' rooms down the long corridor with the prayer room and another lecture room over the kitchen and the mistress's suite over the dining room. One of the rooms over the kitchen was originally used as a recreation room, for dancing or exercise, until a gymnasium was built behind the kitchens in 1874.[34] The attic storey provided more students' rooms but on this storey the women only had one room with a curtain to divide the bed from the rest of the room. The servants' quarters were in the kitchen wing.

It is a very simple plan. The students' rooms are in a straightforward range, separated from the lecture room, reading room and dining room, the more public rooms. Waterhouse pulled out the wall surface to the right of the entrance where the lecture rooms were to be, thereby emphasizing that these rooms were different from the others. The dining room extends still further south. Overall, the plan resembles an elongated, institutional house with the long range of bedrooms and sitting rooms set apart from the communal rooms, which were grouped together at one end and the kitchen areas kept in the back. The effect of the blank wall that faces south was softened by a large bay window to the east, a characteristically domestic feature which elaborated this important room, and was part of a larger gabled extension which provided greater space for the mistress's room above. The stark south wall of the dining hall and mistress's room indicated further plans for extension in this direction.

The facade of Old Hall is relatively uncomplicated (see color illustration 1). The paired sets of arched windows mark the sitting rooms of the students and the single arches light the bedrooms. The dormers, set with three sash windows each, punctuate the roof above the sitting rooms. The entrance is articulated by a large gable pulled out from the wall, which eventually housed a round clock in the center. A spindly fleche, now missing, drew further attention to the entry and embellished what would otherwise have been a rather dull repetition of Waterhouse's very tall chimneys breaking up the long horizontal of the roofline. A modest brick cornice extends the length of the house and is more articulated by shadows in the elevation drawing than in the building itself.

The overall massing, the large blank wall, and the terra-cotta window dressings, all hearken back to one of Waterhouse's earliest commissions—for Hinderton, a house he built in Cheshire in 1859. While Hinderton is more elaborate both in detail and in its silhouette, the clear articulation of parts and the treatment of bay and oriel windows are quite similar. Tile hanging in the dormers on Old Hall at Girton was used in other domestic commissions such as Blackmoor[35] and on what is now St. Andrew's Hall at the University of Reading of 1880. Throughout the entire building campaign at Girton, Waterhouse included dormers and picturesque gables as vernacular quotations which lend a domestic flavor to the whole composition.

Settling into the new building was not comfortable, because the students and

34. Prudence Waterhouse, *A Victorian Monument: The Buildings of Girton College* (Cambridge: Prudence Waterhouse c/o Girton College, 1990), 10.
35. Ibid., 29

LEFT 7. Hinderton, Cheshire (by Waterhouse, 1859). From *The Builder* (15 January 1859), 43.
RIGHT 8. Dormer detail, St. Andrew's Hall, Reading (by Waterhouse, 1880).

Miss Davies moved in in October 1873 before the building was completely finished. That Davies was not at ease with the responsibility of the interior decoration is clear from her letters to Bodichon, asking for advice on curtains, colors and carpets. From these we can glean an idea of what the early rooms looked like. In September 1873, both Davies and Waterhouse were pleased with how the building was progressing, and had discussed interior decor together:

The blue carpets are here and look nice, and Mr. W. is delighted with the Japanese curtains. I could not get blue lining that would do, so they are all lined with white twilled *glazed lining (very nice) and the sitting rooms have a border run on which matches wonderfully and is half penny a yard.*[36]

These letters describe rooms with pretty chintz sofas and chairs, carpets and curtains in blues and greys. The bedroom furniture was painted white "with a suspicion of cream in it."[37] The color schemes and Japanese details fit in with a growing trend in interior decor that was part of the larger Aesthetic Movement taking place in painting, architecture and the decorative arts concurrently. The interest in things Japanese or Eastern was brought from France by Rossetti and Whistler and reflected greater stylistic freedoms which were being explored at the time. E. W. Nesfield and Richard Norman Shaw led the way in architecture and interior design with their collection of Japanese prints and Nanking vases and an altogether brighter and less heavy look in their interiors than was common in the mid-Victorian era.

The main corridor at Girton was painted white, with the wooden window and doorframes stained dark. The floor was paved with a geometric pattern of tiles and the passageway was light and airy, with a window at the far end. The original dining room was at first rather sparse, with a vast expanse of blank wall surface. The large bay window had stained glass, colored in reds, blues and greys amidst the clear glass,

36. Davies to Bodichon, B88, 25 September 1873, Girton College Archives.
37. Davies to Bodichon, B110, 5 September 1874, Girton College Archives.

9. Dining Hall, Old Hall. *Reproduced courtesy of the Mistress and Fellows, Girton College, Cambridge.*

perhaps decided upon by Bodichon.[38] The glass however, has since been removed. Dark beams stretch across the white ceiling of the dining room, embellished only above the bay window by a pretty carving in a leafy pattern. The fireplace (now gone) was tiled in an almost Moorish style, although we cannot know the color scheme. Small tables were arranged around the room, draped with white table cloths and set with flowers, with no attempt to mimic the tradition of High Table which Davies had failed to instigate at Benslow House.

The house was light and cheerful, no doubt in part due to Waterhouse's skill as a planner. The corridors at Girton, no matter how long they may become in some wings, are always open and airy. By keeping the rooms all along one side of the building and ranging the corridors along the other, he avoided the problem of dark and gloomy tunnels, the effect of which can be confusing and depressing. But in this arrangement he sacrificed a compact house system, and in order to get the required number of rooms had to stretch out the length of the buildings. The effect can be institutional and monotonous. However, as we shall see, Waterhouse used several techniques to vary the facades and avoid excessive repetition, thereby eschewing an institutional flavor on the exterior.

38. In the RIBA drawings collection, WAT [A] IF 26 is a color wash sketch of lead lights for dining room with Mme Bodichon's name and address written on it, suggesting that it was sent to her for approval or a decision on the color scheme.

In 1876 more rooms were needed and the first of many additions was begun. This extended to the west, lengthening the corridor and then turning south to form an L-shaped whole (see fig. 6 above). The wing also included a laboratory built at the rear of the range, which formed a simple one storey gabled block. The new range contained three more lecture rooms and students' rooms. The very long corridor which resulted in the addition to the original building worried Bodichon, and in November 1875, when the plans were being worked up, Miss Davies reassured her:

You will see that the plan for the additions includes a staircase, which I suppose removes the fire objection to lengthening the corridors. Have you any others?

According to the plan, we continue our present line for three more pairs of students' rooms per story. Then comes necessarily before turning the corners, a square space, to be occupied by a new staircase, then four more pairs of students' rooms per story. Only that the two pairs on the ground floor which would respectively meet the staircase at the corner, we propose to make Lecture rooms, as we already rather want them, and it is well to utilize some of the ground floor.[39]

It is fitting here to mention the inclusion of the lecture rooms as a constant feature in the plans for Girton and the women's colleges which followed. Traditionally, undergraduates were offered tutorials in the dons' individual suites. When lectures were offered they were given outside college in separate buildings intended for this purpose, which were called the Schools Buildings. It was not until the mid-nineteenth century, when the universities began reforming themselves and their curricula that the issue of lecture rooms was raised. Even then, the demand was usually for new science laboratories. Seldom in the building campaigns of the nineteenth century were lecture rooms included at individual colleges. One of the few exceptions to this occurred in 1869 when St. John's College, Cambridge, commissioned G. G. Scott to build two lecture rooms, which were eventually incorporated into the larger Penrose Building, completed in 1887. More often than not, male undergraduates, if desirous of hearing a lecture by such notables as Ruskin, Pusey or Charles Kingsley, left their college gates.

For a number of reasons, this system would not work for the women's colleges. To begin with, the lectures that were given to the undergraduates were not at first open to women. Tutors traveled to Hitchin and then to Girton and repeated their class to a small group of women. Private tutorials were offered although they were always conducted in the presence of a chaperon. Since women were rarely allowed into lectures and were discouraged from leaving the college walls, especially to go into town, lecture rooms had to be provided. As the number of students increased, so the variety and number of lectures grew as well. Thus every building scheme at Girton for the next thirty years included lecture rooms. This feature of the women's colleges, which resulted from the social conditions attached to the schemes for women's higher education, further sets them apart from the Oxbridge tradition.

A new range extending south from the newly-built corridor was begun in 1878. This became known as the Hospital Wing, as it included a patient's room and a suite for a nurse at the far end of the range. This infirmary could be reached by a separate doorway, thus ensuring that the patient could be completely isolated from the other

39. Davies to Bodichon, B145, 5 November 1875, Girton College Archives.

LEFT 10. Hospital Wing, Girton College (by Waterhouse, 1878).
RIGHT 11. Separate Entrance, Hospital Wing.

students to prevent infection. The inclusion of such a precautionary suite of rooms gives further evidence of the tremendous concern for women's health away from home at college. Sick bays do not appear in the ordinary schemes for men's lodgings at college, because men's constitutions were considered much more robust and resilient than women's. Similar health facilities were included in women's colleges in America such as Vassar and Wellesley College. There too, all elements of the college were housed under one large roof in an attempt to nurture a familial spirit and safeguard women's health. (There is, however, no evidence to suggest that, at this point, Davies and her committee were in touch with the movement for women's education across the Atlantic which was going on concurrently.)

There is evidence that the early female students at Girton did suffer from various maladies, not the least of which was generally referred to as neuralgia, which was believed to be brought on by overtaxing the female brain. In 1874, Miss Welsh, one of the earliest students, was diagnosed with neuralgia. In a letter to Bodichon, Davies described how she consulted her old friend, Elizabeth Garrett Anderson, who spoke out:

strongly about the injuriousness of too much food, especially animal food, for people who are engaged in brain-work. Dr. Radcliffe, who is much resorted to by overworked barristers, at once cuts them down to meat once a day and abolishes beef tea etc.[40]

There was, evidently, some dispute between Davies and Bodichon over what degree of protection was needed for the early students. Davies believed that the students themselves should bear some of the responsibility for their own health and should learn by example and habit how to take care of themselves. It appears that Bodichon would have preferred closer supervision, but Davies defended her policy by saying:

40. Davies to Bodichon, B112, 14 September 1874, Girton College Archives.

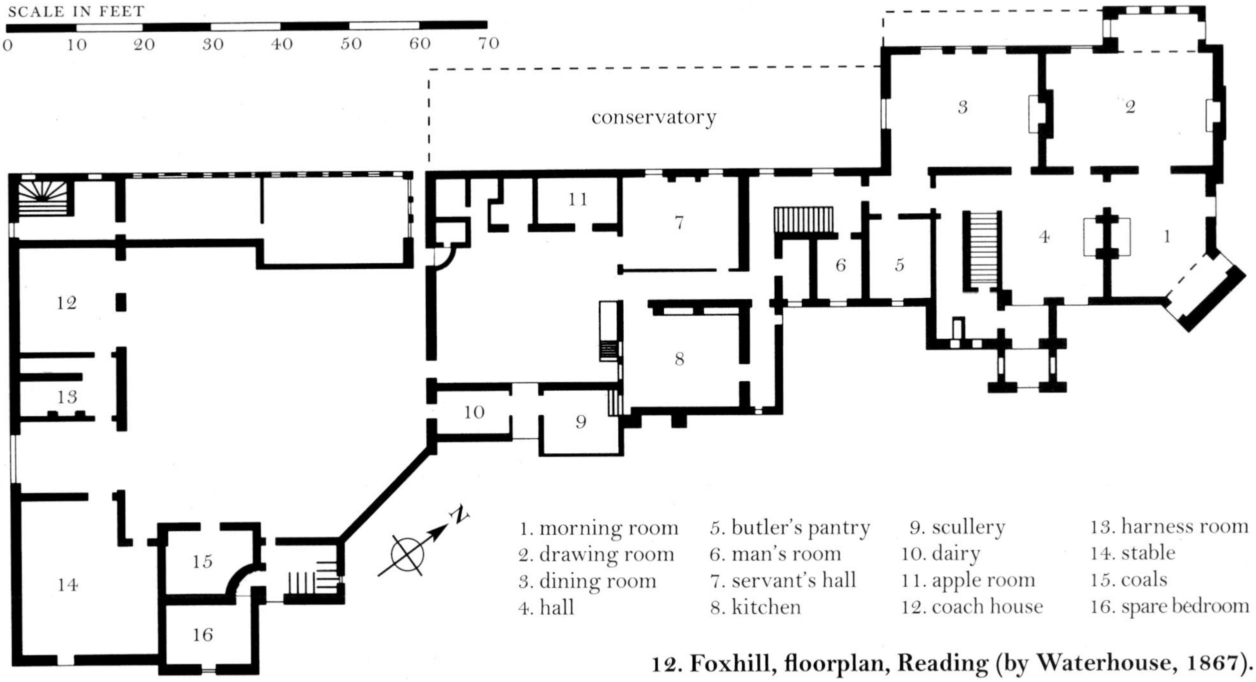

12. Foxhill, floorplan, Reading (by Waterhouse, 1867).

the thing to aim at is not to be constantly looking after them about every detail but to have a generally healthy system going on, and only to put in a word now and then, and to be ready of course to advise and help and even to nurse, when any special need arises.[41]

Davies, whose plans for the college were more ambitious than her committee or society as a whole were prepared to share, did not want her students to be treated like children, but this more casual attitude worried many others involved in the scheme. Given the attention and concern paid to the issue of health in letters and articles, it is little wonder that one of the earliest additions to Girton was a provision for illness. Here again is a clear example in which the architecture reflects the social concerns for women and their health and safety. The planning issues involved in this experiment in women's education were conditioned by widely-held beliefs regarding the fundamental differences between men and women and their respective needs.

The Hospital Wing continued the previous addition for three more sets of rooms per floor, ending in the nursing suite on the ground floor and including a suite for a resident lecturer on the first floor above. The end of this wing was dramatized by a tower that housed a spiral staircase which added a picturesque finality to the range. Once again the dormers are tile hung. Also included in the addition of 1878 was what became known as the Taylor Knob, named after Sedley Taylor. This included two new lecture rooms on the ground floor, extending out beyond the corner, and lengthening the original corridor still further. The first storey included another suite for a resident lecturer. The inclusion of a square bay window breaks up the southern corner of the last lecture room. Waterhouse used a very similar feature in the morning room of his own house, Foxhill, in Reading of 1867. In both cases the square bay breaks what would otherwise have been a very regular corner. From the exterior at

41. Davies to Bodichon, B99, 12 June 1874, Girton College Archives.

LEFT 13. Taylor Knob, Girton College (by Waterhouse, 1878).
RIGHT 14. Jesus College, Cambridge (range by Waterhouse, 1869–70).

Girton, this is an interesting domestic detail, roofed in scalloped shingles with a decorative brick course running between the two floors. It is a significant detail because it is so unnecessary and so calculated, and is one of the many devices which Waterhouse used to soften and vary the outline of the whole.

Bay windows were generally considered to be a vital aspect in the domestic house. Ruskin, who inspired the young Waterhouse, had praised the bay window for its quaint charm in the domestic house in his *Lectures in Architecture and Painting*. He wrote:

> *You surely must all of you feel and admit the delightfulness of a bow window; I can hardly fancy a room being perfect without one. Now you have nothing to do but to resolve that every one of your principal rooms shall have a bow window . . . and you will have as inexhaustible a source of quaint richness in your street architecture, as of additional comfort and delight in the interiors of your rooms.*[42]

That Waterhouse was concerned with including such domestic details in his scheme at Girton is evident from the many bay and oriel windows he included throughout, as well as from the tile hung gables and white trimmed dormers which articulate an otherwise lengthy roofline. The large bay window on the Taylor Knob, which added a cozy, domestic niche to an otherwise uninteresting rectangular room, is a characteristic attempt on the part of the architect to temper the practical and institutional aspects of Girton with an attractive and comfortable domesticity. It is a clear illustration of Ruskin's and other Victorians' belief that the language of architectural elements should be used to communicate the purpose of a building through both appearance and association.

Such details, though they appear in Waterhouse's other domestic work, are not

42. John Ruskin, *Lectures in Architecture and Painting* (1853; reprint, London: George Allen, 1907), 56–57.

LEFT 15. Gatetower, Jesus College, Cambridge (by Bishop Alcock of Ely, c. 1497).

RIGHT 16. Oriel, detail, Jesus College (by Waterhouse, 1869–70).

17. Orchard Wing, Girton College (by Waterhouse, 1882).

prevalent in his Oxbridge commissions. For example, Waterhouse designed a range for Jesus College, Cambridge in 1869–70, using brick, as at Girton. Here however, the stone dressings add a stark outline to the windows and doors. The flat roof, squat crenelated tower and unbroken wall surface are in keeping with the severe, almost fortress-like appearance of the surrounding college buildings. Even where Waterhouse broke the rectangular box with an oriel window, the effect is massive and

18. View of enlarged Dining Hall, Girton College (by Waterhouse, 1882). *Reproduced courtesy of the Mistress and Fellows, Girton College, Cambridge.*

weighty, with the single buttress below and the crenellation above. A comparison with the Taylor Knob makes it clear that Waterhouse borrowed from different sources for Girton and Jesus. At Jesus, the precedent was an earlier collegiate Gothic. For Girton, Waterhouse relied on his domestic commissions as sources for details in order to break up the institutional ranges and add a softer domestic flavor.

Girton continued to grow quite rapidly. By 1882 plans were being drawn up for another wing, the Orchard Wing, which extends back to the north from the Knob. This added four more lecture rooms in addition to more rooms for students. A resident lecturer lived in a gabled extension at the end of the wing, her sitting room articulated by an oriel window decorated with a band of patterned brickwork. The bedrooms in the Orchard Wing have a west and southwest aspect, whereas those in the Hospital Wing face the southeast. In planning this wing, Waterhouse had to choose between facing the rooms to the northeast or the west/southwest. Clearly, the latter was preferred as it allowed the maximum amount of sun possible for this particular addition.

19. Stanley Library, detail, balcony.
20. Tower Wing and gate, Girton College (by Waterhouse, 1886).

Concurrent with the building of this wing came the enlargement of the dining room and the building of the Stanley Library with rooms for the mistress above (see color illustrations 2 and 3). The Stanley Library was made possible by a gift from Lady Stanley of Alderley, who had been an active member of the committee and an early supporter of the college. The dining room was extended south from the original bay window, and afforded a great deal more space, as well as another fireplace and more elaborate mantelpiece. It is, overall, a much grander room for the addition.

The library is across the corridor from the dining hall, and extended the building even further south. It was the most formal of all the rooms built thus far, and is still elegant and well-preserved. The heavy cross-beamed ceiling adds a certain gravity, which is balanced by the full length bay window at the far end which lights up the interior. The windows are leaded with borders of patterned stained glass, but with plenty of clear glass for good reading light. Under every window are cushioned window seats, bound in leather. These are continued beside the fireplace as inglenooks, which provide cozy spots for reading. The walls are lined with bookshelves and in the center of the room was a large table for common study. The fireplace is outlined by tiles and the mantelpiece, similar to that found in the extended dining hall, has a large overmantel within which were placed a clock and two large Japanese vases, very much in the aesthetic style of the day.[43]

The library is reached along a cloistered corridor that runs along the length of the dining hall. At the corner, a spiral staircase leads up to what were the mistress's rooms. Her suite was large, and her sitting room had an ingenious balconied window above the library bay. Also built above the dining hall was a visitor's bedroom and reception room. The wing formed the third side of what is now called Emily Davies

43. This was passed on to me by the Girton College archivist, Kate Perry, and the view in P. Waterhouse's book confirms it.

21. Tower Wing (by Waterhouse, 1886). *Reproduced courtesy of the Mistress and Fellows, Girton College, Cambridge.*

Court. It is more elaborate than the previous additions, with varied gables and dormers and a dramatic and picturesque skyline.

Part of this elaboration may be due to a growing confidence and security on the part of the college and its committee. The number of students was steadily increasing, as the concept of a women's college gained acceptance and support. By 1886, Waterhouse was again at work planning another addition, this time to extend to the east from the library wing. This scheme suggests even greater confidence and optimism. It included a new entrance beneath a large tower, with a room for a female porter. In a certain sense this arched entranceway looks to the Oxbridge tradition of a tower and gateway, with entry through a porter's lodge, into the traditional courtyard. It was envisioned at the time that the courtyard would include a cloister and a large, formal dining hall, all of which were ultimately built. It was, therefore, the beginning of a scheme which would more directly mirror the male tradition.

But where the planning impulse behind this new wing suggests a confident imitation of the male example, Waterhouse's stylistic decisions were based on something different. For it is here that Waterhouse gives play to the tendencies that we have seen at work previously in gable and dormer detailing. These Shavian, 'Old English' elements such as half-timbering and tile hanging, are here given full blown

22. Pembroke College, Cambridge (range by Waterhouse, 1871).

expression in the vernacular treatment of all the gables and dormers. The half-timber work was originally painted brown against a white plaster background and along the base of the gables runs a row of three decorative quatrefoils, also in timber and plaster. Each dormer has a token half-timber treatment. The effect is picturesque and evocative of a domestic tradition which mellows the imposing effect of the tower and arched entranceway (see color illustration 4).

Pevsner grouped these buildings together with Waterhouse's work at Jesus and Pembroke Colleges in Cambridge.[44] But they have little in common with Waterhouse's range for male undergraduates. At Pembroke, Waterhouse stressed the murality of the range with horizontal stone banding amidst the brick. A heavy cornice runs along the facade above the first floor, above which rests a stone balustrade. The roof, so praised by Ruskin for the sense of domestic security which it promised,[45] is set back almost out of sight behind the balustrade and dormers. In contrast, at Girton, as in much of his domestic work, Waterhouse emphasized the roof with scalloped tiles, and a steep pitch. The gables and dormers have overhanging, sheltering eaves. Waterhouse broke up the length of the range at Girton with gables which vary in size, and several bay windows. His work at Pembroke, as at Jesus or Gonville and Caius Colleges, laid stress on the regularity of the wall surface and is representative of a more formal style of building. The use of such a vernacular and domestic technique as half-timbering had no relation to the collegiate tradition of building and would have been considered undignified and thus inappropriate for a men's college.

44. Nikolaus Pevsner, *Cambridgeshire*, 2nd ed. (Harmondsworth: Penguin Books, 1970), 190.
45. "Whatever external splendor you may give your houses, you will always feel there is something wanting, unless you see their roofs plainly."

23. Gatehouse, Blackmoor, Hampshire (by Waterhouse, 1869–72). *British Architectural Library, RIBA, London.*

At Girton, the traditional collegiate formality with all its associations was not yet considered suitable for a women's college. Therefore, Waterhouse did not borrow motifs and styles from his work in Cambridge but tended instead to look to his domestic work. In the 1860s, Richard Norman Shaw and Eden Nesfield began to sketch old houses in Kent for their domestic inspiration. They were looking for alternatives to the Gothic which they considered too heavily laden with religious associations to be appropriate for the ordinary dwelling house. The 'Old English' style, as it became known, offered new creative freedom and an escape from the dogmatism of the previous generation. The picturesque massing of the 'Old English' and its tile hung gables and half-timbering, hearkened back to an older domestic tradition. This became quite popular with the younger middle classes. As Andrew Saint points out in his book on Shaw, half-timbering became so popular because: "It had the right manorial ring; it was medieval and ancestral without being 'cottagey' as half-hipping and tile hanging might be thought to be."[46] By the 1870s, the style had taken off and was being used by many architects for their domestic practice. Both Andrew Saint and Mark Girouard cite Waterhouse as "the first acknowledged imitator"[47] of Shaw's 'Old English' style as evidenced in Waterhouse's work at Blackmoor.

In his own house, Yattendon, of 1876, Waterhouse presented a melange of Gothic, Tudor and 'Old English' elements in a comfortable, picturesque whole (see color illustration 5). The silhouette is varied by three large gables, a half-hipped gabled projection over a double-storey bay window and a square, crenelated Tudor tower to the left of the entrance. It was in red brick with terra-cotta detailing. The surface of the walls is broken up by patterned courses of brick work in the gables, above the ground floor windows and circumscribing the tower. A checker-board pattern just below the crenellation on the tower at the fourth storey serves to lighten the stark surface of the walls. Bay windows and porches add variety and interest to the ground floor.

Waterhouse's treatment of the roofline, windows and gables at Yattendon are seen again, albeit in a simpler form in the entrance wing of Girton. The tower has

46. Andrew Saint, *Richard Norman Shaw* (New Haven: Yale University Press, 1976), 88.
47. Ibid., 143.

ABOVE 25. Mowden Hall, front elevation, Darlington, Co. Durham (by Waterhouse, 1881).

LEFT 24. Tree Court, Gonville and Caius College, Cambridge (by Waterhouse, 1870).

since been altered, but originally it was banded at the top in a white and red brick checkered pattern (see fig. 21). The edges are rounded and the wall surfaces are broken up by white trimmed windows. In detail, it more closely resembles Yattendon than the gateway at Gonville and Caius, also by Waterhouse, of 1870. Furthermore, at Girton, Waterhouse attached a half-timbered gable parallel to, but one storey above, the roofline. This gable adds picturesque variety to the Girton skyline as it is approached from Cambridge, and softens what otherwise would have been a stark transition between the roof and the tower. All these elements combine to give a domestic impression to this new block, and do not suggest the grandeur of collegiate tradition, but rather denote a cheerful, domestic quality, such as Waterhouse had employed for his own home.

Other domestic commissions share stylistic elements with Girton. For example, in 1881 Waterhouse designed Mowden Hall in Darlington for E. L. Pease. This is a simple house designed on an L-shaped plan, much like the layout of Girton's earliest buildings. The entrance front is dramatized by two large gables pulled out from the wall surface to emphasize the rooms within, and a small gabled entrance porch. The small dormer windows at Mowden Hall have since been painted a purplish red (intended, presumably, to match the brick). But close examination shows the overhanging eaves and half-timbering over the set of windows, identical to the dormers provided by Waterhouse in his addition of 1886 at Girton.

Also interesting, especially in the light of Waterhouse's reputation as a Gothicist, is the use of the sunflower motif at Mowden Hall. Throughout the terra cotta decorative friezes that divide the ground floor from the first, are sunflower bosses. The sunflower was a favorite motif of 'Queen Anne' architects and aesthetes. While Waterhouse is generally considered to be a conservative proponent of the Gothic school, the presence of the sunflower strongly suggests that, in his own rather staid

26. Sunflower boss, detail, Mowden Hall.

manner, he too flirted with the architectural and aesthetic trends which were shaking up the establishment in the 1870s and 1880s.

Documentary evidence does not exist to explain Waterhouse's choice of the 'Old English' elements seen at Girton. But the obvious differences between Girton and his ranges at Gonville and Caius or Pembroke Colleges, and the similarity in detail with his domestic work, suggest a conscious decision on the part of Girton's architect, and the patrons, to avoid too close an imitation of the male tradition. By 1888, there was little doubt that Girton was a success. Numbers kept increasing, and new rooms were constantly needed. Why then, do the details and motifs of the most important wing, the entrance, hearken back to a domestic tradition such as Waterhouse was using in his houses?

This question needs to be examined in two parts. In the first place we must look at the general theories of architecture which prevailed in the nineteenth century regarding styles and building types. From Pugin's writings in the 1840s throughout the century, the issue of appropriateness in architecture was a key consideration for architects. Both Pugin and Ruskin wanted architecture to be honest, to express the interior layout on the exterior, to use materials plainly, without pretense, basically to make the architecture speak sincerely of its purpose and composition. Starting from these ideas, writers on architecture elaborated on the issue of the language of buildings, going on to discuss the suitability of certain styles for particular building types.

For example in 1853, in his essay entitled *Principles and Practice of Architectural Design,* George Wightwick carefully outlined which style was appropriate for each building type and included the reasons why. Gothic was to be applied to churches, for obvious reasons of association. Colleges and schools, since they came under church supervision were also to follow the Gothic example. Important civic offices and grand houses, as befitted their imposing function, should be Classical, whereas institutions for the poor or commercial buildings should employ a very simplified, almost coarse version of the Classical style, in no way mimicking the grander example, but rather using the sparse details and plain outlines that such a style afforded.[48]

The debate over styles continued ferociously in the architectural press over the next thirty years, taken up by the likes of Robert Kerr, William Burges, and J. J. Stevenson, to name only a few. As J. Mordaunt Crook explains:

in the Victorian period, architect and patron alike were prisoners of two pervasive socio-aesthetic categories: propriety and association. Associational thinking—that is architecture

48. George Wightwick, "Principles and Practice of Architectural Design," in *Detached Essays of the Architectural Publication Society* (London: Architectural Publication Society, 1853).

as embodied in memory — and the idea of architectural propriety — that is, style as an expression of status as well as of purpose-supplied both explanation and justification of the whole panoply of historical forms.[49]

In the 1870s, architects such as R. N. Shaw and J. J. Stevenson were investigating alternatives to the pure Gothic or Classical styles for the English house. Stevenson's ideas will be investigated in more detail later; it suffices here to say that these architects were continuing the quest for an appropriate domestic style that carried with it suitable associations. The younger generation rejected the Gothic and Classical styles of architects such as G. E. Street and C. R. Cockerell for their domestic work because they saw those styles as too laden with religious or classical rhetoric. In their search for a simple house architecture the 'Old English' and 'Queen Anne' were hit upon for their associations with rural England, and their evocation of a quaint and cozy domesticity.

Waterhouse was a practical architect who took little part in the theoretical debates of his day. But he was also extremely rational, and believed that each commission should be planned according to the demands of that commission. A building should be appropriate for its purpose. While he stressed that the plan must, first and foremost, accommodate the needs of the inhabitants, he believed it was necessary to:

Afterwards clothe the building so planned in the most fitting dress you can devise. That dress may be in many cases extremely simple, in others ornate; it may have to be sometimes severe, sometimes of exquisite beauty, if you can make it so. As you have in the first instance been solicitous that your building should adapt itself in every way to the needs and conditions of the people who are to use it, so now strive that every detail of the dress in which you clothe it shall help to make its purpose clear.[50]

His choice therefore, of the 'Old English' style employed at Girton can be viewed as a conscious decision based on rational motives. Clearly, Waterhouse did not wish the appearance of Girton to be evocative of the male tradition of the Oxbridge colleges. While money was always an issue in the building of Girton, as we have seen, Waterhouse balanced the budget while still including extra inglenooks and bay windows, hipped roof dormers and turreted towers. Girton grew into a vast ranging complex of courtyards and corridors which included all the basic collegiate necessities. But the style in which Waterhouse clothed this college owes more to a domestic tradition than to a collegiate one. This suggests therefore, that Waterhouse saw a domestic style as "the most fitting dress" he could devise for this fledgling college for women. He tempered the dignity and grandeur of the towered entrance wing with a quaint domesticity that he considered appropriate for female students.

The second explanation for the choices made at Girton is that the public voice of Davies differed from the private. For example, in her article, "Some Account of a Proposed New College for Women," she described the discipline and control that would be exerted over the students as that practiced by a "wise mother."[51] The daily routine was described in such a way as to be familiar and very much like home. But her letters to Bodichon present quite a different ambition. In 1875 Davies wrote:

49. J. Mordaunt Crook, *The Dilemma of Style; Architectural Ideas from the Picturesque to the Post Modern* (London: John Murray, 1989), 132.
50. Alfred Waterhouse, "Address to Students," *The Builder* (2 February 1889): 90.
51. Davies, "Some Account," 552.

my 'idea' of the College is that of a society, not a family. The students have their family life already, without us. I think we ought to supply something different from home, not an inferior imitation of it, as a family composed of women only must be. I should not like the College to be a sort of widow with a great many daughters all about the same age.[52]

This was how she personally felt about the issue. However in her article and in other letters, she was very concerned about public opinion and tried to project an image intended to gain sympathizers, not alienate the public. In one instance she argued against putting the final touches on the new house at Girton because in its unfinished state it would remind people that they needed money.[53] She was acutely aware that fraternizing with certain elements in society, namely the 'Radicals,' could frighten away prospective students and their families. As we have already seen, the Hospital Wing itself was, to a certain extent, a propaganda tool meant to assure parents that all their daughters' needs would be looked after, most especially their health.

Davies was painfully aware that modesty and caution were a means of selling her college to the public, and she tempered her own ideas and ambitions for the sake of the venture. While not compromising her ultimate goal of equal higher education for women, Davies did not want to alienate any possible sympathizers in the Cambridge community. As we have seen earlier, Davies was against beginning in Cambridge for reasons of health and discipline. But she also wrote in a letter of 1868, that, given, "the string of feelings against us that we should stir up at Cambridge, just at the beginning . . . it will be pre-eminently necessary to conciliate."[54] By choosing a site away from Cambridge, in Hitchin and then in Girton, Davies ensured that the project would not be seen as ambitious and competitive; a quiet little house for ladies, rather than a daring college for women.

Constance Louisa Maynard, one of the earliest students, wrote of this issue in her memoir of college life, *Between College Terms*. She described how every student was aware of the unwritten rules of propriety and how vital it was to the success of the college to observe society's conventions of propriety and decorum. She pointed out that the pioneers crept "under the shelter of conventionality and [stayed] there as long as we could."[55]

In light of these concerns we can see the domestic vernacular used by Waterhouse at Girton as a further method of propaganda. To have blatantly imitated one of the men's colleges would have insulted and alienated many of Davies' supporters in the University, and infuriated those already against it. Such an appearance might have suggested to parents and critics an overriding ambition to imitate men, which promised not to produce better mothers, wives and teachers, but rather masculine women. Given the importance attached to appearance, association and propriety in the Victorian era, it is not surprising that the face presented by Girton was not laden with elements hearkening back to the ancient academic establishment, but rather used familiar motifs from women's understood environment, the home. While the traditional ingredients of a college, such as quadrangles, a library, and an entrance tower, were included in the early schemes of Girton, they were not dressed to imitate their predecessors. The 'Old English' style was applied to simple, and in some cases, institutional ranges, in order to distinguish Girton from its brothers.

52. Davies to Bodichon, B99, 12 June 1874, Girton College Archives.
53. Davies to Bodichon, B135, July 1875, Girton College Archives.
54. Davies to Bodichon, B17, 23 November, 1868, Girton College Archives.
55. C. L. Maynard, *Between College Terms* (London: James Nisbet, 1910), 190.

27. Chapel and Entrance, Girton College (by Waterhouse, 1900).

28. Hall and Cloister, Girton College (by Waterhouse, 1900).

Such vernacular elements had no connection with a collegiate tradition and thus could not easily be seen as a challenge to the male bastions of learning.

The next additions were built in 1900 and include the hall and chapel. From the start, Davies was firm in her desire to affiliate the college with the Church of England, again in keeping with the tradition of the men's colleges. However, the committee itself was divided on the issue, and Lady Stanley of Alderley, the benefactress of the library, was adamantly against building a chapel in her lifetime. After she died, Waterhouse and his son Paul, who had taken charge of much of the work by 1900, produced plans of a more Gothic and traditional nature. The chapel is of very

29. New Court, St. John's College, Cambridge (by Rickman and Hutchinson, 1825–31).

30. New Dining Hall, interior, Girton College (by Waterhouse, 1900). *Reproduced courtesy of Mistress and Fellows, Girton College, Cambridge.*

31. Woodlands Court, Girton College (by Waterhouse, 1900).

simple, red brick with terra-cotta dressing and a steep gabled roof. The interior is markedly plain and dark with the red brick lining the walls.

Another long wing extends north from the chapel and houses mostly lecture rooms on the ground floor, with more sets of rooms above. Two thirds of the way down this range is a cloistered passage which leads to the dining hall. This ensemble of cloister and hall is Gothic in style, and in the tradition of New Court at St. John's College, Cambridge, designed by Rickman and Hutchinson in 1825–31. The one-storey crenelated cloister encloses Cloisters Court and provides covered access to the new hall which, like the chapel, is made of red brick with terra cotta detailing. An interior view of the dining hall as it first appeared, shows a hammer beam roof with exposed beams rising up from the brick walls. The walls were originally of white plaster up to the base of the windows and have since been paneled. At last Emily Davies got her way, and a platform was included at one end on which the High Table stood.

The final courtyard was begun in 1900 and is known as Woodlands Court. It continued the architectural style and motifs of the earlier buildings, but the darker brick which was used and the orange terra cotta details, effect a harsher appearance. This courtyard was enclosed by Giles Gilbert Scott in the 1930s.

This last building campaign that comes within our discussion is evidence of a new confidence on the part of the college. It boldly asserted its collegiate status in undeniable architectural terms. Prior to 1900, to the casual observer, Girton might have appeared to be a very large house, roaming and picturesquely vast like Eaton Hall. A photograph taken before 1900 shows a large assemblage of gables, turrets and chimneys, a long but varied silhouette. The chapel, cloisters, and hall added elements directly taken borrowed from the collegiate tradition. The appearance of these additions is more stark and regular, both in outline and stylistically. By 1900, the women's college was an accepted fact which could not be ignored. Cambridge was not to grant full degrees to women until 1947, but their success, popularity and

32. Eaton Hall, Chester (by Waterhouse, 1870–82). From *The Builder* (11 December 1880), 695.

presence in the University was no longer to be questioned. While the venture at Girton began modestly, by 1900 the college had existed for thirty years, had established its own traditions and was confident in its future. Thus the additions of 1900 give architectural expression to a new and more assertive phase of Girton's history.

The domestic arrangement and order of the students' lives in Girton were advertised in careful terms which suggested an atmosphere that would be familiar to the young woman leaving home for the first time. As we have said earlier, the founders were very concerned that Girton appear respectable and proper. This meant that the women must be dressed modestly and be well behaved. They were to be chaperoned whenever they went into Cambridge, and parents were assured that their daughters would be carefully looked after in every way, with all the care of a good mother. The routine of the day included time for exercise and fresh air to counter fears of overwork from too much study. Everyone was required to attend dinner in hall and no one was allowed out after dark without specific permission. Tea, which was reportedly popular with the male lecturers out from Cambridge,[56] was brought around by servants at 4:00P.M. A tradition that prevailed at Girton and in the other women's colleges to follow, was the practice of having cocoa parties in the students' rooms after 10:00P.M. The women would invite their friends round and serve cocoa and cakes. This was a pleasant way to socialize and may have been encouraged as a deterrent from overwork. It was also seen as a substitute for the male undergraduates' tradition of "Wines."

The students' rooms were papered and painted to be charming and cozy. One article from 1897–98 described the lives of the students and praised the young women's bedrooms and studies. Each woman had:

her own little sanctum, her 'castle', where she can study in peace, and enjoy for the first time the delights of hospitality in her very own domain. Perhaps it is even the first opportunity of

56. E. A. B. Hodgetts, "Girton and Newnham Colleges," *Strand* (1893): 509.

33. Girton College (by Waterhouse, pre-1900). *Reproduced courtesy of Mistress and Fellows, Girton College, Cambridge.*

exercising her own taste in the arrangement of her surroundings. Most of the little Girton studies are gay with flowers, favorite pictures adorn the walls, favourite books fill the shelves . . . there is usually an easy chair or two for the owner or a friend.[57]

In articles such as the one just quoted, the women's dress is described as simple and modest, and their behavior circumspect. The reader is assured that they do not play billiards or smoke,[58] and that the life they lead is innocent, earnest and feminine.

The reality of the situation was somewhat different. The early students were reported to be rebellious, causing Davies considerable strain and worry by their behavior. When they were still at Hitchin, the students performed a play with some of the women taking male roles. This caused a furor among the committee, as it was feared that the public might hear that women were actually strutting around like men. Constance Maynard recalled another incident with one of the students who "was mentally condemned because . . . she wore an *ulster*, which at that time was a rare and sporting garment and confined to the sex which . . . is designated as 'the more worthy.'"[59] The key issue of concern for the students and committee was that the

57. A. Zimmern, "Women at the Universities," *Leisure Hour* (1897–98): 435.
58. Hodgetts, "Girton and Newnham Colleges," 508.
59. Maynard, *Between College Terms*, 189–90.

college venture should, as much as possible, go unnoticed by the community at large. No publicity was better than bad publicity.

But within the walls of Girton and between the students, the artifice of feminine domesticity was not so strong. In the early days the women called each other by their surnames, a habit borrowed from the male undergraduates. The pioneers believed themselves to be in alliance together against an oppressive society, and looked on their chance at higher education as a right to be granted. In her diaries from her days at Girton, Constance Maynard painted a picture of life at college as exciting and much freer than published accounts suggest. She does not mention being chaperoned everywhere, and her movements were relatively unrestrained. She was staunchly Evangelical, and was tormented by some of the agnostic and atheistic discussions that took place in college, especially around the writings of Darwin. That it was a tightly-knit community, devoted to women's progress is clear from one diary entry from November 1874: "Heard that Woodhead [a past student] is engaged to be married! She wrote a most humble note, in fear of Girton's anger."[60] Such a community of women isolated from University and town-life was almost defensively committed to the success of their venture, believing that through solidarity and single-minded determination they would prove themselves equal to the challenges of higher education.

Considering the history of Girton's early years under Davies' vision, it is little wonder that such isolationism existed, or that some feelings of betrayal may have arisen towards women who rejoined the male community. Davies was determined that her college curriculum should mirror the men's. There were to be no special examinations set up for women, because, she believed, they would automatically be considered to be of a lower standard to accommodate women's so called "weaker" brains. To her mind, and those on her committee, only by exact imitation was equality to be proved. This put her out of step with the other movement for women's education in Cambridge led by Henry Sidgwick, who had little faith in the existing system for men, and saw no sense in women preparing for out-of-date examinations. He and his supporters sought to offer lectures and exams for women which would be more suited to their needs and interests. It was not so much that he did not consider women able to perform at a similar level as men, but that they were unprepared, and sometimes unwilling or unable to complete the full blown course of study.

We shall look closely at the efforts of Sidgwick and the emergence of Newnham College in the next chapter. Suffice it to say here that his work was a bane to Emily Davies' existence. Indeed at one point in her correspondence she wrote to Sidgwick that he was the "serpent that was eating out her vitals."[61] Such strong language is indicative of the tension between the two ventures into women's education taking place concurrently in Cambridge in the early 1870s. Davies could not accept another scheme that vied with her own. In her mind, Newnham was merely a dressing put over the wound, an insufficient remedy to a very grave problem.

Davies' letters to Bodichon are full of disparaging comments about the work at Newnham. As late as 1881, Davies was complaining of having to discuss plans for a shared physiology lab with the Newnham Committee, which she described as a quite unpleasant meeting. She goes on to recount the impressions of a Miss Scott (a Girton student) who had visited Newnham. Their routine was regarded suspiciously

60. Maynard, Diaries, 1872–75, CLM/MSS/D: week of 15 November 1874, Queen Mary and Westfield College Archives.

61. A letter from H. Sidgwick to F. Meyers written between May and June 1871, in Mrs. Eleanor Sidgwick and Arthur Sidgwick, *Henry Sidgwick, A Memoir* (London: Macmillan, 1906), 246–47.

as too protective and communal, with inadequate time for study. Davies concluded her letter:

The opinion at Girton of these arrangements was that they were 'horrid'. *Beatrice Taylor, who had been visiting her friend Miss Winkworth at Newnham, reported herself much disappointed. The room was* very *small, and crowded with furniture. From the accounts, the rooms must be much less comfortable than ours. Girton was looking very nice.*[62]

Such a sense of competition is unusual in the development of the other colleges for women, and served to set Girton further apart. It began with the most determined academic ambitions and would accept nothing less than the standards set for male undergraduates. For the first thirty years of its existence, Girton stood in relative isolation, both figuratively and literally, from the mainstream movement for women's education. With Davies in charge either as mistress or behind the scenes, there was little or no co-operation with the other fledgling women's colleges.

Yet despite its determination to follow the male course of study and adopt certain Oxbridge traditions, the overall picture which Girton and Davies tried to present was not one of alternative, or masculine bluestockings. Public appearance and behavior were carefully monitored. Davies kept apart from the suffrage movement so as not to associate the college with the unpopular and aggressive suffragette. Special considerations for women's health and routine were always made. As we have seen, these concessions to women's health and their traditional role in society were made in the architecture of Girton. Both in planning and stylistic terms, Girton avoided associating too closely with the male examples specifically because women's understood strengths and weaknesses and their future roles in society, were still considered different from men's. While Girton College sought equality on an intellectual level, it consciously hid behind a domestic facade of propriety. How the students disported themselves behind the scenes might have shocked much of society. But a modest and ladylike demeanor and a reassuring domesticity were the fundamental means at Girton's disposal which helped the pioneers to achieve their ambitious academic ends.

62. Davies to Bodichon, B199, 14 May 1881, Girton College Archives.

2 ON DIFFERENT TERMS

Newnham College

Newnham was in those days outside, but not far outside, Cambridge University proper. It had the proportions and atmosphere, with its Dutch red-brick gables, its corridors, landings, solid banisters, and mansarded attics, of a comfortable country house.
A. S. Byatt, *Still Life*, 1985[1]

WHERE EMILY DAVIES' SCHEME FOR A COLLEGE FOR WOMEN BEGAN WITH A determined effort to realize a defined goal, Newnham College evolved in slow and tentative steps, with no grand master plan or ambition to emulate the Oxbridge tradition. The college is made up of individual units; each building is a charming essay in red-brick with white trim, connected to one another by enclosed passages. Built by Basil Champneys in the years between 1875 and 1910, Newnham is important to the study of women's colleges, not only because of the unified and picturesque face it presents, but also because its intimate and small scale set a precedent for some of the women's colleges which followed.

One of Newnham's roots can be traced back to the figure of Miss Anne Jemima Clough. She was the quiet and rather timid sister of the poet, Arthur Clough, whose work, though largely forgotten now, was highly regarded in the literary circles of his day. While Miss Clough did not receive much in the way of formal education, she was very close to her brother and learned as much as she could from him. She was an unmarried woman, and she followed one of the few paths offered to single women, opening up her house as a school between the years of 1852-62 while she lived in Ambleside with her mother. By 1861 she had three boarders and twenty day students. With the death of her mother in 1860 and of her brother Arthur the following year, as well as the inheritance of a small independent income left to her in 1862, Miss Clough was, in a sense, left to her own devices. On various trips to London, she had mingled with the "Ladies of Langham Place," had written several papers for the Social Science Association and had attended meetings of the Kensington Society. Contact with the ideas prevailing in these circles stimulated her to greater action in the field of female education, with which she was already familiar.

In 1866 she wrote an article for *Macmillan's Magazine* in which she complained of the lack of worthwhile education available to girls and offered ideas for improvement. Some of these were realized in the establishment of the North England Council for the Promotion of the Higher Education of Women, founded in 1867 in Liverpool. This was established to co-ordinate a series of lectures for women in the cities in the north of England. These were organized by Miss Clough with the help and encouragement of Mrs. Josephine Butler (see appendix). In 1866 she and Miss Clough established a series of lectures for women on astronomy given by James Stuart, a young Cambridge don, in Liverpool, Manchester, Leeds and Sheffield. The success of these lectures led to the formal establishment of the North England Council, whose members included Mr. James Bryce, head of the Schools Inquiry Commission, Mr.

1. A. S. Byatt, *Still Life* (New York: Collier Books, 1985), 118.

Butler, the President of Liverpool College, and Thomas Markby, who was then secretary of the Cambridge Local Examinations and was later to play a role on the Newnham committee. The lectures were enthusiastically attended and rapidly spread around the north of England.

The popularity of the lectures prompted the organizers to look for some form of final examinations with which to conclude the series. As discussed in the previous chapter, there was very little in the way of formal education for women in the 1860s, and it was this void that Emily Davies so successfully filled at Girton. But working concurrently (if not in concert) with Girton the North England Council for the Promotion of the Higher Education of Women, with Miss Clough and Mrs. Butler in charge, looked to Cambridge University for a series of examinations which would cater to the lecture series being offered, but which would not so closely mirror the examinations for men. For the scheme's proponents such examinations offered women a chance to prove their knowledge, but they were arranged so as to take into account the great disadvantages under which women began their studies. The advocates did not expect the female students to perform on par with men whose education had, from the start, been considerably more thorough.

Working for this scheme in Cambridge was a young and enthusiastic don, Henry Sidgwick. While not involved at the very start of the discussions, by 1867 he could write to his sister, Mary Benson:

I am involved in a project for improving female education: by providing examinations for governesses—an endeavour is being made to form a joint board, consisting of members of the two universities, for the purpose. The plan is at present vague; but I think it may be likely to come to something good.[2]

In the same letter he mentions the work of the North England Council for the Promotion of the Higher Education of Women. It is no surprise that he was aware of Miss Clough's work in the North. He had been friends with the poet Arthur Clough, and kept in contact with Clough's widow through letters and visits in London. It was through these visits that he first met Miss Clough.

Sidgwick was an affable and easy-going character who was remembered for his sense of humor and verbosity despite a stutter. In his letters he often complained that he had not accomplished enough, but by the end of his life he had written extensively on Moral Science, was in the forefront of psychical research with his wife, and had faithfully helped to nurture one of the earliest colleges for women in the country. His less aggressive approach towards women's education infuriated Emily Davies, but her anxieties never seemed to ruffle him. Of his early interest in women's education he wrote again to his sister:

Did you see my letter in the Spectator . . . defending our (Cambridge) scheme for women's examinations[?] A friend told me with an air of surprise that he thought it was very sensible. Common sense is not supposed to be my forte: but the fact is on this question I feel so sure that all the good arguments are on our side that I am inclined to be very moderate . . .

We (the reformers) hold the winning cards: if we play quietly we shall get the game without any fuss.[3]

2. Henry Sidgwick to Mrs. Mary Benson, 26, 13 November 1867, Sidgwick Letters, Trinity College Archives, Trinity College, Cambridge.
3. Sidgwick to Mary Benson, 20, 27 January 1868, Trinity College Archives.

This last statement is indicative of both his and Miss Clough's attitude towards women's education. They were convinced of the logic and necessity of women's higher education, but neither was quite certain what form it should take. Miss Clough wanted at all costs to avoid aggressive and masculine behavior, but to offer women a chance to better their condition and their minds. Sidgwick, amongst many others in the Cambridge community, was dissatisfied with the existing structure of education in the universities, and wanted to avoid passing on an outdated and archaic system of examinations to young women. Similarly, he was not at all sure what academic standards women could attain and regarded the whole scheme as something to be gently worked through, uncertain of where it might lead.

By 1869, Cambridge itself was offering a course of lectures to women from the town, and the Cambridge Higher Local Examinations had been instituted. Meanwhile, the first five students had begun their course of study in Hitchin. Any attempts to combine the two efforts were thwarted on ideological, and subsequently, personal grounds. Where Davies wanted her students to pass every exam offered to the men, Sidgwick wanted a new examination, specially suited to women; Davies wanted her college associated with the Church of England, and Sidgwick, who ran in the new circles of intelligentsia and rebelled against the strict dogma of the past thirty years, wanted a secular and more liberal educational system implemented for women. So the two schemes evolved side by side, but it was to be many years before relations were warm and cooperative.

The lectures for women in Cambridge were a huge success, and were supported by such notables as the Reverend F. D. Maurice, founder of Queen's College, as well as many respectable members of the University who worked on the general committee for the Association for the Higher Education of Women. These men included the Professors Adams and Cayley, Mr. Jackson, Mr. Jebb, and Alfred Marshall, professor of economics, who would later marry one of Newnham's earliest students, Mary Paley. The lectures were held in a small garden building behind the house of a Mr. Clay, who lent the room free of charge. In the early stages, Sidgwick and Mrs. Millicent Fawcett, wife of the blind professor of Political Economy, and sister to Elizabeth Garrett Anderson, had discussed the need for a house for students outside Cambridge, but no action was taken on that matter until the need arose.

It was not long until accommodation was in demand from students not from Cambridge who wanted to attend the lectures. Sidgwick undertook to find a house for students and wrote to Miss Clough early in 1871 asking her to be the mistress of the early students. She was busy with her work in Liverpool but consented to come in the Autumn of 1871. During the summer holidays, Sidgwick tried his hand at domestic matters, hunting about for linen, plate and furnishings, often using his own money, to ready 74 Regent Street for the first five students' arrival. This house was small and not very commodious for five young, lively women. Miss Clough was reported as being frustratingly over-protective, and in such small quarters exerted a stifling influence over the women. Yet her motherly ways were what convinced at least one parent to allow his daughter to come to Cambridge. Mary Paley won a scholarship to come to Cambridge and be one of the first five to live with Miss Clough. But it was not until her father, Mr. Paley, had met Miss Clough and been reassured by her lady-like manner and cautious concern for the students that he gave his consent.[4]

4. Mary P. Marshall, *What I Remember* (Cambridge: Cambridge University Press, 1947), 10.

Expenses were kept to an absolute minimum and the students themselves had many of the domestic responsibilities. There was little formal structure in the women's lives, but their actions were restricted. Sidgwick had several talks with the women, explaining to them the necessity of circumspect behavior. The following year saw them settled much more comfortably in Merton Hall, an old house with a big garden in the back. This could accommodate more students, and gave them ample room and some privacy. Each of the now fourteen students had a room of her own and she was free to roam in the spacious garden and orchard. Also at this time a formal set of rules was drawn up regarding chaperonage, hours of work, religious attendance and so forth. A Committee of Ladies was formed which was intended to help Miss Clough administer these rules and was made up of women from the Cambridge community such as Miss E. Bonham Carter, Miss Julia Kennedy and Mrs. Peile. This eased tensions between Miss Clough and the students by giving everyone clear guidelines to follow.

As the year progressed, more students applied and additional space was needed. Another boarding house was taken on Trumpington Street to accommodate the overflow, but by 1873 the landlord of Merton Hall required the property again, and two adjoining houses were taken on Bateman Street. This yearly migration from house to house was proving unsatisfactory, and talk was begun about building a house for the students. No one on the committee was overly enthusiastic about making such a long term investment in a scheme that had no definitive goal and whose future was so uncertain. But by 1873 the decision had been reached and a company, which was to become the Newnham Hall Company, had been formed to raise money for a hall of residence for women students in Cambridge. Shares were offered nationwide, and the response was hearty and encouraging. Miss Mary Ewart began by offering £1,000, and her subscription was quickly followed by more money, both from those actively involved in the scheme like Henry Sidgwick and Dr. and Mrs. Peile, as well as many others from the north of England who were familiar with Miss Clough and her work there.

The Company chose a site on land owned by St. John's College, Cambridge, in the small neighboring hamlet of Newnham (hence the company's name). This has since been absorbed by Cambridge itself, but at the time was of a rural character, with fields and orchards, but within easy walking distance for the lecturers. Correspondence began in 1873 between the Bursar of St. John's, the Reverend George J. Reyner, and Miss Clough, regarding an appropriate site. In August 1873, Miss Clough wrote to the Bursar inquiring about land on which to build a house for the women students.[5] This is of interest as it clearly suggests that the Association intended to build a boarding house, in no sense abandoning the domestic environment from which the women came. This idea is given further confirmation in a letter of 24 November, 1873, in which Dr. Reyner outlined the terms on which a lease of land to the Association of Higher Education of Women would be possible. The college agreed to grant two acres, along a small footpath in Newnham, near Professor Liveing's house, for a lease of ninety-nine years. The Association was not to spend more than £5,000 on the building. Furthermore,

These Buildings are to be at [sic] the nature of a Dwelling House; of the style and quality of

5. A. J. Clough to Dr. George Reyner, 7 August 1873, Estate Papers, Newnham College, St. John's College Archives, St. John's College, Cambridge.

a Gentleman's House: the details of which are to be settled hereafter more precisely in conference with the College or its Surveyor: and are to be approved by the college [St. John's].[6]

Upon receiving this letter, Miss Clough and her committee expressed concern over the college's requirement that the building be "of the style and quality of a Gentleman's house."[7] To her queries, Dr. Reyner responded:

I cannot say anything more definite than that the buildings to be erected ought to constitute something not unlikely to be let as a Gentleman's House or two Gentlemen's Houses in the event of its being discontinued to be used for the purpose which it is at present intended.[8]

This is a significant requirement in the building history of Newnham College. Neither Sidgwick, Miss Clough nor the Association were at all sure into what form the lecture series for women would evolve. While Girton grew nearby under the eager determination of Emily Davies, those in charge in this case had no desire to compete with her on her terms, much less compete with the male undergraduates. Yet the success of the lectures meant that more ambitious steps had to be taken to accommodate the many women clamoring for a higher education. Their decision to build was made reluctantly and did not inspire tremendous confidence in the scheme on the part of the St. John's College committee. Both Sidgwick and Miss Clough may have shared the Bursar's skepticism to some extent. That is not to say that they were not fully committed to the cause of women's higher education. But neither were they at all certain what form such an education would take, and they saw the process in a more organic and flexible way than those on Girton's committee.

The Bursar at St. John's was also not convinced that this experiment in housing women for educational purposes was destined to succeed, and the college wanted to be certain that they were not left with an unusable white elephant if or when women's enthusiasm for higher education waned. The requirement laid down by St. John's, which stipulated the domestic nature of Newnham's first building, set an architectural precedent at Newnham and in subsequent colleges.

A young architect named Basil Champneys was called in to design the house. He had been an undergraduate at Trinity College in Cambridge, where he had known Sidgwick. In 1873, he was just beginning his architectural career. He had carried out his articles under John Prichard of Llandaff, who worked primarily in the Gothic style. Champneys' first commission was for a church, St. Luke's, Kentish Town, which he designed in 1869. This was a Gothic Revival church with elegant tracery and severe crenelation on the towers.

Champneys was a thoughtful, more ideological architect than Alfred Waterhouse. He was interested in poetry and ideas, and it was not long before he became involved in the artistic circles of the Pre-Raphaelites, probably through his friend the art critic and historian Sidney Colvin.[9] It was within this movement that the Gothic Revival was being challenged by artists and architects reacting against the high moral tone and the pedantic religiosity of the previous thirty years. Just as Shaw and Nesfield had gone off sketching old English vernacular farmhouses in Kent, in 1874 Champneys published *A Quiet Corner of England*, an illustrated tribute to the unspoilt and subtle landscape and architecture of the area around Winchelsea, Rye and the

6. Dr. G. Reyner to A. J. Clough, 24 November 1873, Estate Papers, Newnham College, St. John's College Archives.
7. A. J. Clough to Dr. Reyner, 4 December 1873, Estate Papers, Newnham College, St. John's College Archives.
8. Dr. G. Reyner to Miss A. J. Clough, 16 December 1873, Estate Papers, Newnham College, St. John's College Archives.
9. Mark Girouard, *Sweetness and Light* (New Haven: Yale University Press, 1977), 49.

Romney Marshes. Like Shaw and Nesfield he was advocating a return to a simpler, native English architecture such as could be found in the seventeenth and eighteenth centuries.

It was at this same time in the early 1870s that Champneys was commissioned to build the first house for Newnham College. That he was to build a house is clear from the restrictions set down by St. John's. As the correspondence over the site continued, the stretch of land requested by Champneys was enlarged to two and a half acres and the cost of building raised to £5,500. At a meeting on 25 February, 1874, further stipulations were decided by the building committee. The first was that the house face the south, parallel to the existing footpath, for reasons which Miss Clough explained to Dr. Reyner: "This would give a better aspect to a larger number of the rooms which will be an important point for the health of the future inmates."[10]

Further requirements included one sitting room and a bedroom for the Principal; public rooms including a dining room 36' × 18', a sitting room 20' × 18' and two more sitting rooms half this size; and study/bedrooms which were to be 14' × 12'. The building committee also concluded that "through passages are indispensable on the upper floors" and "that the same arrangement is desirable on the lower floor."[11] To this last request Champneys objected to Miss Mary Ewart (who was an active member of the building committee and had a strong interest in architecture herself),[12] when he wrote:

There can be through passages [a corridor running the length of the building] *on the upper floors by a little sacrifice of accommodation and these passages can be made any width — but to make through passages on the ground floor would destroy the dining hall, and there would be no way of arranging for it except to make it an entirely independent building which would be I think an awkward and certainly very costly arrangement.*[13]

The through passages were considered vital to the planning of the building. Miss Clough was recorded as saying that she liked through corridors because they offered light at both ends of the passages and provided pleasant views out into the gardens and fields.[14] In the first floorplans Champneys drew up, bedrooms were placed at the end of each corridor, thus cutting off the sunlight and views which Miss Clough so desired. As built, however, the corridors on the upper floors are lit at both ends by windows, suggesting that the plans were changed at the building committee's request. These early plans were labeled Merton Hall, in reference to the college's previous lodgings. As time went on the corridors became the basis for the social network of Newnham, and in personal recollections and novels based on Newnham, a woman's corridor was her social lifeline. New students were immediately greeted by their neighbors on the corridor, and as friendships were formed students would request to be placed near their friends along the same passage. Thus the cliques that formed were often based around the residents of each corridor.[15]

The passages in Champneys' first building, which is now called Old Hall, run down the center of the building, providing the spines off which all the rooms open. This "double loaded corridor" system differed from that at Girton where the rooms were kept on one side of the building, and the corridors stretched down the other.[16] While Waterhouse's solution afforded lighter, more open corridors, the central

10. A. J. Clough to Dr. Reyner, 3 March 1874, Estate Papers, Newnham College, St. John's College Archives.
11. Minutes of the Building Committee, 1874–80, 25 February 1874, Meeting in Merton Hall: Newnham College Archives, Newnham College, Cambridge.
12. Miss Ewart was well acquainted with the Pre-Raphaelite circle herself and commissioned Phillip Webb to build her own house.
13. Basil Champneys to Mary Ewart, 9 March, 1874, Building Box 1874–1910, Newnham College Archives.
14. B. A. Clough, *A Memoir of Anne Jemima Clough* (London: Edward Arnold, 1897), 205.
15. Such social organization is described in the various novels about life in a women's college such as Alice Stronach, *A Newnham Friendship* (London: Blackie, 1901) or L. T. Meade, *Sweet Girl Graduate* (London: Cassell, 1891) or Meade, *The Girls of Merton College.* (London: W. R. Chambers, 1911).
16. Dr. Paul Turner mentions this system in reference to Benjamin Latrobe's work on college planning in America in the early nineteenth century. Latrobe rejected the 'double loaded corridor' for reasons of noise, darkness and aspect. While there is no evidence that his ideas had any impact on English women's colleges, it is worth pointing out that such planning concerns were shared across the Atlantic. See P. V. Turner, *Campus: An American Planning Tradition*, revised ed. (Cambridge, Mass.: MIT Press, 1990), 67.

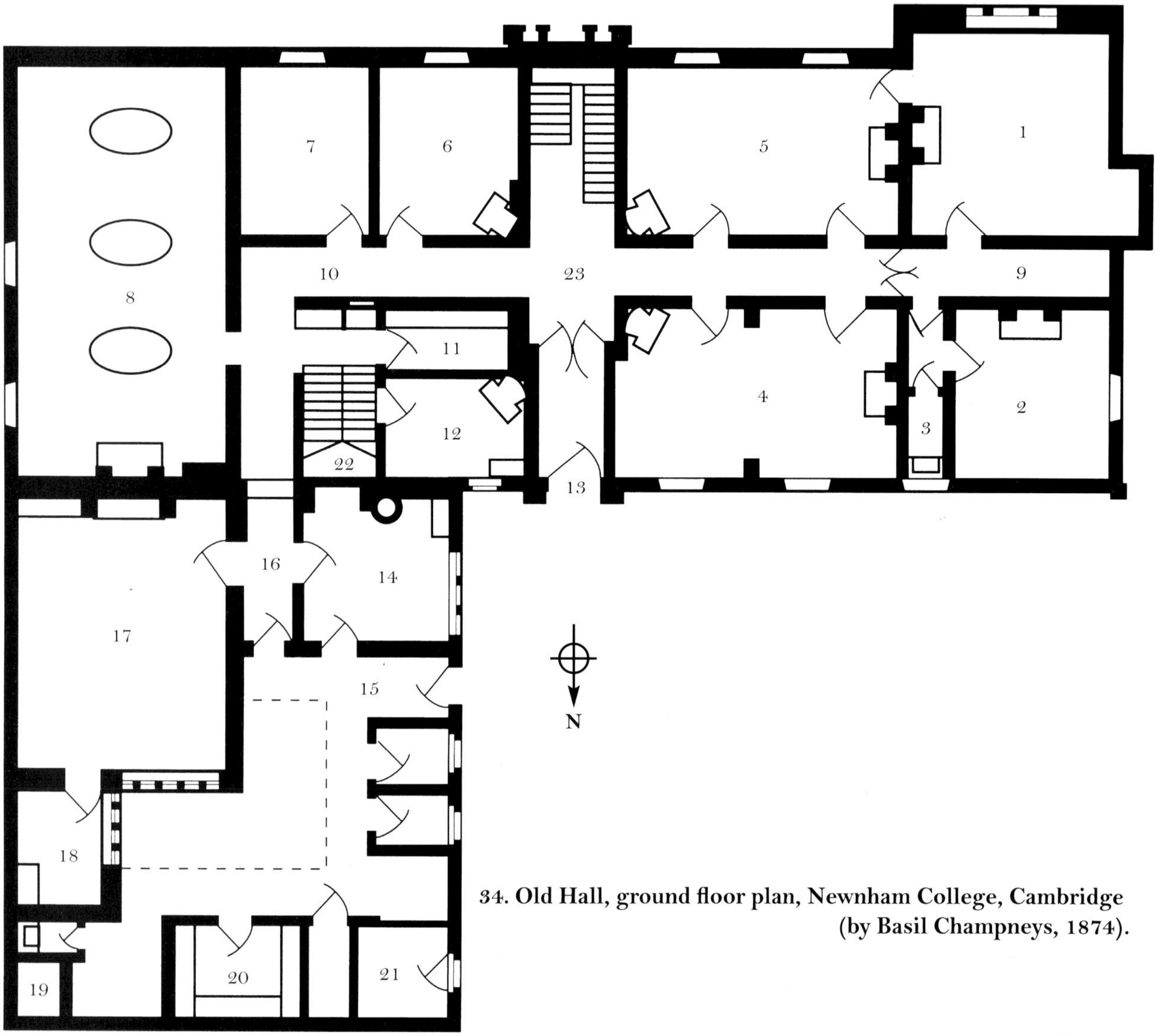

34. Old Hall, ground floor plan, Newnham College, Cambridge (by Basil Champneys, 1874).

1. principal's room
2. principal's bedroom
3. watercloset
4. lecture room
5. lecture room
6. lecture room
7. housekeeper's room
8. dining room
9. principal's entrance
10. passage
11. stores
12. pantry
13. entrance
14. back kitchen
15. tradesman's entrance
16. servant's passage
17. kitchen
18. scullery
19. dust
20. boot & knives
21. coals
22. back stairs
23. principal stairs

system at Newnham offered greater intimacy, and meant that the passages in each house were not as long and institutional as many are at Girton.

Entry into Old Hall was originally through the south front, into a hall from which the main staircase rises. Opposite the main entry is a luggage door. The principal rooms on the ground floor included three rooms labeled lecture rooms on the plan but which became the sitting rooms required by the committee in their meeting in

35. Old Hall, Newnham College (by Champneys, 1875). *Reproduced courtesy of Principal and Fellows, Newnham College, Cambridge.*

February 1874. The principal had a set of rooms which faced each other on the west end of the building. At the other end, the corridor terminates in the dining room. In the plan, three oval dining tables were drawn in pencil suggesting the eating arrangement. These rounded tables facilitated the wish on the part of the Newnham committee that dining was to be an intimate and familial affair. As opposed to the long rectangular tables in traditional collegiate halls, the oval shape of the tables were conducive to a more intimate seating arrangement, and meant that more diners could see each other and carry on communal conversations during their meals.

Also in pencil on the plan were three bay windows added on the east end in 1893 to accommodate more students at three more tables. The back of the house, as at Girton, comprised a servants' wing of only one storey which included the kitchen, larder, tradesman's entrance, scullery, rooms for boots, knives and coals, a small yard, and a larder for cooked and raw meat. There is also a servants' passage which led to the back stairs and opened onto the dining room. The housekeeper had a room of her own beside the dining room.

The next two floors consisted of bedrooms for the students, totaling twenty-six in all, each with its own fireplace. As at Girton, the students were provided with baths on each floor, an advance in civilized, personal hygiene that was missing at the men's colleges. The attic storey, in typical domestic fashion, was for the servants. This was reached by the back stair only and included five bedrooms and some lumber closets. The overall plan is basically symmetrical and compact, yet not as condensed as many of Champneys' houses which tended to be more square in plan. His other houses were, of course, for single families, and did not require accommodation for twenty-six young women. But the basic accouterments of the house and kitchens reflect the Victorian trend in domestic house design. There is no attempt to recreate a traditional collegiate environment with a great hall, library, and chapel, and obviously, if both the committee and St. John's envisioned a house, the staircase system employed at the men's colleges had little relevance for Champneys.

36. Kew Palace, Kew Gardens, Richmond-upon-Thames (by Samuel Fortrey, 1631). *Crown Copyright. Historic Royal Palaces.*

Champneys designed Old Hall in what is commonly called the 'Queen Anne' style. It is a tall house with dramatic curving gables at each end and a smaller one in the center above the doorway. It is symmetrical, with each end pulled out slightly from the main block, and the corners defined by brick quoins. Modified Palladian windows line up in the center, which is also pulled out and articulated by brick quoining. Massive chimney stacks rise above the gently sloping roof which is softened by the white balustrade and vigorous, cheerful segmental dormer windows. Above the main doorway rests a curving open pediment of cut or moulded brick. The whole is an exuberant essay in red brick and white trim, softened by curves, half-circles and ovals in the window frames. In outline and material, it closely resembles the Palace at Kew of 1631, which was often referred to as a source of inspiration for 'Queen Anne' architects, who appreciated its simple charm, picturesque variety, and modified classicism. Champneys' first work at Newnham was an early example of domestic 'Queen Anne' and as such is an important part of a growing movement which began in the early 1870s and flourished, particularly in domestic work, until the end of the century. Champneys continued to build in the 'Queen Anne' style at Newnham until the First World War. Consequently, it is necessary to examine the style in some detail in order to understand its origins, wider associations and relevance for Newnham College.

As mentioned earlier, Champneys ran on the periphery of the artistic Pre-Raphaelite circles. Figures in the movement included the well known Dante Gabriel Rossetti, William Morris, Philip Webb, Walter Pater, Matthew Arnold, Richard Norman Shaw and E. W. Nesfield, as well as many lesser known artists, architects and thinkers, such as J. J. Stevenson, E. R. Robson, Warrington Taylor, and Rhoda and Agnes Garrett. In the 1860s, Webb began to borrow vernacular elements from the seventeenth and eighteenth centuries such as sash windows, window aprons and cut or moulded brick which he combined with Gothic elements in his own individualistic way. As discussed in the previous chapter, Shaw and Nesfield had also begun to seek out a new, more vernacular language for domestic architecture, which they first found in the 'Old English' style. Increasingly, however, their work began to adopt characteristics from the late seventeenth and early eighteenth centuries, with the use of simple red brick with white sash windows, large gables, either curved or straight, certain Classical elements such as pilasters, and capitals used informally, and charming details made with cut brick or pargeting. Proponents of the style sometimes called it the 'free classic' style because of its easy interpretation of classicism in combination with a more Gothic and picturesque skyline.

The style was bound up in a new artistic attitude that valued art and beauty for their own sake rather than a moral and didactic art laden with religious sentiment. Those involved in what became the Aesthetic Movement wanted to discard the heavy, dark and muscular Gothic of their predecessors and replace it with an art and architecture that embodied "sweetness and light" a term made famous by Matthew Arnold. Mark Girouard, in his book on the subject, described it thus: "Sweetness would dissolve the ugliness of their houses and cities, light would smooth away their intolerance and narrow-mindedness."[17] There was a reaction against the confines of the Gothic Revival and a celebration of many different styles, including details from the French Renaissance, Classical Greece, and Japan. In interior design this reaction was manifested in bright, sunny rooms, often hung with Morris paper, and furnished with delicate furniture inspired by the eighteenth century. It was with the 'Queen Anne' style that blue and white china vases and plates became popular, and in which the sunflower was picked up as a motif, to be used over and over again in 'Queen Anne' houses and at Newnham for the next thirty years

Shaw was one of the first to employ the full-blown style in his New Zealand Chambers of 1871 (now demolished). In the same year, J. J. Stevenson built a house for himself called the Red House (now demolished). Both buildings combined all the elements which were to characterize the 'Queen Anne' style. Shaw's work for the New Zealand Chambers created an uproar with its unorthodox use of traditional architectural elements. The building was dominated by graceful oriels of small paned glass and elaborate decorative pargeting panels between floors. Pargeting was a technique of exterior plastering in molded designs that was generally found in half-timbered, vernacular architecture. While certain aspects in Shaw's work were borrowed from a Classical vocabulary, such as the pediments and engaged piers, the profusion of details which cover most wall surfaces is too fanciful and delicate to be called either Classical or Gothic. Stevenson's house was equally unrelated to either style in particular. While he adopted an asymmetry from the Gothic, and certain motifs from the Classical such as volutes and pediments, his treatment of them as well as his use of Dutch gables, and the sunflower motif in the ironwork, all combined into a fresh and novel design.

Stevenson was one of the most vocal proponents of the 'Queen Anne' style and defended it in several articles, as well as in his book *House Architecture.* In an article published in *The Architect* of 1874, Stevenson explained the reaction of architects like himself, who, trained in the Gothic camp, had looked away from the Middle Ages for their inspiration:

17. Girouard, *Sweetness and Light,* 4.

37. New Zealand Chambers (by Richard Norman Shaw, 1871). *Building News* (5 September 1873). *British Architectural Library, RIBA, London.*

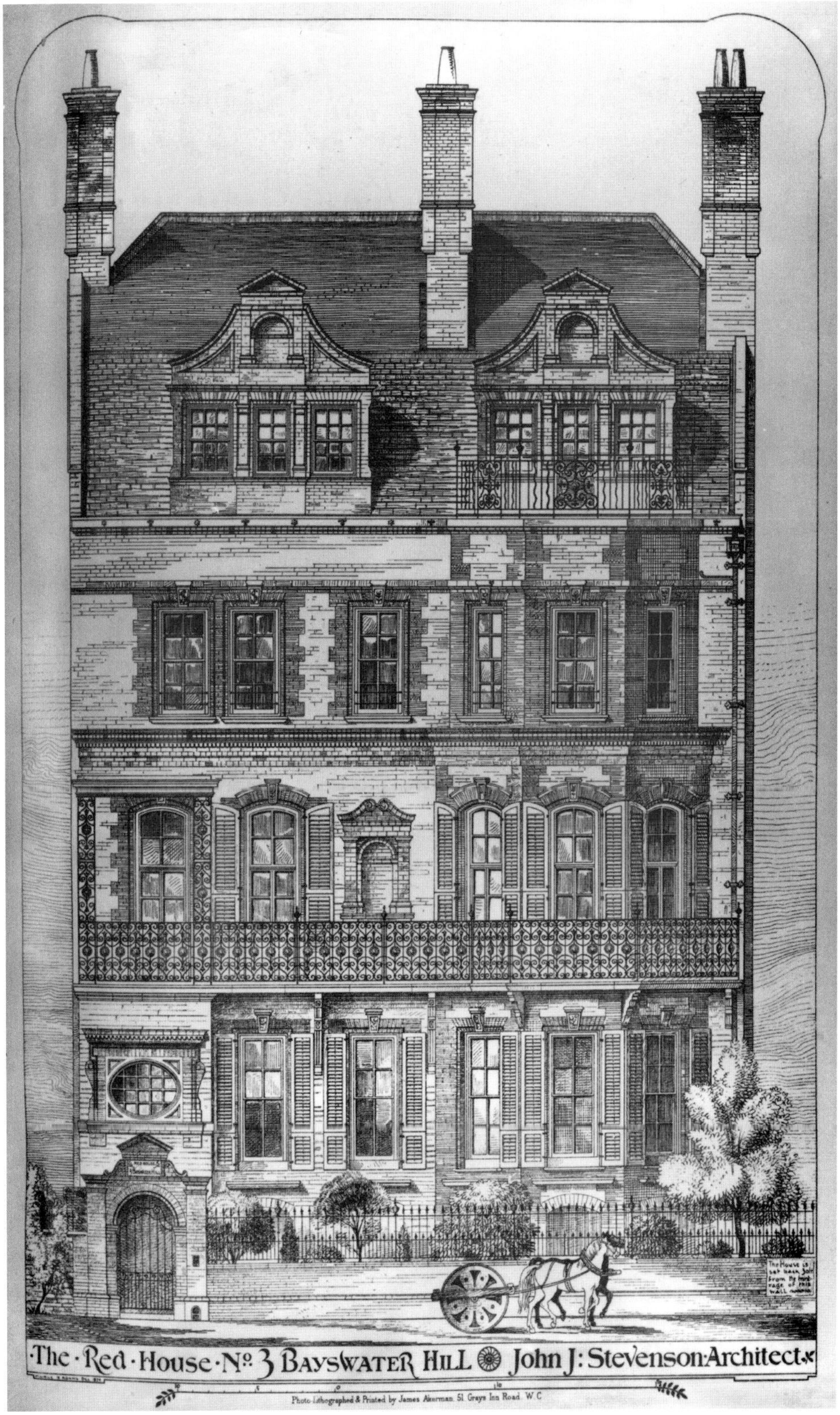

38. Red House (by J. J. Stevenson, 1871–73). *Building News* (18 September 1874). *Reproduced courtesy of the Trustees of the Boston Public Library.*

> *In England this reaction to Middle Age ideas has strongly influenced the more imaginative minds; since the time of Sir Walter Scott their religion, poetry and art have been Medieval. It was a natural and living movement, and for this very reason subject to the law of all living things, change, growth and development. The feeling grew that there are elements of modern life which not Middle Age chivalry nor asceticism, nor Gothic architecture, were fitted to satisfy. The naturalism and emotionalism, the absence of restraint and conventionality, and also of refinement, began to pall, and men turned, . . . to the classic conception of life, glorying in full, healthy, natural outcome, yet moving in measured rhythm, and to the art which is the manifestation and expression of such life.*[18]

Stevenson continued in this essay and the others which followed to praise the 'Queen Anne' as a stylistic solution for the domestic house. While claiming that he and architects like him, if faced with a commission for a church, would still employ the Gothic, he argued that an alternative was needed for domestic buildings. The 'Queen Anne' style was humble, not laden with religious associations or derived from a Greek temple. Rather it was a modest and English vernacular style. The domestic house, he declared, did not require "grandeur or sublimity" and "to express our domestic life, it should be more pleasing than impressive, more beautiful than grand, characterised by refinement rather than by state."[19]

Champneys shared Stevenson's opinions about Gothic and 'Queen Anne'. In various articles he looked back over the search in the 1860s and early 1870s for a domestic architecture more suited to the needs of modern man. While he too advocated Gothic for church architecture, he argued that: "As a style suitable to the ordinary dwelling house, Gothic may be said to have been tried in the balance and found wanting, though many have attempted its adaptation to modern ends with various degrees of ability."[20] He praised the architecture of the eighteenth century for its charm and simplicity, and believed that it more closely related to life at the end of the nineteenth century than did the style of the Middle Ages. That Champneys, Stevenson, Shaw and others, found a recipe for the domestic house offering charm, originality, and comfort, is clear from the popularity among the 'artistic' middle classes, of the new 'Queen Anne' suburbs, such as Bedford Park in west London.

The 'Queen Anne' style was vehemently opposed by the staunch Gothicists of the previous generation. In 1873, William White blasted the movement in an article published in *The Architect.* Where Stevenson and Champneys defended the style for its "'Englishness", White saw it as an application of corrupt French draftsmanship, which excelled at picturesque ornament but falsified principles of construction. He considered Shaw's New Zealand Chambers a sad example of "rhyme without sense or reason."[21] Over G. F. Bodley's London School Boards Offices, he worried that the nation was descending into an enjoyment of the "burlesque" with their acceptance of meaningless and false ornament, such as swags, pilasters and volutes. Hugh Stannus accepted the style if it suited someone's taste, but he warned against trying to make it more than it was. Students should only study an architecture of logic and proportion and function. Therefore to make a study of the 'Queen Anne' which was "admitted, even by its upholders, to be an unformed and corrupt style," would, he feared, "become ludicrous."[22]

In 1872, Bodley presented the public with the Office of the Board Schools in a

18. J. J. Stevenson," On the Recent Reaction of Taste in English Architecture," *The Architect* 11 (20 June 1874) (supplement): 9.
19. J. J. Stevenson, *House Architecture* (London: Macmillan, 1880), 1: 69.
20. B. Champneys, "The Architecture of Queen Victoria's Reign," *Art Journal* 39 (June 1887): 208.
21. William White, "The Dolly Varden Rediviva," *The Architect* 10 (13 and 20 September 1873): 128.
22. Hugh Stannus, "The Queen Anne Style," *The Builder* (27 March 1875): 285.

39. Board School, Eel Brook Common, Harwood Road, Fulham (by Champneys, 1872). *The Builder* (18 October 1873). *Reproduced courtesy of the Trustees of the Boston Public Library.*

'Queen Anne' style and shocked many who expected a more formal treatment for such a large public building. Examples of the style were also seen in designs the early London Board Schools. The Board Schools were the result of the Education Act of 1870 and were an attempt to bring basic levels of education to the poorer classes in London. They were part of a social philanthropic movement to educate the lower classes and improve their lives, and were intended to be havens of "sweetness and light" in the midst of grim urban surroundings.

In the early 1870s there was debate as to what sort of face the Board Schools should present to the public. The first few designs were in the Gothic style, but this proved controversial because of the association of Gothic with the Church of England. Champneys was one of the first to submit designs for a school in the 'Queen Anne' style. His design in 1872 for a Board School was not accepted but was praised as being both very English and very school-like.[23] Again in 1872 he submitted a design for the Hardwood Road School in Fulham which had "red brick and white sash windows, large chimney stacks, and Flemish gables — features which were to become hallmarks of the "London School Board" style."[24] This was one of the first Board Schools to be built in the 'Queen Anne' style.

The architects J. J. Stevenson and E. R. Robson shared a practice in the early 1870s and designed some of the earliest of the London Board Schools. Eventually,

23. Deborah Weiner, "The Institution of Popular Education: Architectural Form and Social Policy in the London Board Schools, 1870–1904," (Ph.D. dissertation: Princeton University, 1984), 105.
24. Ibid.

Robson took over as chief architect and established a type still recognized in the streets of London today. Like Champneys and Stevenson, Robson had definite ideas about the propriety of certain architectural styles for certain building types. He believed:

'A Board School should look like a Board School and nothing else . . . Some may . . . think that . . . [Art] *has no right to trouble herself where only ragged children are concerned, and that in doing so she is, in some way, derogating from her lofty mission. Yet there is a sense in which she may exert her influence in the highest and best manner. She may suitably mark a great social movement if invited to be present in its buildings, may show what can be done in the merest plain brickwork if her fundamental principles of truth and common sense be adhered to throughout; and, in making her mark on the schools of the people, show in some wise what the homes of these people ought to be.'*[25]

Thus for Robson and the Board Schools' committee, these schools were to have a didactic mission, not only teaching the children the basic three Rs, but also providing an example of the correct manner in which to live and fashion oneself.

The 'Queen Anne' style, with its refined, middle-class, domestic connotations, was considered to be the best means of transmitting middle-class values of taste and hygiene into the slums. As Deborah Weiner points out in her thesis on the Board Schools: "The style with its associations of middle-class comforts and domestic values corresponded as well to the ideology of a rescue mission which ran through the rhetoric of the period."[26]

The architects of the Board Schools sought an architecture for a brand new institution that was free of religious associations and rich in domestic ones. Very similar requirements were considered when Champneys was commissioned to build a house for Sidgwick, Clough and the Newnham committee. For what was to become Newnham College, Champneys chose a style which was purposefully associated with a charming English domesticity and which was thus deemed suitable for a boarding house for young women. As we shall see, as Newnham grew and developed, and other women's colleges followed, the 'Queen Anne' style successfully satisfied the requirements of this new female institution.

In 1874, circulars were sent out advertising Newnham Hall as a boarding house for young women attending the lectures offered by the Association for the Higher Education of Women in Cambridge. Parents were assured that the students would be under the careful management of Miss Clough. Life was begun in the new hall and was described by Henry Sidgwick in the following letter to his mother of 1876:

The reason why I should have been glad if you could come to Cambridge now is that I should like you to see Newnham Hall with, so to say, the first bloom on it. The house is full, and everything is going on satisfactorily so far, and we have all of us the sense of repose and tranquil pleasure with which one reaches the top of the first stage in climbing a hill.[27]

Between 1874 and 1876 certain modifications were made in the arrangement of rooms in the house to accommodate more students.

Talk of the need for a new building was begun as early as 1877, when the

25. Ibid., 137.
26. Ibid., 129–30.
27. Eleanor Sidgwick and Arthur Sidgwick, *Henry Sidgwick, A Memoir* (London: Macmillan, 1906), 300.

40. Student's Room, Clough Hall, c. 1900, Newnham College. *Reproduced courtesy of the Principal and Fellows, Newnham College, Cambridge.*

overflow of students meant that the Association was required to rent space in other boarding houses around town. As the discussions continued, it was decided that it would be advantageous to amalgamate the Association for the Higher Education of Women with the Newnham Hall Company, thus forming one unit to be called Newnham College. The second house was to be much like the first but was to include lecture rooms, thereby replacing those rented in town by the Association. This was a bold step and it took two years of discussion to reach the final decision. But on 15 February 1879, Sidgwick reported to the building committee that the decision to build a "new house for women students"[28] was supported unanimously by the main council. It is important to point out here, that throughout the early building campaigns, even after Newnham College was established formally, the council and building committee often called their buildings houses. In both semantic and architectural terms, the evolution of Newnham College was primarily domestic. This was due to several factors conditioning the growth of this early institution for women, which we saw affecting Girton's development and which play an important role in the colleges which followed.

In the nineteenth century women's assumed sphere was the private and domestic environs of the house. This domesticity was understood to play a key role in conditioning behavior and social attitudes. The pioneers at Girton threw off many of the domestic shackles that had bound them previously, but as we have seen, they perpetuated obvious elements of domesticity in order to pre-empt criticism.

In the case of Newnham we find less evidence of a surreptitious rebellion against accepted patterns of behavior and their accompanying environment. More commonly, the founders of Newnham seemed happy to consider their college as a home, modified and enlarged in order to afford women access to higher education. Just as the curriculum was devised to accommodate each woman's individual needs without

28. Minutes of the Building Committee 1874–1880, 15 February 1879, Building Box, 1874–1910, Newnham College Archives, Newnham College Cambridge.

pressuring her to achieve the same standards as the men, so was the atmosphere of Newnham consciously constructed to be more homey and domestic. No doubt this domesticity is partly the result of the personalities involved with the foundation of the college. Anecdotes abound regarding the motherly nature of Miss Clough, who watched over her flock of young women with a careful and acutely sensitive eye. Sidgwick, while enthusiastically supporting the venture, had no great scheme in mind when he started, and seemed to accommodate change when it happened rather than planning for it as Emily Davies did. The vision motivating Newnham from the start was that of an advanced and enlightened household—women dressed in Pre-Raphaelite garb, expanding their horizons in sitting rooms decorated with Morris papers with prints, fans and peacock feathers adorning the walls.

Champneys was called in and designed the second house, which came to be called Sidgwick Hall (see color illustration 6). This is another, more elegant essay in the 'Queen Anne' style which was growing ever more popular in the late 1870s and early 1880s. Like Old Hall, the facade is symmetrical with the two gabled ends pulled out from the main block. The center is emphasized over the door with another gable pulled out from the wall. This time Champneys took more liberties with his curving Flemish gables. All three are elaborately articulated by pilasters, quoins, curving or broken pediments and graceful festoons in cut or molded brick. Palladian windows light the rooms in the wings. The windows of the main body of the house are slightly more squat, without the ebullient curves which topped those at Old Hall and increased its verticality. At Sidgwick brick apron curtains soften the wall surface beneath the windows and continue the curvaceous energy of the whole. Once again dormer windows are segmental, and a white balustrade eases the transition between the roof and sky. Tall chimney stacks at six regular intervals dominate the skyline.

The plan of the building was also much like that of Old Hall, where a simple body expands in back into more elaborate wings. Once again, the dominant aspect is south, the facade is parallel to the back of Old Hall, and a small footpath originally passed between the two. The dining room is in the southeast corner on the ground floor, and behind it stretch the kitchens and servants' area. A spine-like corridor runs through the center of the whole, with the main staircase running up opposite the main door. On the southwest corner was a suite of rooms first lived in by Henry Sidgwick and his wife Eleanor (née Balfour), who volunteered to give up their house in Hillsides, and move in in 1880. This began as an experiment in administration. Mrs. Sidgwick had been actively involved with Newnham since her marriage in 1876. She was appointed Vice-Principal in 1879 and by living in Sidgwick Hall could oversee the smooth workings of the new house. Extending north from their suite were more bedrooms for the students. Ranged along the ground floor were the much-discussed lecture rooms.

On the western front the ebullient treatment of windows and gables continued. The first two bays are marked by simple window frames with brick apron curtains. Above them jut two, small curving gables. Beside these relatively sedate bays the third breaks out into a dynamic bay window of white trim and small panes of glass rising up two storeys with a balustraded balcony on top. Behind the balcony is another Palladian window, and a larger more elaborate gable. In the fourth bay is tucked a small, unobtrusive doorway, most likely included to afford a more private

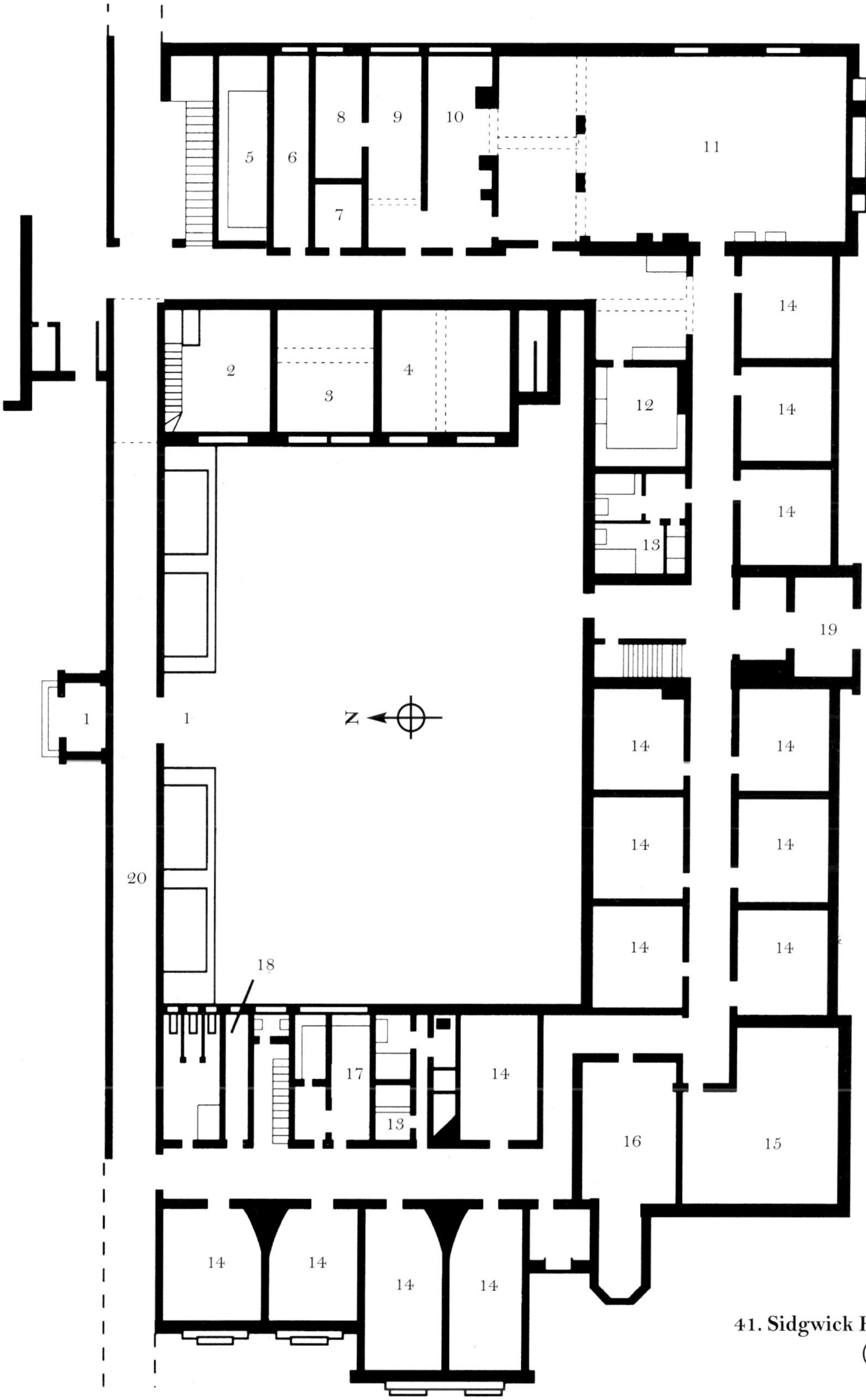

1. entrance
2. luggage and boots
3. housekeeper
4. maid's sitting room
5. linen store
6. linen
7. store
8. larder
9. scullery
10. service kitchen
11. dining room
12. pantry
13. bath
14. students' room
15. tutor
16. common room
17. pantry and ironing
18. drying
19. garden entrance
20. corridor

41. Sidgwick Hall, ground floor plan (by Champneys, 1880).

42. Sidgwick Hall (by Champneys, 1880).

entry for the Sidgwicks to come and go. Beyond this the wing projects out one bay and begins another range of rooms, this time marked by two larger and elaborate gables with pretty oriels windows defining the third story and ending with two smaller, relatively quiet bays. In typical 'Queen Anne' style, the building is a charming essay, combining picturesque irregularity with diluted and playful quotations from classicism.

The two houses existed as very separate entities, united only by the common use of the lecture rooms in Sidgwick, each surrounded by iron railings. Old Hall, under the supervision of Miss Clough, was generally regarded as more 'Aesthetic' with Morris wallpapers and students who tended to dress in Pre-Raphaelite clothes. Sidgwick, on the other hand, generally accommodated students who were attending college for more professional reasons, and had less money and time to spare, thus their walls tended to be plain white, and their dress much more simple.[29] Dining was kept separate as each house had its own dining room and kitchens, which maintained a more intimate, familial atmosphere. This was a tradition adhered to throughout the building campaigns at Newnham because of the contact it provided between the principal, tutors and students.

The 1880s saw many new developments in the young college. In 1881 the students at Girton and Newnham were formally admitted to the Little Go and Tripos examinations, these being the first examinations which undergraduates took, and the honors exam, respectively. This did not mean the women obtained degrees, but until this time they had been allowed access to the exams purely on the sufferance of the University. By legally admitting the women to the examinations, the students' place on the fringes of the University was guaranteed, which was very encouraging for those involved.

In 1883 additions were planned for Sidgwick Hall. Drawn up by Champneys, these included sixteen more rooms for students and a hospital wing. As we saw in the case of Girton, the issue of health was very much on the minds of those involved in

29. K. M. Rathbone, "A College with Status," in Anne Phillips, ed., *A Newnham Anthology*, 2nd ed. (Cambridge: Newnham College, 1988), 21.

43. Clough Assembly Hall, Newnham College (by Champneys, 1886).

the scheme for women's education. The inclusion of hospital wings or infirmaries expressed a commitment in architectural terms to safeguard the health of women away from home who were involved in "brainwork," as it was so often called.

By 1885, the success of the venture called for new discussions of another house. This time it was decided that accommodation for fifty more students was needed, as well as a large assembly hall which could unite the college under one roof for large lectures, dances and other special occasions. This marks a new phase of confidence on the part of the college founders, who no longer considered their scheme as tentative, but rather recognized its potential permanence as a college for women. With the building of this third hall, the existing names, South and North Halls, were changed to Old and Sidgwick Hall respectively, with the latest hall being called Clough.

Clough Hall also faces south, and presents a symmetrical facade with two projecting gabled wings and the central doorway highlighted by an elaborate gable (see color illustration 7). In this case, two oriel windows dramatically light the center stairs above the doorway, their mass of white trim standing out starkly against the red brick. In the gables, Champneys used a more elaborate Classical vocabulary. The pilasters of the first two buildings have here developed into semi-detached columns, with finials and urns standing out more starkly against the sky. At the top of the two end gables, he quoted from Italian sources in the Classical pediment couched on either side by scrolled volutes. The main body of the building has become more regular and stable, with simple bays of white sash windows, but the dormer windows project out with the same energetic, curved force as those of Sidgwick Hall. To the western end, set back two bays is another, small entrance set within a double gabled facade which is dramatized primarily by a rounded, double-storey bay window.

The large hall, or assembly room attached to Clough Hall provides the greatest visual impact. This was set on the eastern edge of the hall, closest to Sidgwick. On each end to the west and east are curving gables topped with finials. The south front runs the length of the hall and is broken up into seven bays marked by slender buttresses and semi-detached columns with spiky finials silhouetted against the roof. Large arched windows, above which hang graceful festoons, light the interior. The

Classical rhythm of the facade is broken up in the second and fifth bays by huge bow windows, each crowned by a dome and a pediment decorated with plasterwork. The exuberance of these great windows, trimmed in white and projecting out so far as to suggest almost a full circle, seems to epitomize the 'Queen Anne' style of Newnham, which never, even in its great hall, seems to approach the serious or formal, but is always inviting, gracious, "sweet" and "light".

The interior of the hall is open and airy, thanks to the ample windows (see color illustration 8). It has a wagon roof with elaborate plasterwork, which was chosen over the alternative of a paneled roof.[30] The ornate plasterwork was hotly debated in the meetings of the building committee by some members for reasons of cost, but Champneys firmly insisted on its inclusion.[31] There is a gallery on the east end, a side gallery to the north, and a moveable platform for high table was included at the west end. The kitchen facilities extended out in a wing between the assembly hall and Clough Hall itself, thus providing services for both large events and for the more intimate dining room in Clough.

In a general committee meeting in 1886, the minutes record a discussion of the building of Clough Hall when it was agreed to give the students a choice of rooms varying in size and cost. Thus the wealthier students had the option of double rooms or one very large room, and those less well off could choose the cheaper and smaller rooms.[32] This decision was integrated into the plans of Clough Hall, and some rooms were altered in the older buildings to accommodate the change. Sidgwick and Clough were both built as independent, self-sufficient entities. However, in keeping with the serious concerns over the health of the students, a covered, glazed corridor was built in 1888 connecting the two houses. Whereas Girton had long corridors which unified the whole in order that the women would not need to venture outside in inclement weather, Newnham addressed the same concerns but in a slightly different way. These covered passages, which connect each house to the next and could keep the women safe and dry, act as a unifying thread that binds the disparate units into one. It was in this way that the founders of Newnham maintained separate, familial houses while ensuring healthy interaction without creating a large impersonal institution.

In 1891, the public footpath that ran between Old Hall and Sidgwick was finally closed. This had been a baneful issue for the college for years. When Sidgwick was built it faced the rear of Old Hall. The two were kept separate by the footpath, thus interaction between the houses was minimal, and there was no satisfactory route of access. With the closure of the footpath, a new road, Sidgwick Avenue, was opened; this runs behind Sidgwick and Clough Halls and is now the main means of access to the college. The arrangement has always been somewhat awkward, as it rendered redundant the original entrance to Old Hall. Consequently, Old Hall seems isolated from the others. Similarly with the removal of the footpath and the creation of the new road, the main entrances of Sidgwick and Clough became the garden fronts, and access from the road was gained through what were intended as the back doors. Of this confusion of entries and backdoors, Dr. Peile, Master of Christ's College who had been active on the Newnham Council said:

Newnham has twice executed that often fatal manoeuvre — a change of front. The beautiful front of Old Hall looks now, not as we expected, upon busy streets, but on quiet fields. The

30. Minutes of the Council Meetings and of the General Meetings of Newnham College 1880–97, 19 February 1887, Newnham College Archives, Newnham College Cambridge .
31. Minutes of the Building Committee, 1886, Newnham College Archives.
32. Minutes of the Council and of the General Meetings of Newnham College 1880–97, vol. 2, 13 February 1886, Newnham College Archives, 118.

44. Covered corridor connecting Clough with Sidgwick Halls (by Champneys, 1888).

avenue which preserves another name which will live in the memories of Newnham, does not command the most attractive view of either of the other Halls. But the new gateway can hardly be turned inside out.[33]

However awkward this might be for people on the street, it serves an important role for a woman's college. Where at Girton the facades face outward towards the public, here at Newnham all is inward looking, with the primary focus on the private world of the garden and orchard. Ironically, while the founders of Newnham had little interest in mimicking the men's colleges, this private, inner sanctum, completely hidden from the outside world, is more in keeping with the collegiate tradition of quadrangles than are the long ranges of Girton. Girton's first quadrangle was formed in 1900, and while it is enclosed and private, the main architectural interest is still to be found on the street side.

With the closure of the footpath, a covered corridor was built to connect Old Hall with Sidgwick. In 1892–93, plans were drawn up for a new building, the Pfeiffer Building, which would provide a gateway into the garden where the path used to be. In a sense this wing, like the tower wing at Girton, proclaimed the collegiate status of Newnham — but it did so in very genteel terms. As at Girton, the gateway contained a porter's lodge, but here two towers flank the central arch which leads into the garden. Once again, Champneys used a Classical vocabulary with semi-detached Ionic columns on the three central tiers and an almost baroque open pediment in the center. Curved fanlights rest above each window over the archway. The towers, capped with domes, are much like the splendid bay windows which Champneys used on the assembly hall. There are four in all, two on the street facade and two on the garden front, and they come out from the wall as almost complete circular units. On the street facade the tower on the right, which contains the staircase, is half a story

33. Dr. Peile, "A Change of Front," in Phillips, *A Newnham Anthology*, 37.

45. Pfeiffer Building (by Champneys, 1892–93). *Reproduced courtesy of Clare Browne. Photograph by Brenda Norrish.*

higher than its mate. It is crowned with an arched, brick balcony with ball finials and a weathervane. It is slightly larger in circumference and offsets the classical symmetry with picturesque irregularity. The twinned towers on the garden side, however, present a balanced facade.

To the south of the block, Champneys connected the Pfeiffer Building with Old Hall. To the north, he softened the formality with a two-storey projection in the manner of Richard Norman Shaw. As we can see from a print of the building, Champneys used a steep hipped roof with a dormer window, and a large, oriel window with a pediment. Its easy informality acted as a suitable transition to the covered passageway that then linked Pfeiffer up with Sidgwick Hall. The connecting units on both sides of the Pfeiffer Building were replaced in 1946 with large and institutional blocks designed by Buckland and Haywood, two Birmingham architects.

The Pfeiffer Building contained more rooms for the students and a suite for Mr. and Mrs. Sidgwick. Mrs. Sidgwick had become principal in place of Miss Clough, and thus she and her husband once again returned to live in Newnham. Their accommodation was relatively self-sufficient, but they made it a practice to dine once a week

46. Clough Memorial Gates, Newnham College (by Thomas Elsley, 1894).

with the college, and invited the third or fourth year students to breakfast during which Professor Sidgwick regaled them with his stories and ideas. Sidgwick had a small study of his own, and their apartments were described as "pretty, well-proportioned rooms."[34]

To complete the gatehouse, Champneys designed the bronze gates which were dedicated to the memory of Miss Clough who died in 1890. These were made in London by Thomas Elsley. Acanthus leaves are entwined throughout the whole while sunflowers, a motif common in 'Queen Anne' architecture of the time, dominate the borders. The building committee discussed these gates and the issue of protecting them by a second set in 1894. It was reported that:

The Committee consider that the position of the gates, close to the porter's lodge is in itself a great protection and are not clearly convinced that anything further is needed. They are of the opinion that outside gates would cause great inconvenience and they are also unwilling to regard the bronze gates as purely ornamental.[35]

It was at this time, in the early 1890s, that the issue of fencing was much discussed in the council meetings. What with the opening of the new road and new buildings being built nearby, concern was mounting over the protection of the female students as Newnham no longer seemed as isolated from the University as it had been in 1875. An iron fence was erected to the west of the property, beyond Clough, while a smaller oak fence ran along the boundary line to the south. A large brick wall was built along Sidgwick Avenue, which served the dual purpose of keeping unwanted visitors out, and preventing them from seeing into the college grounds. That the building committee was concerned about the women's safety is

34. Sidgwick and Sidgwick, *Henry Sidgwick, A Memoir*, 529.
35. Report of the Building Committee, 17 November 1894, Newnham College Archives.

47. Library, interior, Newnham College (by Champneys, 1896–98). *Reproduced courtesy of the Principal and Fellows of Newnham College, Cambridge.*

clear from a report of 1893 which stipulated that the fences should not be easy to climb.[36] The fences which circumscribed the whole increased the protection afforded by the covered corridors.

By the 1890s the University had continued to spill over its boundaries into the area known as Newnham. Selwyn College, designed by Arthur Blomfield, had opened its doors in the 1880s around the corner, and the area to the north and west was developing a suburban aspect with a decidedly 'Queen Anne' flavor, with houses by both Champneys and Stevenson. The increased activity around the college, along with the growing numbers of students who could not be so carefully watched, made increased security crucial in order to avoid any unpleasant mishaps or embarrassing or dangerous occurrences.

A purpose built library was added during the years 1896–98. This small addition is tucked behind the covered corridor which connects Sidgwick with Clough. It has since been altered and enlarged in the twentieth century, but the main reading room and stacks have survived intact. Like the larger assembly hall, the library has a wagon roof, with skylights and decorative plasterwork. The stacks form small reading areas and a narrow ledge provides access to the gallery level. It was an important

36. Report from the Building Committee, 18 November 1893, Newnham College Archives.

48. Kennedy Building, Newnham College (by Champneys, 1905).

addition to the college, and, together with the large college hall, served as a common area for all the students.

By 1905, another building was needed, and Champneys was called in once again. This time it was to build the Kennedy Building which was to be a house for lecturers and fellows of the college, not an ordinary student residence. It is sited just west of Clough Hall, and connected by a covered corridor. Perhaps because of its older inhabitants, the Kennedy Building has more somber and Classical characteristics than any of the other buildings which Champneys designed for Newnham. It is a solid rectangular block with a dominant gambrel roof. The only elaboration on the garden front is in the center where two bays project from the wall and are elaborated by curving gables, cheerful festoons and Ionic pilasters. Two oriel windows break the regularity of the whole. The chimneys are stout and the dormer windows are subdued and rectangular compared to those of the other buildings with their forceful, tunnel-like shapes.

The floorplan of Kennedy is also a departure from the established precedents. There is no independent dining room as the fellows and lecturers would take their meals in the various other halls. The entrance faces the road, under an italianate arcade, and brings the visitor into a foyer lit from above by an oval skylight. The central passages which connect the whole are broken up by this open, central area. The rooms are set up in suites with a bedroom and sitting room provided for each lecturer. It is a quiet and private building appropriate for the individual pursuits of the professional women.

The last building to concern us here is Peile Hall, built in 1910. This was Champneys' last work for Newnham, although he was to live on for another twenty-five years. It is sited on the far western edge of the property, perpendicular to Kennedy and Clough and facing in towards the garden with another entrance on Grange Road. It is in effect the third and final leg of a very loose U, with the garden stretching out to the south. Newnham has not developed into quadrangles, but Peile Hall gives a similar sense of enclosure. It is the largest of the halls, arranged like

49. Peile Hall, garden front, Newnham College (by Champneys, 1910).

Clough with two projecting wings on the ends and one large center gable which dominates the garden front. The central gable is a mass of white trim and small panes of glass with a bold, two-storey oriel window in the middle and a large Palladian window above that. On each side of the central curving gable are large balconies, which were requested by the building committee for the students to enjoy in good weather.[37] Their inclusion points to a new, more relaxed attitude towards women's health; with the confidence gained by experience, new liberties could be taken.

On the north end of the building is a dining room, with its own kitchens and servants' areas stretching out behind it. It is lit by a large bay window. The floor plans of Peile show a similar system of corridors, bedrooms and common rooms but on a more extensive scale than in the other halls. On the ground floor near the entrance is a small waiting room for visitors. The hall is connected with Kennedy by a covered corridor which follows the corner of Sidgwick Avenue and Grange Road.

What is striking about Peile Hall is the difference between the garden and street facades. Where the garden front continues the 'Queen Anne' in an almost frilly way, the street side is dramatically different. Even more severe than the Kennedy Building, this facade is stark and simple. This is more in keeping with Champneys' other work at this time, such as the new buildings for Bedford College in Regent's Park of 1913, in which he abandoned the 'Queen Anne' style for a more institutional classicism.

Peile Hall enclosed the grounds of Newnham into a private and isolated world. The development of the garden within this private sphere had been the concern of Miss Clough when the first house was built, and she played a responsible role in its early phases. Most particularly around Old Hall Miss Clough "supervised the arrangement of the garden in a mid-Victorian style that was familiar to her, with

37. Minutes of Building Committee Meeting, 8 March 1909, Buildings Box 1874–1910, Newnham College Archives.

LEFT 50. Peile Hall, street front, Newnham College (by Champneys, 1910).

BELOW 51. Bedford College, Regents Park, London (by Champneys, 1911–13). *Reproduced courtesy of the Archives, Royal Holloway, University of London, RF121/1/4.*

serpentine paths through the shrubberies and orchard trees."[38] Amidst all this was a croquet lawn and a tennis court, and pigs were kept behind the laboratory.

When Miss Clough died, her niece Blanche Athena Clough took over and was responsible for the gardens for the next twenty-two years. It was during this time that three movements in garden design were vying for supremacy. The first was led by Reginald Blomfield, who advocated a return to the formal gardens of the Renaissance. William Robinson led the second movement. He was a popular proponent of naturalistic gardens consisting of meadowlands and woods. The third was led by Gertrude Jekyll, who is well known today for her collaborative work with the architect Edward Lutyens. Their philosophy of garden design, "demanded that the design of house and garden must be interlocking; every door to have its rosemary bush, every wall its sweetbriar, every path its purpose and purposeful ending in an enclosed vista."[39] Newnham was closely connected with Jekyll and her work. As mentioned earlier, Mary Ewart was an important figure on the council of Newnham. Her own house, Coneyhurst, was designed by Philip Webb, and Jekyll had visited her

38. Jane Brown, *The Making of the Gardens: Newnham College* (Cambridge: Newnham College, 1988), 3.
39. Ibid., 9.

52. View of Garden, Newnham College.

there and seen the house. There was also a connection with Lutyens through marriage. In 1897, Lutyens had married Lady Emily Lytton, whose older sister had married Gerald Balfour, Mrs. Sidgwick's brother. In 1900, Lutyens designed a house for the Balfours, called Fisher's Hill and Jekyll laid out the garden. Jekyll had also designed gardens for two houses built by Arthur Clough, Blanche Athena's brother, an amateur architect designing in the Arts and Crafts style.

Thus the Arts and Crafts approach to garden design, perpetuated by Jekyll and Lutyens, was well known to the Newnham council. In 1900, when Henry Sidgwick died and a memorial was to be erected, Miss Ewart recommended Alfred Hoare Powell, a disciple of Jekyll, to design a sunken rose garden in front of Sidgwick Hall. A small pool is in the center, the rim of which is carved with the following inscription: "The daughters of this house to those that shall come after them commend the filial remembrance of Henry Sidgwick."[40]

Similarly, when Mrs. Sidgwick retired in 1911, Jekyll herself was asked to design a garden scheme in memory of Mrs. Sidgwick's work for the college. Designs for the layout exist and include a pagoda designed by Lutyens, but for reasons as yet unclear, the college abandoned Jekyll's scheme and called in a Mr. Watson instead. Watson designed a garden house and memorial for the southwest end of the garden. At present the garden is a delightful mix of formal paths beside herbaceous borders, and meandering routes through the now overgrown orchard and wood. Because of the way Newnham evolved, all the buildings except Kennedy open directly onto the gardens and facilitate the easy interaction between house and garden that was the key to Jekyll and Lutyen's philosophy.

The gardens perpetuate the genteel, domestic nature of the college. This domesticity was noticed when the first three houses of Newnham College were described in *The Builder* in 1889. Champneys exhibited sketches of the halls at the Royal Academy, one of Old Hall, one of Sidgwick and two of Clough. In discussing them the reviewer noted: "The main front is a very quietly-treated building of Queen Anne type, thoroughly 'Collegiate Domestic' in character."[41] This is an early use of the term which Champneys was to reverse to "Domestic Collegiate" to describe his work

40. Ibid., 11.
41. "Architecture at the Royal Academy II," *The Builder* (11 May 1889): 350.

at various women's colleges.[42] In a paper read to the Royal Institute of British Architects in 1903, Champneys wrote about the requirements of the fledgling women's colleges:

It is clear that the life in these must necessarily be of a more domestic character than in colleges for men, and if the style of architecture follows the requirement, the result will be something which may be called 'Domestic Collegiate.' Access to the several students' rooms can no longer be from staircases entered direct from the open air: the approaches must be properly enclosed, and the passages warmed. In the building I illustrate — Newnham College Cambridge — the deviation from the original type is greater, because the system of the college is that of subdivision into halls, each of which is on the whole complete in itself. . . . The only features used equally by the entire college being the great hall and the library, the lecture rooms and the laboratories. Moreover, the scheme as it now stands has been developed piecemeal; has started from small beginnings and grown up step by step, each installment of the group of buildings having been supposed, at the time of erection, to be the last, until the pressure of applicants suggested a further extension.[43]

This is a rare exposition of one architect's theory behind the architecture of women's colleges in England, and, as we shall see, Champneys' role in the designing of these institutions was a dominant and important one. Champneys pointed out that the women's colleges should differ from the established men's colleges in both planning and stylistic treatment. The domestic nature of the first building at Newnham was a requirement of St. John's College, but the members of the Association for the Higher Education of Women in Cambridge, had, from the start, intended solely to build a house, nothing more. Newnham developed into one of the earliest colleges for women, and as it did so, Champneys developed a theory of architecture which he saw as perfectly applicable to women's colleges.

As stated above, Champneys was an early disciple of the 'Queen Anne' movement, led at first by Shaw and Nesfield, and taken up eagerly by a younger generation of architects in the 1870s and 1880s. It was *the* style which Champneys used for his domestic work, and as he suggested in his article in 1903, he believed the 'Queen Anne' style "followed the requirement" of a women's college. In an age of propriety and association, when Champneys and others sought a domestic style of comfortable modesty, the 'free classic' or 'Queen Anne' filled all the recognized domestic needs of the day, and carried with it the associations of cozy, tasteful, English homes. Significantly, these were the associations which Champneys regarded as suitable and appropriate for a women's college. He and his patrons, the council of Newnham, wanted the buildings of Newnham to be recognized first as domestic and only later as collegiate.

As at Girton, the reasons behind this domesticity have to do with public perception of, and tolerance for, a scheme for women's education, as well as a belief, firmly held at Newnham, in the differences between men and women; Newnham's educational curriculum was not directly modeled on the male example, nor did its buildings bear any strong resemblance to their male counterparts'. The 'Queen Anne' style offered a fresh, domestic vocabulary with which to realize a women's college. In a very real sense, Champneys' whimsical mixture of classicism with the picturesque,

42. Champneys, "The Planning of Collegiate Buildings," 209.
43. Ibid.

53. Range at New College, Oxford (by Champneys, 1896).

in which exuberant finials interrupt pediments, bright white windows practically obliterate the wall surface, and the rules of severe classicism or moral Gothicism are randomly flouted, reflected Newnham's educational development. Not that it was in any sense a frivolous enterprise. But the founders had no set curriculum or timetable; students came for two terms or nine; they took classes for the joy of learning or in a determined effort to gain high honors; they attended to improve themselves before marriage; or to prepare themselves for a life of teaching or philanthropic work. The only overriding goal behind the foundation of Newnham was, figuratively speaking, to open the windows of learning for women and to let their minds respond to the light as best they could. Miss Clough and Henry Sidgwick did not intend to revolutionize women's lives, just to improve them. Champneys housed the students in residences that resounded with associations of a new enlightened aesthetic; a clear departure from Gothic or Classical architecture which itself harkened back to age-old traditions of religion, morality or scholarship.

Champneys was proficient in designing in these other traditions and was aware of their associations. In order to put his work at Newnham into context, it is helpful to examine some of his other work. He built extensively in Oxford for the University, including ranges for New College, Merton and Oriel. In his range for New College of 1896, he completed the front of a quadrangle, connecting the buildings of G. G. Scott with the Warden's Lodge. This work included Robinson's Tower and a two-storey range of students' rooms. Here he employed a severe Gothic style in Oxford stone, with projecting bays, their balconies crenelated to harmonize with the castellated tower. For Merton College, Champneys designed St. Alban's Quad in 1904–10. This L-shaped range is articulated by gables and oriel windows in a restrained Tudor style. The facade he designed for Oriel College's Rhodes Building is in an imposing late seventeenth-century style with heavy rustication on the ground floor

54. Rhodes Building, Oriel College, Oxford (by Champneys, 1908–11).

and blocked columns flanking the entrance. The upper two storeys received more delicate treatment, with gently curving bays on the first floor and curving gables on the second. Overall there is a grandeur and dignity which blends in subtly with the surrounding architecture of Oxford.

At Mansfield College, Oxford, the 'Queen Anne' did battle with the traditional Gothic. In 1887 Waterhouse competed with Champneys for the commission to build Mansfield, a theological training college for Congregationalists. This was a new type, a non-residential college, intended to be a place for students (especially the Non-Conformists) throughout the University to assemble for lectures, use the library, and attend chapel services. Perhaps because of its alternative origins and purpose, Waterhouse submitted a design more or less in the 'Queen Anne' style with a large French mansard roof over the tower. The chapel and hall had curving, Flemish gabled ends, surprising from an architect known for his Gothic towers and spires. The founders of Mansfield were in agreement with Champneys when he said that it was necessary that the buildings of Mansfield "reflect the character of Oxford collegiate buildings,"[44] and they chose his design, which was of a purely Gothic origin. While this new college was not typical in its organization, the founders wanted an architecture rich in traditional associations which Champneys provided and Waterhouse did not.

Perhaps Champneys' masterpiece in the Gothic style is the Rylands Library in Manchester, a commission that came to him through his work at Mansfield (see fig. 57). Mr. and Mrs. Rylands of Manchester had contributed to the building of Mansfield, and Mrs. Rylands was impressed with the library there when she saw it. Upon her husband's death, she commissioned Champneys to design a building to house "an ecumenical theological library"[45] as a memorial to her husband. Champneys produced an imposing building in Decorated Gothic of red, Penrith sandstone. The interior contains an impressive spiral staircase and a great vaulted reading room.

44. Ibid.
45. David Watkin, *The Architecture of Basil Champneys* (Cambridge: Newnham College, 1989), 36.

55. Design for Mansfield College, Oxford (by Waterhouse, 1887). *Reproduced courtesy of the Mansfield College Archives.*

56. Mansfield College, Oxford (by Champneys, 1887).

That Champneys was an adept and highly regarded architect in the Gothic Revival is clear. But he chose a very different style when building for families or for women. Before leaving this discussion of Champneys' work in relation to Newnham, it is necessary to look again at his commission for Bedford College (see fig. 51 above). Throughout the nineteenth century, Bedford had gone through various difficulties as it struggled to find its role in female education. By the turn of the century it was a flourishing college affiliated with the University of London, and in 1911 it required new buildings in which to house its student body and conduct lectures. Bedford hired Champneys to build on land the college had acquired in Regent's Park.

As was pointed out in the analysis of Peile Hall, by 1913 Champneys' 'Queen Anne' had mellowed into a more restrained classicism, often referred to as a 'Wrenaissance' style because of its quotations from Wren and other various Classical elements. The buildings at Bedford are of red brick with white casement windows, but the effusive oriels and bows have been replaced by large, ordinary windows flush with the wall surface. The overall scheme is more imposing than anything built at Newnham. The

57. Ryland's Library, Manchester (by Champneys, 1890–99).

ground floor elevations are rusticated, and even the arching pediments over the entranceways are solid and heavy. The main entrance bears a resemblance to the facade he built at Oriel College, Oxford, with the ground floor arches and windows, the empty niches just above the doorway and the columns set into the wall. The library, with its white stone dressings and oeil de boeuf windows (since replaced) in the gallery level, is more reminiscent of Wren at Hampton Court than Champneys at Newnham.

However, echoes of Newnham are clear. Champneys laid out the college in seven independent blocks, each with its own identity; two residential halls, a dining hall, two science blocks, arts lecture rooms, and a library. The buildings are aligned in an L shape, with the large residential halls forming the shorter leg, and suggesting, in a loose manner, half a quadrangle. The layout of the individual units closely resembles Newnham with its series of houses aligned in a row with the short arms of a U formed by two more houses. Between each block at Bedford ran small covered corridors, with arched glazed windows, an obvious quotation from Newnham. Thus, as at Newnham, it was considered crucial that the women could pass from building to building under the protective cover of heated passages. Although the function of the buildings had changed dramatically over the thirty-odd intervening years, the need to protect women was considered the same, and Champneys continued to look back to his work at Newnham for inspiration in planning if not in stylistic matters.

The founders of Newnham were acutely aware of the pioneering task which they shared with Girton in spearheading higher education for women. Accounts of Miss Clough's reign as principal are full of praise for her devotion to the job, but also mention her extreme sensitivity to the students' behavior and her overriding concern that the students should always appear ladylike, modest and demure. Her niece Blanche Athena described her in a memoir:

she meant to show that a desire for education, and even the possession of it, did not involve any departure from recognised customs and conventions. These considerations were constantly before her mind, and made her nervously anxious about every detail in the conduct of the women students.[46]

At times her fussy attention put a strain on relations with students, particularly in cases where the women were independent and strong minded. But it appears that even amidst the tension it was hard to dislike Miss Clough as her attentions were so well-meant and her affection so motherly.

She was particularly valued by those women who needed help settling into college life, those who were shy, frightened or unwell. Through the letters of Winnie Seebohm, a student who attended Newnham in 1885, we get a picture of the role which Miss Clough played and how valuable it was in certain circumstances. Winnie's letters describe a tragic life; she was intelligent and eager, and wanted nothing more than to go to college like her brother, and eventually to teach. She expressed the complaint of many young women in the nineteenth century when she wrote to her friend Meta Tuke: "'I often feel inexpressibly weary but I do not think rest is what young people long for, but rather work and power to work—fuller life and activity.'"[47] She was eventually spared at home and given the opportunity to attend Newnham. But just before the term started she fell mysteriously ill. She had trouble speaking and swallowing and suffered terrible asthma attacks. However she protested that she had recovered and was allowed to go to Cambridge. Her letters paint a lovely image of life at Newnham. Her room was in Old Hall, and she described the process of changing the sitting room into a bedroom each night, a lengthy procedure which required much moving of furniture and changing of linens to make room for the bath brought in each morning and to switch the sofa into a bed. She frequented a common room, called the "Blue Room," which contained a library and piano.

Because she was ill, her working hours were even more limited than most, and she wrote to her old teacher that she was "forbidden to read after dinner"[48] and instead she spent many evenings in Miss Clough's room where she was looked after carefully. If she had had a bad night, breakfast was brought to her room by the maid Harriet, and again, Miss Clough would look in on her regularly. In spite of her illness, she was terrifically glad to be at Newnham with a chance to learn. She held up Mrs. Mary Paley Marshall as the ideal new woman, feminine, beautiful, intelligent and successfully fulfilling her career goals.

After a month during which her condition did not improve, her parents and Miss Clough decided to send her home again. They did not consult her, and she suddenly found herself home, and ordered by the doctor to avoid reading and to have "complete rest of brain."[49] She was to die a couple of weeks later, still obsessed with Newnham and determined to return to her golden opportunity for education and advancement.

Her story highlights many issues in the foreground of women's education with which the founders of Newnham struggled. As has been made clear through architectural discussions, domesticity was considered crucial to the success of the women's colleges. Winnie's letters home are full of reassurances; she is not suffering from overwork; she is carefully looked after; she has chaperones to town and lectures;

46. B. A. Clough, *A Memoir of Anne Jemima Clough*, 195–96.
47. Victoria Glendinning, *A Suppressed Cry: Life and Death of a Quaker Daughter* (London: Routledge & Kegan Paul, 1969), 54.
48. Ibid., 74–75.
49. Ibid., 87.

and she was offered plenty of proper food, had she been able to eat much of it. Her surroundings were pretty and comfortable. Except for the lectures and new friends, life was much as it had been at home.

It was cases like Winnie's that caused Miss Clough and the Sidgwicks so much concern, not just because of her individual plight but for the sake of the college as a whole. Had Winnie become sick at Newnham, or died there, the publicity and scandal could well have closed the college doors forever. Victoria Glendinning, editor of Winnie's letters, suggests that much of Winnie's ailment was psychosomatic, brought on by the tension she felt between her duty to her family and her desire for self-fulfillment. Whatever the medical causes, Winnie was aware of the unhealthy effects of too much rest and languid days. She, like so many of her contemporaries, wanted action, interest and something to stimulate her mind. Yet even while at Newnham, she was forever cautioned about too much 'brain-work', and the pat cure offered by the doctors was to avoid mental activity. Thus the founders of Newnham, had the difficult task of providing eager, receptive minds with knowledge, yet always tempering enthusiasm with modest caution.

As a result of these concerns, Mrs. Sidgwick published *Health Statistics of Women Students of Cambridge and Oxford and of their Sisters* in 1890. This was the result of a survey, modeled on a similar questionnaire sent out to female students in American colleges, intended to discover whether education had any real affect on the health of women. In her conclusion she stated:

That any serious alarm as to the effect of university education on the health of women is groundless, is clearly shown by the fact that the net amount of increase in good present health as compared with health between fourteen and eighteen years of age, is greater in the case of students than of their sisters.[50]

It was not just health that Clough and the Sidgwicks had to protect. In 1884, Mrs. Sidgwick defended the education of women at universities in a conference at the International Health Exhibition in London. In the published report, she discussed the career choices made by students, and their reasons for wanting an education. She goes on to praise the social opportunities afforded by college life: making good friends, gaining some independence, learning to live with others. About the issue of overwork, she assured the reader that it was carefully guarded against, and that "There is . . . among the students at Newnham, a healthy and growing public opinion against overwork."[51] She also adamantly denied that women developed any masculine tendencies while away from home, and argued that they would be better prepared to take on domestic duties after college. She concluded: "Nor finally, has the supervision of the conduct of our students been rendered materially more difficult or anxious by the proximity of the seventeen colleges of undergraduates."[52] Thus the protective qualities of home life, such as supervision, care and attention to the lady-like conduct of students was publicly admitted time and time again, in order to allay the public's fears about women's education.

As graduates continued to leave Newnham for careers in teaching, or for marriage, they wrote and lectured about their experiences at college in glowing terms. Katharine St. John Conway wrote an article "Life at Newnham" for the *Young Woman*

50. Mrs. Henry Sidgwick, *Health Statistics of Women Students of Cambridge and Oxford* (Cambridge: Cambridge University Press, 1890), 91.
51. Mrs. Henry Sidgwick, "The University Education of Women," a paper given to the International Health Exhibition Conference, 8 August 1884 (London: William Clowes), 8.
52. Ibid., 10.

in 1895. She described finding her way around the first two halls at Newnham when she first "came up;" ringing her bell and meeting the maid, finding the lecture rooms, principal's rooms, the dining room and library.

Upstairs we found corridor after corridor of Study-bedrooms, each the property of one student, and made her own by visible sign and seal. Here the bed lurks under the dainty draperies of a wildly aesthetic sofa; quaintly carved bureaus and black oak chests make room for all such clothing as is not hung behind a curtain of Morris chintz, which drops from a wide corner shelf. . . . Carefully chosen wall-papers, carpets, and hangings prove the will of the authorities to make the students' surroundings bright and full of variety.[53]

Conway goes on to describe the other two halls, Sidgwick and Clough, pointing out their individual qualities. The large hall in Clough was used for dances once a week in the winter, between seven and eight at night, before the evening's work began.

She related how the students were encouraged to entertain each other, inviting friends round to their rooms for tea in the afternoons and cocoa after ten in the evenings. These events were much written about by other students and included in novels about Newnham that began to appear in the 1890s. They were customs which encouraged habits of social etiquette; playing hostess to friends, and introducing the new students to their colleagues. One former student wrote about the habit of "paying calls," a custom obviously carried on from ordinary home life. For the first three days on arriving at college, visitors dropped in to the new student's room to introduce themselves, or in the case of older students to renew old friendships.[54] In the novel *A Newnham Friendship* by Alice Stronach, published in 1901, these calls were rather traumatic for the "fresher" of limited means who was awed and intimidated by the beautifully decorated rooms of the older and wealthier students. The older girls would descend on the fresher with suggestions of how to make her room look warm and homelike, much like Betty Leslie's room which "was as pretty a den as the most fastidious of 'third years' could desire. It boasted both the corner fireplace and the capacious window seat, which, as the woman student soon discovers, are the first essentials of a pretty room."[55] Betty was the daughter of a millionaire, but she wanted to work hard at Newnham and was not there on a whim. She left behind an anxious aunt who was worried that college would spoil Betty's complexion and ruin her chances for marriage. But Betty defied the critics' charges and those of her aunt, and was pretty and feminine, as well as bright and intelligent.

Such novels became popular between 1890 and the First World War. While some, like *A Newnham Friendship* were about specific colleges, others like *A Sweet Girl Graduate*, or *The Girls of Merton College* by L. T. Meade, changed the names of the colleges, but still described specific examples. The plots are generally formulaic, depicting the adventures and trials of a few of the students, usually one poor girl, who has scraped enough money to come to college intent on earning money as a teacher, one wealthier girl, who is not always sensitive but has a good heart, and one or two girls who are driven by jealousy or foul humor to try to hurt the poorer girl. There is usually a love interest introduced, a young undergraduate who is swayed by the evil girl or led down a wayward path by another undergraduate, but who wins the heart of the wealthy and good girl in the end. In a worthy variation on the theme, the hero-

53. Katherine St. John Conway, "Life at Newnham," *The Young Woman* III (October 1894–September 1895): 100.
54. Edith Colman, "Newnham," in *Laurel Leaves, Edgbaston High School for Girls Magazine* (31 January 1900): 4.
55. Alice Stronach, *A Newnham Friendship* (London: Blackie, 1901), 12.

ine of Walter Besant's novel, *All Sorts and Conditions of Men*, a pretty Newnham graduate, sets off to found a settlement house in the heart of London's slums which she wants built in a 'Queen Anne' style, much like the Newnham home she left.

This spate of novels inspired by Newnham and the other colleges for women is illustrative of a growing interest in and recognition of women's higher education. The novels idealized life in the college, showing the good lessons to be learned from three years of communal life. They painted a pretty life of sentimental and sometimes saccharin characters, who ultimately learned and grew from their experiences in college. In general the love interest was highlighted and at least one of the heroines married, her only hesitation being that she would have to give up her philanthropic, social goals. Her doubts were eradicated by the assurance that through marriage and family, she would being doing a great service to society and her country. The other heroine generally went on to a satisfying career as a teacher or social worker.

While these novels were, in a sense, good publicity, they were also, arguably, a perpetuation of the feminine stereotype that existed before women's colleges were founded. The options which they offered to women were similar; either marriage, philanthropy or teaching, with the exception of three pleasant, if sometimes traumatic years of college thrown in before donning life's duties. They illustrate quite clearly the disparity between students at Newnham who were seriously intent on a career and those who wanted knowledge for its own sake, but they never suggest that the women in these fledgling institutions were rebellious, courageous pioneers, who were in many ways breaking out of society's conventions.

The emphasis on a genteel, domestic life that thrived within a women's college at Cambridge was useful in countering critics' arguments about the wisdom of sending women away from home. But it worked against them in 1896 when a movement for degrees was set afoot by Newnham. Old students and the members of Newnham's staff claimed that women who had successfully completed their courses at Newnham or Girton were still at a disadvantage when applying for jobs because they did not have a Cambridge degree. Girton had led a crusade for degrees in 1887. It had been quietly conducted and caused little notice in the University community. In contrast, the plea for degrees in 1896 finally brought the women's colleges to the attention of the University, but it also elicited a threatening wave of hostility from old students, male undergraduates and fellows. On the day the vote took place, undergraduates hung an effigy of a bluestocking from the window of Macmillan's bookshop, and when the result was announced against the women's cause, the undergraduates stormed the Pfeiffer Gates, causing some damage. The women's colleges were not ultimately hurt by these events, but nor were they in any way helped, and they remained on the fringes of the University for many years to come.

Significantly, in the run-up to the deciding vote, one of the arguments put forward against women taking a Cambridge degree referred to the different residential systems for men and women. Austen Leigh, provost of King's College, posited that women were unfit for degrees because the lives they led at college did not prepare them for the real world. In his words:

The value attached to the B.A. degree depends to a large extent on the fact that for three years our undergraduates have undergone a severe ordeal of character and conduct. They have been in a position of freedom and responsibility. Their share in the common life of a large and miscellaneous body of men has tested and developed their capacity for self-control and self-reliance. They have gradually trained themselves for the duties and opportunities of later life. There is little of this in the life of a Girton or Newnham student. It may be liberty compared to her home life; but it is a very faint copy of the wider opportunities and severe trials which an undergraduate must face.[56]

In effect, Leigh's argument was an attempt to discredit one of the essential ingredients that helped to make the women's colleges in Cambridge successful, their protected domesticity. Had this domestic element been abandoned, and women students allowed the character-building freedom to which Leigh alludes, the outcry against them would have been even greater. It is, however, ironic that the normal, domestic appearance which silenced so many critics in the early years of the colleges' existence, should be used against them as a reason not to grant women degrees.

In the aftermath of this debate, the feminine nature of Newnham was not abandoned, despite Leigh's complaints. Mrs. Sidgwick's treatise on *University Education of Women,* and her report on the health statistics of women, together with the articles by past students in women's magazines and the novels discussed above, worked to present a face recognizable to the general public as feminine, modest and ladylike. Unlike Girton, where domesticity was more or less a veil used to hide a more ambitious and alternative goal, Newnham's domesticity was integrated with its overall approach to women's education. Certainly the founders of Newnham, the Sidgwicks, Fawcetts, Cloughs and Mary Ewart, ran in the liberal, and less conventional circles of their day, as their association with the leaders in artistic and social movements attests. But Newnham's rebellion was quietly understated. Like the 'Queen Anne' architecture which it so charmingly adopted, the movement for women's higher education at Newnham admitted the light of education into women's lives, in a gracious, artistic, and always feminine fashion.

56. Austen Leigh, quoted in Rita McWilliams-Tullberg, *Women at Cambridge* (London: Victor Gollancz, 1975), 122.

3 FOLLOWING THE PRECEDENT

Lady Margaret Hall, Somerville, and Westfield Colleges

There seems to me to be such a spirit of energy in her, that if she does not act, she will either speculate or theorize, or pine and prey on herself. I do believe that hard homely work, such as this school-keeping, is the best outlet for what otherwise might run to extravagance—more especially as you say the hope of it has already been an incentive to improvement in home duties.
Charlotte Yonge, 1856 [1]

During the first decades of their existence, Girton and Newnham were run by principals or founders who nurtured the colleges from their early stages of infancy into their more mature and established years. Their first purpose-built houses were designed by architects who continued to build for them for the next thirty years. Consequently, these colleges present a unified architectural face expressive of the goals and interests of the founders. In contrast, the architecture of the three colleges discussed in this chapter, Lady Margaret Hall, Somerville, and Westfield is less cohesive due to the use of different architects, changes in principals, or lack of money. All three began in pre-existing houses which were then added onto as the student population grew, with additions which did not necessarily harmonize with the existing building. Their architectural and social histories are more checkered than those of the two Cambridge examples, and therefore serve to shed further light on the issues which confronted founders of women's colleges and which ultimately conditioned the colleges' appearance.

The movement for women's higher education was slow to take off in Oxford. It was nine years after Emily Davies had begun her efforts to educate women at what was to become Girton College, that the issue gained real momentum in Oxford. This was largely the result of the efforts of the Reverend E. S. Talbot, then Warden of Keble College, who, inspired by Girton after visiting it with his wife, determined to instigate a similar system for women in Oxford. He recorded this inspiration in the following passage: "We came back to Oxford with this thought in our minds of starting a small residentiary enterprise, for which I suppose 'Hall' was the natural word."[2] As a result of his energetic campaigning, the Association for the Higher Education of Women in Oxford, commonly called the AEW, was founded on 22 June 1878. Talbot visualized a residence governed by the principles of the Church of England but this met with vehement resistance from a large faction of supporters of women's education who wanted a non-denominational enterprise. As a consequence of this religious conflict, it was decided to found two halls of residence, Somerville and Lady Margaret Hall, which opened their doors to students in 1879.

In accordance with Talbot's ideals, Lady Margaret Hall, named after Lady Margaret Beaufort, the pious mother of Henry VII, was established as an

Academical House [based] *on the Principles of the Church of England (with provision for the liberty of members of other religious bodies) which will secure to students the following advantages: a common life with the ways and tones of a Christian family; the protection of*

1. Charlotte Yonge, *The Daisy Chain: or Aspirations, A Family Chronicle* (1856; reprint, London: Macmillan, 1899), 135–36.
2. Rev. E. S. Talbot, "The Foundation," in *Lady Margaret Hall: A Short History*, ed. G. Bailey (London: Oxford University Press, 1923), 20.

certain rules as to hours, society, etc.; general supervision of studies, definite religious instructions and the advice and assistance of a lady of experience and other high qualifications, acting as Lady Principal.[3]

The first principal was Elizabeth Wordsworth, niece of the poet and daughter of the Bishop of Lincoln. Her ties to the Church were impeccable, and she was familiar with Oxford society, having visited and occasionally kept house for her brother, the Reverend John Wordsworth, fellow and tutor at Brasenose College. She was well suited to her post as mistress of a household of young women because of her connections and her reputation as a lively, intelligent lady from an upper-middle class background. Yet, somewhat surprising to twentieth-century perceptions of the women's movement, she had little or no interest in ambitious schemes for women's rights and education, although she saw the value of solid education in women's lives.

Wordsworth was very much a woman of her time and insisted that her students should be as adept in domestic skills as in intellectual pursuits. In an address she delivered to the Church Congress at Exeter in 1894 she outlined her ideal education for women:

the education of girls should disregard nothing. The minor graces of life, such as neat handwriting, skillful needlework, even the folding of a letter, or the way of opening and shutting a door, all the indescribable things the neglect of which often makes a really clever woman intolerable, are quite worth far more attention than they often receive.[4]

Such an attitude was fairly typical of the many early leaders in women's education, such as the Reverend F. D. Maurice at Queen's College, who, like Wordsworth, sought to improve women's lives through a more thorough education but not to alter social roles. Indeed, Wordsworth was vehemently opposed to women who tried to behave like men or model their lifestyles and behavior on the male example.

With the appointment of Wordsworth as principal came the search for an appropriate residence for the first students. Since the 1860s, St. John's College had been developing its Norham Manor estate in North Oxford into a residential suburb. The primary architect involved with this development was William Wilkinson, a pragmatic and somewhat provincial architect who designed many of the villas on the Estate in the Gothic style. Although he was not responsible for all the individual villas, he did have an important say in the laying out of the streets and the sites of the houses.[5]

In her book on the development of North Oxford, Tanis Hinchcliffe points out that in the 1860s through the 1880s seventy-five percent of the residents in this suburb were female. Many of these were servants or young girls attending school at the nearby convent, but in 1881 "a third of the heads of households were women, and they tended to preside over predominantly female households."[6] These women were often widows or spinsters with their own independent income.

The large suburb of North Oxford was broken up into smaller areas, each dominated by residents from particular classes or trades. Families in trade tended to be in one part of the suburb, whereas

3. Minutes of the Hall Committee, 1878–79, Lady Margaret Hall Archives, 37.
4. Elizabeth Wordsworth, "First Principles in Women's Education," in *Church Congress* (Exeter: James Parker, 1894), 16.
5. Andrew Saint, "Three Oxford Architects," *Oxoniesia* xxxv (1970): 53–102.
6. Tanis Hinchcliffe, *North Oxford* (New Haven: Yale University Press, 1992), 169.

58. Norham Manor Estate, North Oxford (by William Wilkinson, c. 1860). *Reproduced courtesy of the Bodleian Library, Oxford, MS. Top.gen. A. 22, fol. 27r.*

The houses women chose were for the most part in Norham Manor . . . and they were more likely to live in the smaller houses in streets like Museum, Norham, Bevington, and Winchester Roads. These houses were in those areas of the suburb favoured by University families, and the perceived shortage of suitable houses experienced by young tutors may have been because they were in competition with female heads who would also have been looking for the smaller, less expensive houses.[7]

In 1877, Parliament passed the Universities of Oxford and Cambridge Act which withdrew the requirement of celibacy for fellows of the universities. This meant that individual colleges were at liberty to allow their fellows to marry. This was a controversial issue, but by the late 1870s and early 1880s those Oxford fellows who did marry were settling with their young families in North Oxford, most particularly in the Norham Manor estate, near the University Parks.

Mrs. Humphrey Ward, herself the wife of an Oxford fellow, described this fledgling community in her autobiography. Although no one was very wealthy:

we all gave dinner parties, furnished our houses with Morris papers, old chests and cabinets and blue pots . . . Most of us were very anxious to be up-to-date, and in the fashion, whether it was in aesthetics, in housekeeping, or education.[8]

In general then, this area of North Oxford consisted of young University families

7. Ibid., 170.
8. Mrs. Humphrey Ward, *A Writer's Recollections* (London: W. Collins, 1918), 119–20.

59. Old Hall and the 1880 addition by Champneys, Lady Margaret Hall, Oxford. *Reproduced courtesy of Lady Margaret Hall, Oxford.*

and of women. It was in this setting that the early advocates of women's education, such as Mr. and Mrs. E. S. Talbot, Mrs. Bertha Johnson, Mr. and Mrs. Arnold Toynbee and Elizabeth Wordsworth met, discussed plans for the venture and sent out circulars to advertise the college and recruit students.

Not surprisingly, the house found most suitable in which to begin this venture was tucked away at the end of Norham Gardens. No. 21, built by Pike and Messenger, was described as an "ugly white villa,"[9] but was considered to be a convenient and suitable house for the first nine students, with ten bedrooms and commodious public rooms. It was here that Lady Margaret Hall began, where life was conducted along the lines of an efficient and protective Christian household.

By 1880 correspondence had begun between Lady Margaret Hall and Mr. Omond, the bursar of St. John's, concerning an addition to the existing house in order to accommodate more students. Basil Champneys, the architect of Newnham College at Cambridge, was called in and designed a red brick house in the 'Queen Anne' style. Work was begun in 1880 but did not proceed smoothly. According to the letters from Mr. Omond, the college had several reservations regarding the building. One concern was whether such a building would be appropriate "on an estate laid out for purely residential purposes."[10] In a sense this concern is much like that expressed by the Reverend G. Reyner, bursar at St. John's College, Cambridge, in his correspondence with Miss Clough over the building of Newnham's first hall of residence. In both cases the men's colleges did not want an institution to be built on their land, and they stipulated that the buildings be of a domestic character in order to be used for residential purposes if these ventures into women's education did not succeed.

9. Rev. E. S. Talbot, "The Foundation," 23.
10. T. S. Omond to Basil Champneys, 1 October 1880, Letterbook 1880, St. John's College Archives, St. John's College, Oxford, 184.

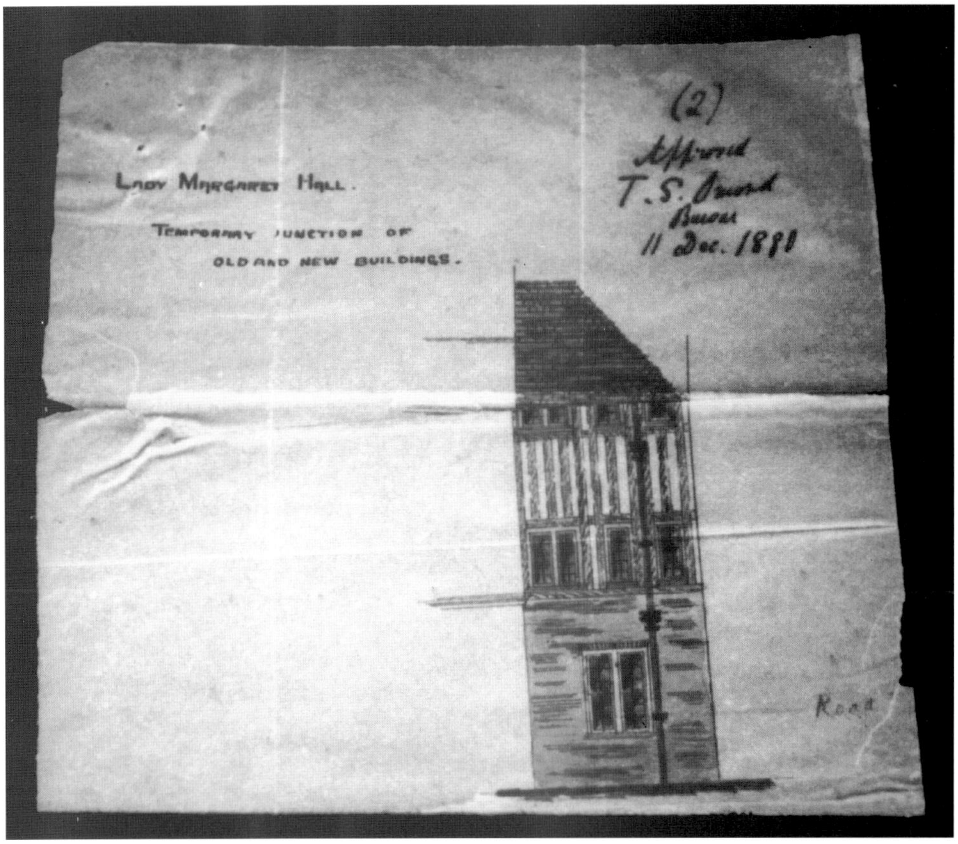

60. Connecting Piece (by Champneys, 1880), Lady Margaret Hall. *Reproduced courtesy of the Archives, St. John's College, Oxford.*

The problem of Champneys' addition was solved in two ways. The first was to connect the two buildings with a temporary structure, thereby enabling the houses to be divided and sold separately should the college fail. Much discussion was given to the manner of linking the two buildings. St. John's insisted that it be easily dismantled so that the new "house [could be] convertible into a decent single house, though perhaps not a very commodious one."[11]

The other concern of the bursar and the committee at St. John's was with the Champneys building itself. By November 1880, the work had begun, and evidence of the red brick, 'Queen Anne' house was emerging. Mr. Omond's letters to Champneys express obvious concern over the style and materials used in the addition. In a letter dated 12 November, Omond pleaded with Champneys:

there still remains the point of outward appearance, and I wish you could suggest something to mitigate the harshness of the contrast. I should be very sorry to ask you to stucco over your Reading brick, or paint the existing house red! But can nothing be done to soften or break the intolerable glare of the difference?[12]

Unfortunately, the response from Champneys in which he defended his choice of style and material has not survived in the archives. But this conflict highlights the architectural debate surrounding the 'Queen Anne' style which was discussed in detail in the previous chapter. We cannot know exactly what Champneys wrote to

11. Omond to Champneys, 12 November 1880, Letterbook 1880, St. John's College Archives, 266.
12. Ibid. 239–40.

Omond in defense of his addition to the house at Norham Gardens, but it is safe to assume that he saw his choice of the 'Queen Anne' style and its materials as the most suitable both for an individual house and as a residence for women. It did not matter to Champneys that the new clashed with the old; the new was appropriate and continued a precedent that Champneys had set at Newnham.

The bursar and the committee at St. John's resigned themselves to Champneys' addition but continued to plead for a smoother transition in the building connecting the two houses. Finally, Champneys sent in a drawing showing a half-timbered connection which would combine red brick with white stucco, thus blending the two colors of the houses. Omond considered the half-timber work "the best thing yet proposed"[13] and the work continued.

Champneys was called in again in 1884 to make some alterations to his addition, but after that no more building was done at Lady Margaret Hall for about ten years. Instead, the overflow of students lived in nearby houses, under the charge of an assistant principal. But in 1893 correspondence was begun over obtaining the freehold for the land to the east of Champneys' addition for the purposes of future expansion. The architect Reginald Blomfield was chosen to be in charge of the new developments at Lady Margaret Hall.

Blomfield began his career under the influence of Richard Norman Shaw, and his early work was in the 'Queen Anne' style. In 1887 he joined the Art Workers Guild and consequently knew many of the Arts and Crafts architects such as E. S. Prior, Ernest Newton, and C. F. A. Voysey. By the late 1880s he had become interested in the work of English Renaissance architects such as Inigo Jones and Sir Christopher Wren, who served as profound influences on him throughout his career. He turned away from the eclectic blending of styles that characterized the 'Queen Anne' and developed an architecture based on balance, symmetry and Classical details. Between 1890 and the First World War, his work was primarily domestic, including small and mid-sized houses for the middle classes as well as larger country houses. It was in this domestic 'Wrenaissance' style that Blomfield designed the new buildings for Lady Margaret Hall.

The plans he drew up in 1895 included one new block of students' rooms directly to the east of the Champneys house. But he also presented a scheme for future development which included "a more elaborate and ornamental block containing library, dining hall and kitchen premises, and beyond that again another block of rooms to be built when and if required."[14] This scheme was laid out in a meandering, incomplete H-plan, with no attempt to create the quadrangles that so characterized the men's colleges. Nonetheless all the blocks were to be connected so as to facilitate communication between the halls and eliminate the need to journey outside. Old Hall and Champneys' house were to be connected to the new south wing by a row of cloisters.

This south wing, which came to be called Wordsworth, is a modest and graceful essay in the late seventeenth-century style that Blomfield preferred for his domestic buildings (see color illustration 9). Built of red brick with white stone dressings, it is a solid rectangular block, with the three center bays pulled out from the main body of the building to highlight the middle. The corners are boldly emphasized by quoins and the cornices interrupted by curving pediments, elaborating the entrances. It had

13. Omond to Champneys, 17 November, 1880, Letterbook 1880, St. John's College Archives, 253.
14. Georgina Battiscombe, *Reluctant Pioneer, A Life of Elizabeth Wordsworth* (London: Constable, 1978), 150.

61. Heathfield Park, Sussex (by Reginald Blomfield, 1896–97). *Reproduced courtesy of the Royal Commission for Historic Monuments.*

rooms for twenty-six students and two tutors and included a common room and a drawing room, with a temporary dining room built on its north side.

It was opened for students in 1896 and was praised by the college. The *Brown Book*, which recorded the events and development of the college through its history, described certain aspects of the house in the following passage:

A most successful feature in the building is its pleasant corridors, through the windows of which there are delightful views of the Cherwell and the parks. The students' rooms are larger than in the Old Hall, and each have two windows with low window seats; the dining room has a floor and arched ceiling of green stained wood. . . . The whole building is lit with electric light, and charmingly furnished under the superintendence of Mrs. Toynbee.[15]

The design of Wordsworth bears striking resemblance to Wittington, a house Blomfield built in 1897 in Medmenham, Buckinghamshire, for Sir Hudson Kearley (see color illustration 10). Though slightly smaller in scale, and with two wings projecting from the rectangular block, Wittington is also built in a style derived from the late seventeenth century. Here again the corners are defined by stone quoins and the doorway articulated by smooth rustication. Dormer windows punctuate the third storey and the center of the roof is emphasized, by a cupola in the case of Wittington and by a widow's walk at Lady Margaret Hall. Blomfield used similar detailing in his restoration work on Heathfield Park, Sussex, of 1896–97, where the solid rectangular block was articulated by quoins and the central entrance was emphasized with Classical simplicity.

The ground floor plan of Wittington which has a spacious hall and servants' wing, is slightly more elaborate than that of Wordsworth, where the simple hall and

15. "The Brown Book, 1892–1907," Lady Margaret Hall Archives, Lady Margaret Hall, Oxford, 17.

62. Wordsworth Hall, ground floor plan, Lady Margaret Hall (by Blomfield, 1897).

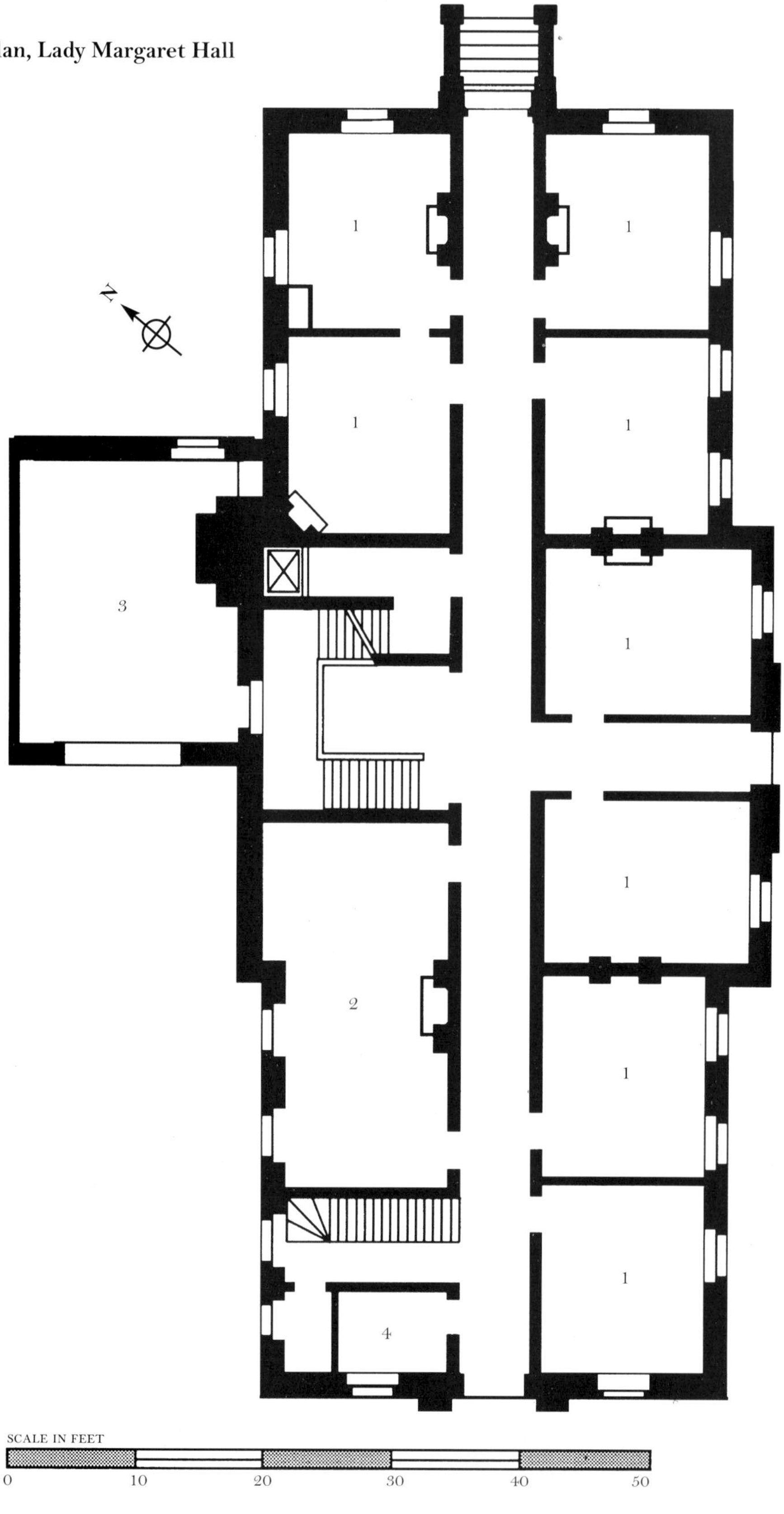

1. students' bedrooms
2. common room
3. temporary dining room
4. lavatory

63. Wittingdon, ground floor plan (by Blomfield, 1897).

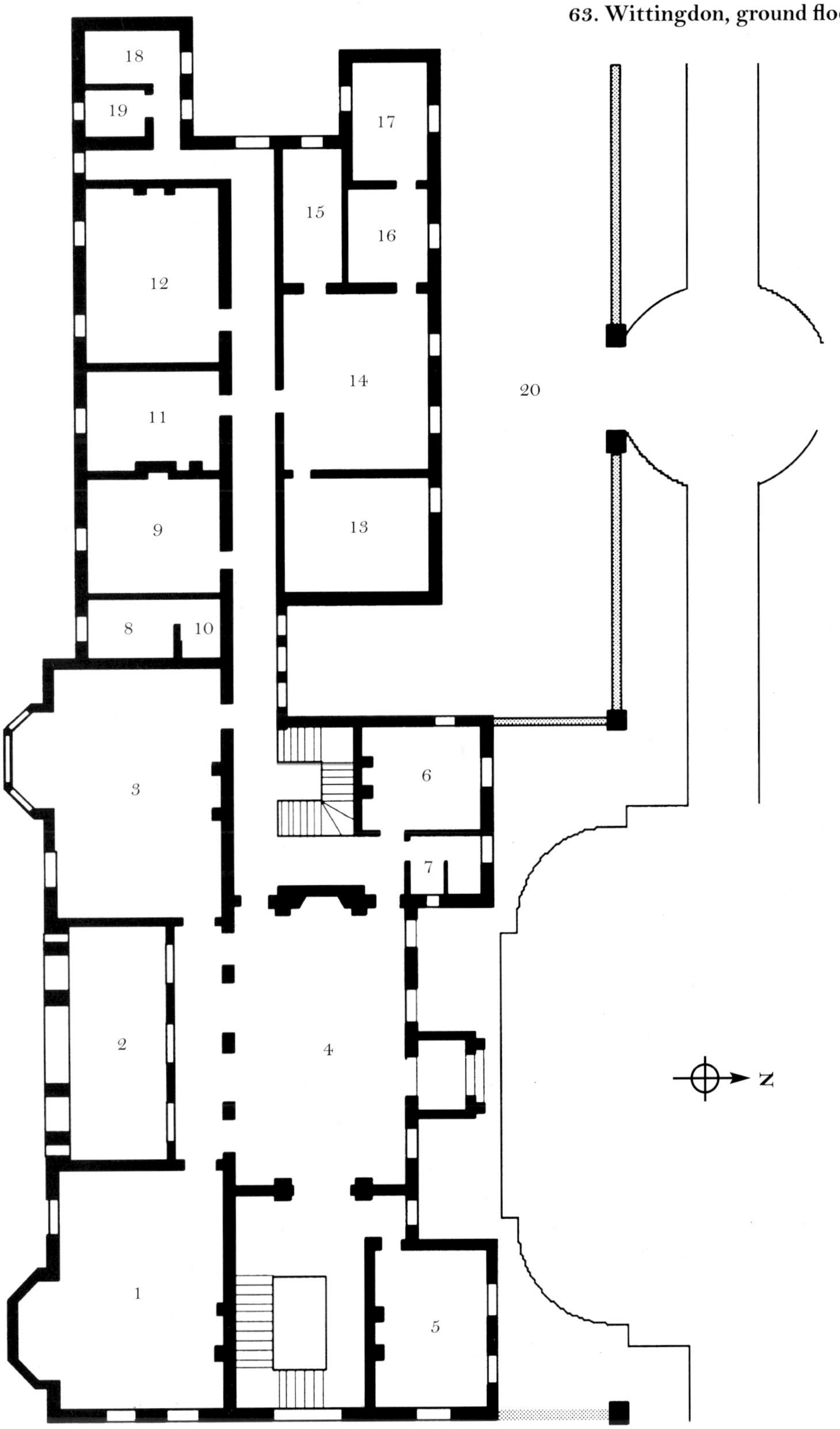

1. drawing room
2. loggia
3. dining room
4. hall
5. smoking room
6. gun room
7. lavatory & water closet
8. butler's bedroom
9. butler's pantry
10. strong room
11. housekeeper
12. servants' hall
13. scullery
14. kitchen
15. larder
16. larder
17. dairy
18. lamps
19. boots
20. backyard

64. Talbot Hall, garden facade, Lady Margaret Hall (by Blomfield, 1905).

65. Wretham Hall, Norfolk (by Blomfield, 1913). *Reproduced courtesy of the Royal Commission for Historic Monuments.*

staircase mark the center of the building. Even so, the similarities are striking. A central corridor runs through both, which establishes a strong axis of communication and the main stairs are highlighted, while the back stairs are kept off to the side. This continues the precedent set at Girton and Newnham of using a system of corridors rather than the staircases of the traditional men's colleges.

The similarities between a house built for a private client and that built for a fledgling college are not surprising in view of the ideals held by the founders of Lady Margaret Hall. Champneys built in a domestic genre for both Newnham and Lady Margaret Hall. Elizabeth Wordsworth had definite ideas regarding the structure of a college for women. In an address given in 1894, she outlined her perfect college which was one "consisting of moderately sized groups of students, each of them small enough to have somewhat of a homelike character."[16] Blomfield's plans for Wordsworth Hall, which maintained an intimate scale and continued the scheme of

16. Wordsworth, "First Principles in Women's Education," 14–15.

66. Goldsmith's College, London (by Blomfield, 1911). *Reproduced courtesy of the London Metropolitan Archives, ref. 81/9067.*

separate, simplified domestic blocks, were well suited for a college endeavoring to maintain a "homelike" atmosphere.

The next building campaign at Lady Margaret Hall was begun in 1905 with the erection of the center block, which is now called Talbot Hall, named after one of the founders, the Reverend E. S. Talbot (see color illustration 11). This is the grandest of the halls. With its formal, Classical facade, pulled out in the center, and the semi-circular stairs that gracefully spill down from the half-domed entranceway, this building greets the visitor with the gracious elegance of a large country house. The eastern facade has a row of four buttresses which accentuate the vertical and frame the full length windows. It is slightly more imposing in character than the front, but the volutes above the buttresses, the finials, and the detailed carving beneath the second floor windows break up and soften the surfaces. Its outline, window treatment and use of finials on the roofline present a facade much like that of Wretham Hall in Norfolk which Blomfield designed in 1913. It also bears some resemblance to Blomfield's work at Goldsmith's College from about the same time, with the vertical emphasis and round, Wren-like windows. But the heavy murality and sparseness of detail at Goldsmith's give an institutional flavor which is avoided at Lady Margaret Hall and Wretham Hall.

The 'Wrenaissance' style which Blomfield developed for his houses and his work at Lady Margaret Hall has little in common with the style of traditional Oxbridge colleges. Not only are the materials, red-brick with stone dressing, atypical of most of the colleges at Oxford, but the Classical vocabulary is also different. The classicism of Worcester College or Magdalen College is severe and monumental, built in the yellow stone which is so typical of Oxford University. There is none of the gracious warmth and intimacy which characterizes the buildings at Lady Margaret Hall.

It is not just in the corridor system that Blomfield broke with traditional collegiate plans. Upon entering Talbot Hall for instance, the visitor finds him/herself in an open and airy foyer of small but elegant proportion. Small rooms branch off of this. On the first and second floors are the dining hall and library respectively. Unlike the

67. Worcester College, Oxford (by Henry Keene, 1753–59).

68. New Buildings, Magdalen College, Oxford (by Dr. Clarke, 1733).

grand, double storey halls and libraries in which men ate and read, these rooms were modest and though paneled, are more like similar rooms in large country houses.

Blomfield's work at Lady Margaret Hall was influential in the planning of women's colleges in the twentieth century. The contained Classical blocks which he designed proved to be a comfortable and elegant solution for women's halls of residence. In these early designs at Oxford, Blomfield created a building type which had echoes of a grand tradition of English building under Sir Christopher Wren, but

69. Talbot Hall, entrance hall, Lady Margaret Hall, Oxford. *Reproduced courtesy of Lady Margaret Hall Oxford.*

which borrowed architectural traditions from a domestic vocabulary deemed suitable for a residence for women.

Talbot Hall marks an important shift in the organization of the college. With the erection of a large library and a formal dining hall some of the intimacy of the individual houses was lost, at the expense of creating a more comprehensive and self-confident community. While the students continued to live in the smaller blocks under the care of a lady principal, the college was unified by the new building. As discussed in more detail later, this symbolized a new phase in women's colleges, during which women's presence in the University was generally more obtrusive and assertive.

The evolution of Somerville Hall from very modest beginnings into Somerville College, with its more confident approach in the twentieth century, closely parallels that of Lady Margaret Hall. As stated earlier, Somerville Hall was the result of the work of those involved in the AEW who wanted to see a non-denominational hall for women students in Oxford. Some of their founding members included the Reverend J. Percival, President of Trinity College who became the first President of Somerville,

70. Walton House, Oxford (by Daniel Taunton, 1826). From the *Graphic* (31 July 1880). *Reproduced courtesy of the Principal and Fellows, Somerville College, Oxford.*

Mr. Arthur Sidgwick, brother of Henry Sidgwick at Cambridge, Mr. and Mrs. Vernon Harcourt, and Mr. and Mrs. Humphrey Ward, all prominent members of the University community. The first principal was Miss Shaw Lefevre, who was highly regarded in Oxford society and was remembered as at all times gracious and ladylike, expecting similar behavior from her students.

The committee's search for a proper residence led them north of Oxford and west of the Woodstock Road to Walton House. The house had been built by Daniel Taunton in 1826 on land owned by St. John's College. The leasehold that Somerville took over was due to expire in 1884, but in 1881 the Somerville Council successfully negotiated the purchase of the freehold.[17] The house was set on two acres at the end of a long lane shaded by big trees on one side and a stable and small row of cottages on the other. Behind Walton House was a large field, with an orchard and kitchen gardens beyond. It was described as having a "very countrified aspect," especially because:

> *for the first few years two Cows and a Pig formed part of the establishment but these were replaced later by a Pony and Donkey which might be seen disporting themselves in the field, adding to the picturesque and homey look of the place.*[18]

There was room for the first twelve students, as well as for the principal. With help from members of the council such as Mrs. Harcourt and Mrs. Humphrey Ward, as well as gifts from the students, the drawing room and dining room were prettily decorated, and with the gift of a piano from Miss Ewart, (from Newnham's committee) the house was praised for being quite "home-like" and comfortable.

By 1881, conditions had become cramped and T. G. Jackson, a fellow of Wadham College and an eminent architect responsible for many important works for the University, was hired to build an addition with eleven rooms for students and a sitting room for the principal. For the elevation, Jackson departed from the existing late Georgian solidity of Walton House, and designed in the Jacobean style. This style was more indigenous to Oxford than the 'Queen Anne' and can be seen on a grand scale in buildings such as the Examination Schools built by Jackson in 1876–82. The style shares certain similarities with the 'Queen Anne' of Champneys' work, particularly in its curving gables and white sash windows. But Jackson's work

17. Hinchcliffe, *North Oxford*, 154.
18. Somerville College, Log Book, 1879–1907, Somerville College Archives, Somerville College, Oxford, 14.

71. Addition to Walton House (by T. G. Jackson, 1881). *Reproduced courtesy of Principal and Fellows, Somerville College, Oxford.*

72. Examination Schools, Oxford (by Jackson, 1876–82).

73. West Building and floorplan, Somerville College, Oxford (by H. W. Moore, 1885). *Reproduced courtesy of Principal and Fellows, Somerville College, Oxford.*

lacks the delicacy of Champneys' addition at Lady Margaret Hall, due in part to the choice of grey stone with red brick trim which was more in harmony with the existing house. The Log Book praised Jackson's addition and appreciated that Mr. Jackson

took pains to plan at our suggestion for flower-balconies outside the windows and for (cushioned) window seats inside, with lockers below them for boots etc. while the windows in the passages were arranged for coal bunkers under the seats.[19]

The success of Somerville Hall in these early years can be measured architecturally. Once Jackson's wing had been filled, the overflow of students lived in the little cottages which lined the drive. By 1885 a new house was begun, this time by the architect H. W. Moore. Moore was then the architect for St. John's College and the North Oxford estates, having succeeded his uncle, William Wilkinson. Many of the villas which Moore built on the North Oxford land were of a domestic Gothic, in keeping with the precedent established by his uncle. But for Somerville, Moore built with red brick in an Elizabethan manner with oriel windows emphasizing the first floor and stone details outlining the gables. The simplicity of detail and the stable horizontality of the roof-line is shared with another house by Moore on Pullen's Lane in Oxford and is quite different from the strong verticals and more elaborate Gothic details that are more often associated with the villas of North Oxford, especially those by William Wilkinson.

The plan of Moore's building bears close resemblance to a private house with a central staircase and a simple spine-like corridor. In accordance with contemporary

19. Ibid., 20.

74. Pollock House, Pullen's Lane, Oxford (by Moore, 1889).

guides to planning houses, the drawing room faces south-east with a large bay window for sunlight, while the dining-room is sited on the north-east corner, this being a room in which sunlight was not considered as important. The building was illustrated in *Building News* in 1887 and described in the following:

The idea of this scheme is that the students should live as members of a large family under the care of a lady principal, each being provided with a separate apartment, fitted up as a sitting room and bedroom. Hence the arrangement of the plan corresponds somewhat to that of an ordinary residence.[20]

This illustrates the underlying ideology of the women's colleges in their early years. They were designed to reflect the home physically, and therefore act as a domestic supplement for the young female students.

This idea was also enforced by a passage in the Somerville "General Report" of 1884–85 in a discussion of plans to build a new house. The report justifies a separate building because it was believed that:

a very large addition to the numbers under one roof would have seriously modified the relations between the Principal and the students, and gone far to destroy that intimate, personal knowledge and care, those constant and easy opportunities for influence and advice, which have been hitherto possible, and to which we attribute so much of the success of our Hall.[21]

Such concerns bear a close resemblance to Miss Wordsworth's concept of a federated college which consisted of a small number of students who lived under the protective supervision of a lady principal. Both Somerville and Lady Margaret Hall, in their early years, preferred a domestic scale for their colleges, as did Newnham at Cambridge.

20. "Somerville Hall, Oxford," *Building News* (9 September 1887): 394.

21. Somerville College, "Somerville Hall, Oxford, General Report 1884–5" in *The Report Book. 1879–99* (Baxter Pointer: Oxford), 11.

The reasons for this preference are complex and many. They have to do with the nineteenth-century concept of the home as the root of social stability and women's subsequent role within that home. The Victorian household was structured according to a clearly-defined hierarchy with the father and husband at the head and domestic help at the bottom. But although the husband ultimately controlled the purse-strings and made the most important decisions, the home itself was considered to be the wife's domain. In her charge were the decisions regarding the smooth working of the house and the moral development of the children. As the helpmate of man she was considered, not less important than man, but different, with special, innate skills that were best employed in nurturing roles, such as mother and wife or, failing that, nurse or teacher.

As discussed previously, a woman's mental and physical health was held to be far more delicate and susceptible than that of her male counterpart, and therefore needed greater protection. Elizabeth Wordsworth cautioned in 1894:

It is no secret among medical men, that many of our young women have already fallen victim to the over-strain which an eager nature, acted upon by that esprit de corps which is so strong in school and college girls, has often led them to undergo in playing, when a sensible mother would have insisted on their declining to do so.[22]

Hence girls and young women needed the special supervision that was found in good homes, to protect them from mental strain and physical decline.

Both Somerville and Lady Margaret Hall took pains to establish routines that closely mirrored the domestic environment from which the students had come. In 1914, Miss Shaw Lefevre's sister recounted an important belief held by the first principal regarding the workings of her college:

I remember . . . that she thought our daily intercourse in college should be something like that of a country house party — many independent hours, much cooperative occupation, all the deference to 'the College' which we should accord to a hostess and all the care to contribute to the common life which would be given by fellow guests.[23]

Thus the domestic model was relied upon for both the physical and social environment of the colleges for women in the first decades of their existence.

After the first part of Moore's building, which was called the West Building, was completed in 1886, the growth of Somerville was haphazard until the turn of the century. In 1890, a gymnasium was added by Moore to the West Building and in 1891 a house on the Woodstock Road was purchased to house an additional six students. In 1894, Moore was recalled to add onto the West Building nineteen more rooms for students, a charming little porter's lodge facing onto Walton Street and a music room. In 1893, Walter Cave, a London based architect specializing in domestic work, was called in to replace the cottages and stables which fronted the Woodstock Road with a gate-house, a porter's lodge, and a music room.

Concurrent with these additions, Walter Cave was hired to rebuild the Old Hall. He built a wing extension on the north side which echoed Jackson's, and he pulled out the entrance wall and raised the roof, adding another storey. In 1897–98, Cave

22. Wordsworth, "First Principles in Women's Education," 12.
23. E. Shaw Lefevre, "Miss Madeline Shaw Lefevre, First Principal of Somerville College, Oxford, 1879–1889, died 1914," Shaw Lefevre File, Somerville College Archives, 1914.

was also responsible for what were called the Eleanor Smith Cottages (see color illustration 12). These connected with the existing cottages on the north side of the property and were in a simple but intimate red brick. Very little of these cottages remains at Somerville now although there is still a small chunk wedged in between the later buildings from the 1950s. All these works were on a small scale and did little to change the intimate character of Somerville.

In 1889, Miss Shaw Lefevre retired and was replaced by Miss Agnes Maitland, whose tenure as principal coincided with several changes in the college. Miss Maitland was chosen out of a long list of potential candidates. She had been an examiner to the Northern Union of Schools of Cookery for twelve years and was well qualified in hygiene and "domestic management." In addition she had a sound knowledge of English literature and had good social connections, both in London and in Edinburgh. Interestingly, Miss Maitland's domestic qualifications seemed to have more influence over the committee in charge than the academic achievements of other candidates. For example, Miss Moberly, who also applied for the post, was not chosen, despite having been educated at Newnham and holding a job as headmistress of a public day school. The choice of Maitland is not surprising considering the concern of the committee and Miss Shaw Lefevre that domestic efficiency be maintained and that the principal be a lady of good social standing. Miss Maitland's knowledge of hygiene may also have been a reassuring element in convincing parents that their daughters' health would be carefully looked after.

As principal, Miss Maitland proved to be more ambitious for Somerville's future than her predecessor. It was she who pushed to have the status of Somerville changed from that of a Hall to a College. This was accomplished in 1894 and marks an important shift in the attitude of the college towards itself and towards women's education in general. While the women's colleges at Oxford continued to exist in a quiet and modest fashion, an increasing number of voices crying for greater recognition from the University were being heard. In 1895, demands were made to grant women degrees if they had passed the same examinations as the men. This request was not granted, nor was it even supported by all those concerned with women's education, such as Elizabeth Wordsworth. But the move signified a new degree of confidence and ambition on the part of the women's colleges, an ambition which Miss Maitland encouraged, albeit in a ladylike manner.

The next major building campaign at Somerville was the raising of the Pfeiffer Library (see color illustration 13). In 1902, Basil Champneys was called in to design an independent block. This was sited between Old Hall and the West Building and connected to both via a covered walkway. It is in a simple Renaissance style, with blocked pilasters and Ionic columns and an open central loggia along the ground floor. The oriel windows subtly hark back to Champneys' 'Queen Anne' work at Lady Margaret Hall, but the use of stone trim and the orders give a more somber tone to the whole. There is none of the exuberant and curvaceous energy found in his work at Newnham, and the strong horizontals of the string-course and roofline are suggestive of a more formal and non-residential function for the building. In spite of this formality, the Pfeiffer Library is a distinct contrast to Champneys' other libraries such as the Rylands Library in Manchester of 1890–99 and the one he built for Mansfield College in 1887–89 in Oxford (see figs. 57 and 56). For both of these he built in the

75. Maitland Hall, Somerville College (by E. Fisher, 1913).

76. Maitland Hall, interior, Somerville College (by Fisher, 1913).

Decorated Gothic style which was rich in its associations with the ancient tradition of education and learning. But for Somerville, a young college for women, he deliberately avoided Gothic and chose a style less laden with academic connotations.

The library was symbolically important for Somerville. Just as the Talbot building at Lady Margaret Hall marked an important shift in the organization of the college, so the Pfeiffer Library was the first step in a similar process of unification at Somerville. It served to connect the two separate halls physically. But more significantly, it was a communal place where all the students could meet and study and it was quite obviously, not a house. The Pfeiffer library had no domestic purpose, but was intended solely as an academic library. As such, it suggests a new confidence on the part of the college; a clear assertion that Somerville was more than just two halls of residence, but a college in its own right.

This idea was more clearly advanced in the building of Maitland Hall. The concept of this hall was originally put forward in a letter of 1910 from a group of old students. In this correspondence, the alumni pointed out

that there was need of a hall large enough for all the College to take its meals in and to accommodate a large audience for lectures, also of a new suite of Principal's rooms, and finally, that it was desirable, in the interests of women's education in general, that additional accommodation should be provided, sufficient to bring the members of the College up to a hundred.[24]

The Hall was designed by Edmund Fisher, brother of H. A. L. Fisher, a well known historian who was then president of Somerville's governing council. Edmund Fisher was killed during the First World War, having built very little. But he won the competition for Maitland and was able to see it opened in 1913. It was built of dark red brick in a very simple, streamlined 'Wrenaissance' style. Plans had originally been suggested to build in stone, but lack of funds meant the tradition of red brick at women's colleges continued. It consisted of a large hall with dark wood paneling and a barrel vaulted ceiling, which was considered to vie with the traditional men's college halls in both size and dignity. It also included kitchens, better rooms for the principal, improved common rooms for the staff and students and more bed-sitting rooms for students. It is large and severe and makes no attempts to include the dainty details that so characterized the earlier buildings.

The formal dining halls in Maitland and Talbot mark an end to the practice of the women students dining together in small groups in their individual houses. This was a practice consciously adopted from Newnham by both Somerville and Lady Margaret Hall. It had facilitated the homelike intimacy considered such a vital part of the women's colleges, by offering regular occasions for the principals to meet and chat with their students. But by the early twentieth century, this tradition was abandoned for the sake of greater formality and in imitation of the male precedent.

The erection of Talbot and Maitland Halls in 1906 and 1913 respectively, highlight a crucial struggle under way in women's education by the turn of the century. For the first twenty years women's education at Oxford had been conducted in a quiet and unobtrusive fashion. The movement began with tentative and cautious steps. It was not at all clear to the men and women involved in this experiment what form it should take and whether it would prove worthwhile. Critics and skeptics

24. H. A. L. Fisher, Vice Chancellor of Sheffield University, "Address from the President of the College," 1913, in Log Book, 1907–, Somerville College Archives, 2.

77. Views of Somerville College, from the *Graphic. Reproduced courtesy of Principal and Fellows, Somerville College, Oxford.*

were scathing in their analyses of the venture and prophesied catastrophic results such as infertility, lunacy and the basic breakdown of society if women were trained at a university level. Such fears were not voiced merely by men who felt their social supremacy threatened. Some women were just as opposed to the prospect, concerned that if women were educated like men they would begin to behave as men, thus eliminating the differences between the sexes which were so celebrated in the nineteenth century. The idea of an aggressive bluestocking, loud and unladylike, made the majority of society uneasy. Both Miss Wordsworth and Miss Shaw Lefevre saw the masculine woman as abhorrent, indeed Miss Wordsworth was quoted as saying that in her youth, she would have "preferred occupying the stiffest of upright chairs, in a thorough draft"[25] to sitting beside a woman from a ladies' college.

As at Cambridge, the most immediate and therefore threatening obstacle facing these fledgling colleges at Oxford, was the University itself. Although some of the most energetic and enthusiastic supporters of women's education were eminent dons at Oxford, the majority were opposed to the idea, or at least indifferent. At the start, these women's colleges existed on the generosity and goodwill of the University. When Balliol College first allowed women to attend certain lectures with male undergraduates, it did so voluntarily, and was under no official obligation. Not until the women's colleges actively began to demand degrees, in 1895, was the issue of women's education given much attention from the University. The women were allowed to exist on the sidelines as long as they did not noticeably threaten the male bastion. But the issue of degrees involved the governing of the University as a whole and, as at Cambridge, it was to that issue that hostility towards the women's colleges became open and vocal.

These obstacles to women's higher education had a profound impact on the shape of the women's colleges at Oxford. As we have seen, their architectural form was

25. Battiscombe, *Reluctant Pioneer*, 102.

78. Common Room, Old Hall, Lady Margaret Hall, Oxford. *Reproduced courtesy of Lady Margaret Hall, Oxford.*

domestic. In their first buildings the domestic character was of course taken for granted. But the subsequent buildings maintained the domestic tradition, both in their plans and their architectural style. They did so in order to counter the arguments of their critics. Fear of criticism also conditioned the routine of the women's lives, which was carefully laid out with hours set aside for study, meals, entertainment and exercise. By 10:30P.M., the women were to be in their rooms, preferably sleeping. Students who stayed up late studying were reprimanded for risking their health by overwork. As at Girton and Newnham the corridor system made it possible to monitor the women's movements and keep track of their habits.

Care was also taken to furnish the buildings in a comfortable and homey manner. William Morris papers covered the walls of the drawing and dining rooms, blue china rested in the cupboards, donated prints and photographs hung on the walls and above the mantel. The author of an article in the *Lady's Pictorial* of 1892 described the drawing rooms of Somerville as "particularly cheerful, cozy and homelike,"[26] thus reassuring parents and skeptics that their daughters would continue to live in a domestic environment.

While constructing a domestic atmosphere in which the women would study, the principals also took great pains to see to it that the behavior of the students was that of middle class ladies. In the early days, Miss Wordsworth insisted that her students wear gloves and a hat whenever they went outside, even if they were in the privacy of their own garden. One anecdote passed down through the years, describes an incident in which one rebellious student at Somerville thought to defy the principal, Miss Shaw Lefevre. Knowing that Miss Shaw Lefevre insisted that her students dress modestly, she wore a rather gaudy hat. When the principal asked her to change,

26. L. T. Meade, "English Girls and Their Colleges," *Lady's Pictorial* v (2 January 1892): Somerville College Archives.

she replied that this was the only hat she had; whereupon Miss Shaw Lefevre offered the student one of her own hats, and would not let her leave until she had changed.[27] In a similar incident, Mrs. Bertha Johnson, secretary of Lady Margaret Hall, was asked by the committee to install a large, full-length mirror in Old Hall "in the interest of tidiness as to skirts and shoes."[28] Women were chaperoned everywhere they went and were never allowed to have a private session with a male tutor. Lady chaperons followed the women to lectures and excursions, ever vigilant of the students' safety and behavior.

All these concerns for the appearance of life in a ladies' college, from the residential character of the buildings to the gloves which the students wore, were of vital importance to the success of women's higher education. It was crucial in this first phase of the women's colleges in Oxford that nothing be done to fuel criticisms of the experiment. It is almost possible to match the critics' fears regarding the results of women's education with efforts on the part of principals, students and planning committees to allay those fears. For example, the more voices heard against bluestockings, the more care and attention was paid to the students' appearances and evidence was given that the ladies in college could still pour tea, do needlework and play the piano. Similarly, the greater the outcry against direct, academic competition with men, the greater was the emphasis on the feminine quality of life in the halls and the specially arranged course of study which was best suited to a woman's needs. Mrs. Bertha Johnson summed up these worries in the following:

It was a vital necessity for the ultimate success of our work that nothing should at first happen in any way to make College authorities anxious, or to strengthen the very decided initial prejudice of the undergraduate against the supposed 'bluestockings' who were invading Oxford. There was not one amongst us who did not feel the absolute necessity of great care.[29]

Nestled on the outskirts of the town of Oxford and the University itself, Lady Margaret Hall and Somerville spent the first twenty years of their existence in quiet and ladylike modesty. As Annie Rogers described them:

They were within easy reach if you wished to visit them, or to keep an observant eye on them, and yet they did not thrust themselves upon you. No one could possibly suppose that such modest establishments could rival the men's colleges. In the early days, at least, they had a domestic character. Their whole attitude was most suitably feminine, and it is, I believe, safe to say that they have never been unpopular even if they have roused unreasonable alarm.[30]

But as the women's presence in the University became more established, and a new, more confident generation of students enrolled, the shape of the colleges began to change. With their own halls and libraries, Somerville and Lady Margaret Hall began to assert themselves as colleges in their own right and to insist upon physical manifestations which proclaimed their status.

This was not a smooth or rapid evolution. By 1913, when Maitland Hall was opened, the younger generation of students and alumni were growing increasingly impatient with the modesty and what they saw as outmoded rules that had structured Somerville College from the beginning. They began to take for granted the

27. "Miss Shaw Lefevre Obituary," in *Journal of Education* (November 1914): 793–94.
28. Bertha Johnson, "The First Beginnings 1873–90", in *Lady Margaret Hall: A Short History*, 48.
29. Ibid., 51.
30. Annie Rogers, *Degrees by Degrees* (Oxford: Oxford University Press, 1938), 157–58.

existence of women's colleges and to claim for women in more strident voices the rights of suffrage and full admission to the University. This did not sit well with the older generation, who had seen their quiet and humble methods blossom into respected places of learning. This struggle is described in the book by Muriel Byrne and Catherine Mansfield on Somerville, when they discuss the tenures of Miss Maitland, the second principal and her successor, Miss Emily Penrose:

If Miss Maitland led enthusiasts, Miss Penrose had the far more difficult task of governing a community critical of the position that had been won . . . As long as the cause of women's higher education was a cause to be fought for, the present was less important in itself than as a starting point for the future. The audience that met in the Maitland hall divided itself into two—the old generation and the new . . . the past thought of the future, the present thought of itself.[31]

Yet this new confidence of the younger generation did not result in a radical approach to building. Certainly, with large, formal dining halls, and the tradition of the high table, some aspects of the men's colleges were borrowed. But even after the War, Blomfield continued to build his blocks at Lady Margaret Hall in the late seventeenth-century style that characterized his early work there as well as his larger country houses. The next block built for Somerville, Penrose Hall, designed by Harold Rogers is, both in outline and style, much like Maitland Hall. These buildings will be discussed in more detail in Chapter Five with regard to the 'Wrenaissance' style and twentieth-century halls of residence for women. It was not until the 1930s in the case of Somerville and the 1960s at Lady Margaret Hall that the closed quadrangle was adopted from the traditional male colleges; the corridor system has never been abandoned in favor of separate stairways, both for financial and security reasons.

While the college halls at Somerville and Lady Margaret Hall provided residence for women away from home, they perpetuated an environment in which the codes of domesticity were rigidly enforced. This domesticity was considered a crucial tool in the experiment in women's education, and made the women's colleges a reality. For it was clearly the domestic environment which served to allay the critics' fears and which softened the dramatic reality of women's higher education.

The founders of Lady Margaret Hall and Somerville were put under tremendous pressure by their position on the sidelines of Oxford University, and domesticity was used as a means of gaining a foothold there. Westfield College, Hampstead, was founded on the outskirts of London, away from the critical eyes of a traditional university. It also used the domestic model for its organization. Westfield was begun close on the heels of Lady Margaret Hall and Somerville, in 1882. The ideas behind its foundation date back to 1880, when a small group of evangelicals began to consider the idea of intellectual training for women along Christian lines. In her book about the history of Westfield, *Castle Adamant*, Janet Sondheimer describes in thorough detail the slow and gradual evolution of Westfield and the key figures involved in its genesis. Two of these were Miss Caroline Cavendish and Major Charles Hamilton Malan. They were working to promote a scheme for the Higher Christian Education of Women in order to better train women for philanthropic,

31. Muriel Byrne and Catherine Mansfield, *Somerville College 1879–1921* (Oxford: Oxford University Press, 1921), 35–36.

evangelical work among the poor. Malan became involved through his work abroad with missionaries. During these years he had met female missionaries who had been trained at Mount Holyoke Seminary for women in western Massachusetts. Upon learning of this college for women, he determined to start up a similar venture in England, and published *The Higher Christian Education, Mental and Practical, of the Young Women of Britain*, in 1880. He was working with Cavendish towards the realization of this scheme when the Petrie family joined in the crusade.

Lieutenant Colonel Petrie was a semi-retired army officer with two intelligent and energetic daughters. In 1878, his oldest daughter, Mary, attended University College in London which was affiliated with the University of London. This was the first year that the University offered degrees to women and it was the first English university to do so. Both Colonel Petrie and his daughter became interested in women's higher education and when Mrs. Petrie introduced Mary to Cavendish and Major Malan, she enthusiastically volunteered to help with their work. Cavendish and Malan had already been in touch with a woman who was to be essential to the establishment of Westfield College, Miss Constance Louisa Maynard.

At the time when her correspondence began with Cavendish and Malan in 1880, Miss Maynard was teaching in St. Andrews, Scotland, at what was to become St. Leonard's School for Girls. She taught there with Louisa Lumsden, with whom she had studied at Girton. Maynard has already been mentioned in connection with Girton and her valuable record of life first in the iron rooms of Hitchin and then in Girton's first building. While she was intoxicated by the education she was receiving on the fringes of Cambridge, she was constantly worried by the irreligious attitude that prevailed amongst the early students. She attempted, without much success, to bring her fellow students round to more Christian ideals. It was through these experiences that she began to see the need for a college of higher education for women which was based on Christian principles, through which a woman might train her intellect for the good of others and the honor of God.

Thus it is not surprising that she was receptive to the early ideas of Cavendish and Malan, although she had certain reservations about the scheme. She disagreed with Malan's insistence that the college follow the example of Mount Holyoke, which admitted girls aged fifteen and older, and included an emphasis on domestic, as well as intellectual, training. Maynard had hoped for a religious version of Girton. While she worried over the differences during a holiday in Italy, Cavendish and Malan had a falling out, which freed Maynard, upon her return, to work more closely with the scheme and avoid what she saw as the unsatisfactory aspects of Malan's proposal.[32]

In the Autumn of 1880, Maynard left St. Andrews and came to London where she took drawing courses at the Slade School of Art and helped Miss Cavendish with her scheme. By this time, Cavendish had organized the Christian Women's Education Union, whose members shared four goals:

to permeate existing schools with Christian teaching; to promote 'among young ladies in their homes' the cultivation of their intellects to Christ; to establish a college on a Christian basis; and to start a periodical to give news of efforts in support of Christian education in all parts of the world.[33]

32. Janet Sondheimer, *Castle Adamant in Hampstead: A History of Westfield College 1882–1982.* (London: Westfield College, University of London, 1983), 13–14.
33. Ibid.,15.

Both Maynard and Mary Petrie were active in the Union; their earliest contributions being the mailing of course papers for the "College by Post" which was begun to satisfy the second of the Union's objectives.[34]

In January 1881 Maynard organized a meeting of prominent Christian schoolmistresses in order to garner support for a college and work out its requirements. It was decided that the college would prepare students for degrees from the University of London, making the London Matriculation (the standard entrance examination for the University of London) the prerequisite for entry. One of the headmistresses who attended the meeting was Miss Fanny Metcalfe. She and her sister ran Highfield, a well respected boarding school for girls. Fanny had been involved with the organization of Girton and she offered valuable support and advice to Maynard.

Throughout 1881, Maynard lectured to evangelical groups about the need for such a college, hoping that it might be realized within a few years. In December 1881, Maynard wrote in her diary about the possible genesis of the college and about her introduction to Holloway College, the subject of the following chapter, which was still in its infant stage, but which she found sufficiently intimidating:

The proposed College seemed the fixed point from which to act, and though distant, the schemes seemed clearly defined enough—Holloway College to be inquired into, if promising to be applied for, if hopelessly secular a whole new field in Miss Metcalfe's plan, which becomes more possible and more solid each time I heard of it. Yet it is not all so simple. The daring expedition to 'Holloway' was nearly fruitless, and the information collected around it very discouraging; yet it is so vast, so well backed up, so enormously rich, that it would be sheer folly to start an opposition.[35]

She had considered applying for the post of mistress of Holloway College, but Thomas Holloway, the founder, insisted on a non-denominational college for women. This was unacceptable to Maynard, who wanted to see an evangelical, thoroughly Anglican alternative to women's higher education; but it is no wonder that she was tempted by the great wealth behind Holloway College, and was not a little overwhelmed.

Maynard persevered and in early 1882 found a benefactress in Miss Ann Dudin-Brown, whose financial support made Westfield a reality five years before Holloway College ever opened its doors. Miss Dudin-Brown became involved in the college through the Petrie family. A wealthy woman and very religious, she gave liberally to many charities but by 1882 was searching for a cause related to religious education towards which she could direct some of her money. The Petries introduced her to Maynard and to the scheme for a college conducted along Christian lines.[36]

Miss Dudin-Brown was advised in her work by three men of importance in evangelical circles at the time. These were Canon James Fleming, vicar of St. Michael's Chester Square, Dr. Boultbee, who was familiar with religious education through his work as principal of St. John's Hall in Highbury, and Dr. Barlow who ran an institution for training missionaries. None of these figures, including Miss Dudin-Brown, was particularly committed to women's higher education, but all were drawn to the scheme because of its ardently religious basis. Rather than training women for new careers, they were intent on educating women along strict Christian principles in

34. Ibid.
35. Constance Louisa Maynard, The Green Books, CLM/ MSS/GB 18. 1881, Westfield and Queen Mary College Archives, 28–29.
36. Sondheimer, *Castle Adamant*, 18.

order that they might go out into the world and better help those in need and spread the Gospel.[37] Such a scheme was more like the example of Mount Holyoke which inspired Miss Dudin-Brown, who was not as interested in founding a religious version of the more academic Girton.

Miss Dudin-Brown's conservatism caused some conflict with Miss Maynard's desire to found a serious academic college, not a religious training school for young girls aged fifteen and older. But Maynard made a sound case for a college for women working for degrees from the University of London, with the strong Church of England base which Miss Dudin-Brown so wanted. By March of 1882, a council was formed, with Miss Maynard as Honorary Secretary. The council's task was to raise support for the scheme and more funds to add to Miss Dudin-Brown's £10,000 investment.

Several well-connected, leading members of the educational community were invited to one of the early meetings of the council when the scheme for the college was put forward. One of the guests was the Earl of Shaftesbury who was an active campaigner for improved conditions for the poor and insane, and whose influence in matters of social reform must have attracted the council. However, he came out strongly against the idea of a new college for women, indeed for higher education for women in general. Shaftesbury's powerful influence could have dealt a crippling blow to the scheme. However, Miss Maynard recorded in her diary how she brought tea to Shaftesbury and spoke calmly to him, asking him please not to speak out publicly against the college. He was apparently impressed with her enthusiasm and energy, and encouraged her to go forward and not to worry about his reaction.[38]

Thus reassured and at least privately encouraged, the founders pressed on with their plans. In March 1882, the council decided that:

It is not enough to guarantee a comfortable boarding-house where students can live while attending to lectures; we want something more, something that is not to be attained so easily; we want the many influences that flow from working together with one interest and one aim, we want the public spirit, the order and energy of a true corporate life.[39]

Teaching was to be according to the principles of the Church of England, and while there were no restrictions on who could apply, those with connections to the Anglican faith were more strongly encouraged.

The domestic arrangements, as laid out in the Council Minutes, borrow from the other colleges discussed so far. Not surprising for an early alumna of Girton, Maynard insisted on two rooms per student, a bedroom and sitting room such as she had enjoyed both at Hitchin and Cambridge. In common with all the other colleges considered, the internal discipline was organized so that: "Rules will be few, being only such as are necessary to the order and comfort of every large household, but it is expected that they will be perfectly obeyed.[40]

In the Minutes of 3 April 1882, Dr. Boultbee raised the point that a college so dependent upon spiritual values would be reassuring to religious parents whose daughters sought a higher education. He pointed out that these women

may be sent where Christian companionship may be had, where spiritual advice and sympathy

37. Ibid.
38. Ibid., 23.
39. Westfield College, Minutes of the Council 1882–87, 1882, Westfield and Queen Mary College Archives, 23.
40. Westfield College, Minutes of the Council 1882–87, 1882, 25.

may draw out latent spiritual life, and where the secularizing influence[s] of scientific study may find their true safe-guard in the atmosphere of a true Christian life.[41]

In several ways the aims of Westfield have much in common with the foundation of Lady Margaret Hall. The founders of both wanted to create truly Christian households in which academics and religion were equally stressed. It is somewhat surprising that there is no suggestion of co-operation between the two fledgling colleges. This may be due in part to the modest scale on which both these colleges began, but it is unlikely that Maynard was completely unaware of Lady Margaret Hall. A more probable explanation is that each college discussed thus far was begun by a small number of people who were all equally committed to their own personal vision of what a woman's college should or could be, and who tenaciously held onto their own particular ideals. We have already seen Emily Davies' response to Sidgwick and Miss Clough's scheme for higher education for women in Cambridge, and how their slightly different goals bred competition in what was otherwise a shared ambition. In the case of Westfield and Lady Margaret Hall, the strong evangelical conviction of Maynard and Dudin-Brown, and the need which Maynard saw for a women's college affiliated with the University of London, probably precluded any real co-operation with the Reverend Talbot and Miss Wordsworth's early work at Oxford.

Similarly, Miss Wordsworth and the advocates of women's education in Oxford, in the early 1880s, had no definite plans for a college per se offering full university degrees. While working to offer lectures and improved options for women, they would not have been particularly enthusiastic about ambitious plans for another college, much less one which set degrees from the University of London as one of its goals. Thus Westfield, while it borrowed some inspiration from other precedents in women's education, evolved along its own individual lines.

The main committee at Girton received the news of Miss Maynard's venture without much enthusiasm. Maynard recorded that Davies was lukewarm about the idea, but wished her old pupil luck.[42] Lady Stanley of Alderley, who had been a strong voice on Girton's committee from its inception, was not so gracious. She accused Maynard of being a "'traitor in the army,'"[43] and harangued her for her evangelicalism. Such criticism was difficult for Maynard to bear. She was a highly sensitive woman, who took criticism badly and was tortured throughout her life by self-doubt and feelings of guilt.

Regardless of the hostile reception from some quarters, the small council of what was to become Westfield College pressed on. As soon as the council had been formed, the search began to find a suitable house in which to begin. It was decided that this should be near to London, but with a healthy prospect. On one occasion a doctor was asked to inspect a house to establish whether or not it was a salubrious site.[44] The quest for the proper residence was long and drawn out. At a meeting of 17 July 1882, the council

agreed that it was desirable that the College bear as much resemblance as possible the aspect of a country house with all the numerous attendant advantages, such as could in no way be gained by residing in London.[45]

41. Westfield College, Minutes of the Council 1882–87, 3 April 1882, 32–33.
42. C. B. Firth, *Constance Louisa Maynard: Mistress of Westfield College* (London: George Allen and Unwin, 1949), 186.
43. Ibid., 196.
44. Westfield College, Minutes of the Council 1882–87, 11 February 1882, Westfield and Queen Mary College Archives.
45. Westfield College, Minutes of the Council 1882–87, 17 July 1882, 51.

This desire is strikingly like that recorded by Miss Shaw Lefevre's sister quoted above. That the country house served as a model for these early schemes in women's education is not surprising. As we have seen time and again, the founders of these women's colleges followed the domestic example for reasons of familiarity, security and propriety.

Westfield College began in a pair of semi-detached villas, which were combined by adding connecting doors between them. The address was numbers 2 and 3 Maresfield Gardens in the rural but developing suburb of Hampstead. Considering the criterion of the council for a suitable house, near enough to London, yet maintaining a rural and healthy aspect, it is little wonder that the borough of Hampstead proved so appealing. Until the 1870s and 1880s Hampstead was a rural village, made up of several large estates. The rail lines which were reaching north by this time brought more development. Care was taken, however, to preserve a large park, known as the Heath. Even today, this great expanse of parkland with its lakes and rolling hills can trick the visitor into believing that the vast sprawl of London is miles away.

Maresfield Gardens was favored because it was near the Finchley Road which provided easy access into London, but maintained a countrified feeling. The name Westfield was adopted at first from the name the landlord had already given the two houses. The college signed a lease for seven years and preparations were made for the first five students' arrival on 2 October 1882. For the first year Miss Maynard, the mistress, was assisted by Miss Tristam, a resident lecturer, who had studied at Cheltenham Ladies' College but had never gone on in higher education and thus had no college experience on which to draw. The second year brought Miss Frances Ralph Grey, who had passed the Cambridge Classical Tripos during her tenure at Newnham. Another Newnhamite, Miss Richardson, became a resident lecturer in 1887. Both Miss Grey and Miss Richardson brought with them the influence of Newnham's example, which they welded to Westfield's evangelical position.

The report of the first year praised the success of Westfield and described it as comfortably settled in "two convenient and nicely built houses, made to communicate on every floor, and affording separate studies for fifteen students, beside the necessary lecture rooms, and rooms for the Mistress and Miss Tristam."[46] Though the college began with only five students, by the end of the year the number had risen to ten. Throughout the early years of its existence, Westfield did not insist that its students adhere rigidly to a three year course, or insist upon the London Matriculation exam as a pre-requisite for attendance. Instead a woman could attend for as many terms as she could afford, with the freedom to leave or return according to family or financial demands.

As the seven year lease came due at Maresfield Gardens, the council at Westfield began to look for a new residence. The search was begun in the Spring of 1889 and once again, location, convenience and health were key factors in the search. From the start, it was acknowledged that whatever house was found would inevitably need to be enlarged; thus ample space around the house was considered crucial.

Concern for the quality of the neighborhood also occupied the committee. In April 1889, the council minutes record a discussion of one house on Fitzjohn's Avenue, Hampstead. Here the house of a Mr. Anderson was for sale, and was praised

46. "College for Ladies at Westfield: for the Preparation of Students for the Degrees of London University. Report of the First Year," 1883, Westfield and Queen Mary College Archives, 3–4.

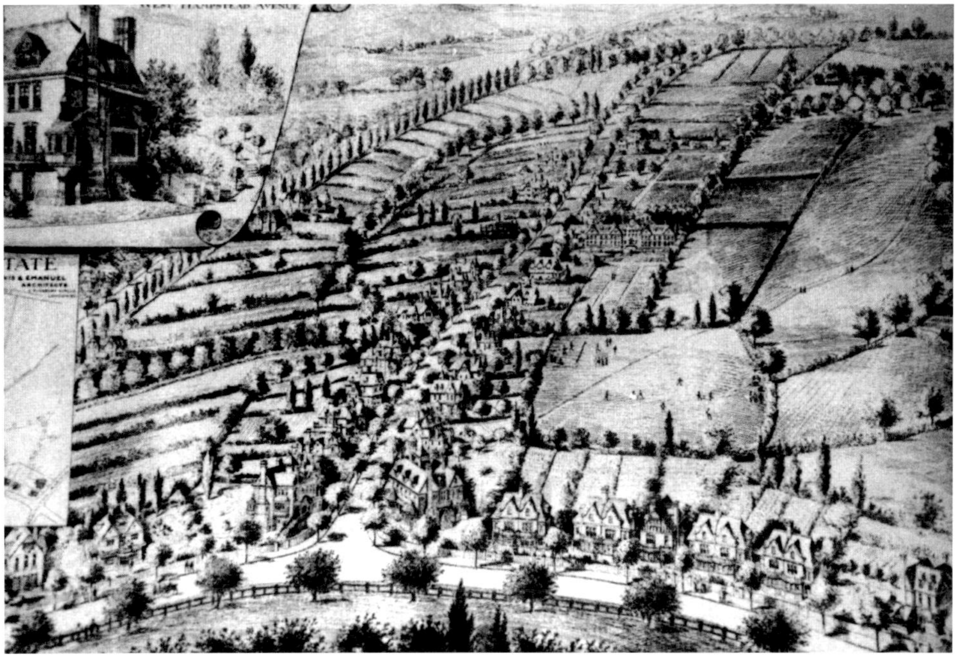

79. Kidderpore Estate, c. 1890. *Reproduced courtesy of Queen Mary and Westfield College, University of London.*

because "The situation is a good one, the thoroughfare of Fitzjohn's Avenue being well known as an important residential position in which only houses of a first class character have been erected."[47] In spite of the very respectable neighborhood, this house was rejected on the grounds that there would not be adequate garden space for recreation after building an addition, and too many alterations would be needed to the existing house to make it a feasible option.[48]

By October 1889 the council was favorably inclined towards buying a house, also in Hampstead, called Kidderpore Hall. The village of Hampstead had seen irrevocable development in the 1880s, when Londoners flocked to buy the trend-setting 'Queen Anne' houses being built there. The larger estates were gradually being sold off and divided, developing into suburban communities. On one such estate was Kidderpore Hall. This was a Neo-Classical house built in 1846 for Charles Cannon, a wealthy businessman who made his money as a dyer in London. He named his estate after the Kidderpore district in Calcutta where he had business connections. He died in 1876 and left his estate to his three daughters, dividing it among them. By 1889 the land had been further reduced and developed until the Hall itself was put up for sale with just two and a half acres of grounds. It was this house that the council of Westfield agreed to buy. A bird's eye view of the Kidderpore Estate from 1891 shows how rural the area still was, but the line of houses along Kidderpore Avenue foreshadow the development to come.

Kidderpore Hall itself was described in the freehold papers as an "elegant modern mansion . . . commanding rich and extensive views on all sides."[49] Built in the Classical style with a symmetrical facade and a porch supported by simple Ionic columns and stuccoed a pale green color, it stands out dramatically against the red brick, 'Queen Anne' of the surrounding development. The ground floor has a large entrance hall with an elegant double stair, and spacious public rooms commanding

47. Westfield College, Minutes of the Council 1887–89, Queen Mary and Westfield College Archives, 188.
48. Letter of Canon Fleming, Minutes of the Council 1887–89, Westfield College.
49. Freehold Papers; describing the Particulars of Lot 1.16A.2R.25p, 1892, Queen Mary and Westfield College Archives.

80. Kidderpore Hall, Hampstead, 1846.

views of the garden. The first and second storeys provided sixteen bedrooms; those on the first floor fitted with dressing rooms and bathrooms, and connected by a "handsome Corridor."[50] One of the most attractive features was a conservatory which stretched along the rear elevation of the house and offered a pleasant area for recreation or reflection for the early students.

From the start, additions to the existing house were needed. In a meeting of 28 October, 1889, the council decided to investigate Kidderpore Hall in more detail. One item under consideration was the "class of house to be built on the land adjoining Kidderpore Hall."[51] As discussed in previous chapters, the use of the term "house" for many of the additions or new buildings for the women's colleges is significant. It strongly suggests that the councils or committees perceived their college buildings as domestic, even though in the case of Westfield, the addition would have made a large and institutional home.

In November 1889, the final decision was made to buy Kidderpore Hall, and a competition was held for an architect to design the addition. Instructions were drafted for the architects, including the stipulation that each student was to have two rooms. These guidelines were sent off to five competing architects: Mr. Falconer MacDonald, Mr. Fenning, Mr. Luck, Mr. Williams and Mr. Creed. All were requested to send back "plans showing economy combined with good effect."[52] How these five men were chosen is unclear, and the archival material sheds no light on the issue.

By February, the plans were received by the council, and were exhibited in two venues in London over two weeks. The council's choice was unanimously in favor of designs by Robert Falconer MacDonald. MacDonald was the son of the writer George MacDonald[53] and had been articled to J. J. Stevenson for three years. He had then been a draftsman in the office of George and Peto for two years, thus his background was primarily domestic and his grounding in the 'Queen Anne' strong. After his work for Westfield he went on to forge a partnership with Herbert Read, with

50. Ibid.
51. Westfield College, Minutes of the Council 1887–89, 28 October 1889, Queen Mary and Westfield College Archives, 233.
52. Westfield College, Minutes of the Council 1889–94, 10 December 1889, Queen Mary and Westfield College Archives, 9.
53. Sondheimer, *Castle Adamant*, 41.

81. Maynard Hall, garden front (by R. F. MacDonald, 1890).

whom he worked until his death in 1913. He was made a Fellow of the Royal Institute of British Architects in 1899.

MacDonald's addition to Westfield was one of his earliest works. It replaced the stables and gardening sheds of the existing house (see color illustration 14). The building is a long simple range of red brick with a Roman cement cornice.[54] It is symmetrical, with the entrance emphasized by twinned gables, a cupola and a central stair leading to the door. It does not front Kidderpore Avenue, but in 1890 it looked out over what was then a large expanse of fields and countryside. This has since been developed into a residential suburb, and the Maynard Wing, as it came to be called, now faces a loose quadrangle of later residential halls.

Although the stipulation of careful economy meant the resulting building appears more institutional than the other colleges discussed, MacDonald did employ certain architectural elements which added interest. In the long, regular range MacDonald placed Palladian windows in the gables. White casement dormers relieve the otherwise uninterrupted roof-line. The garden facade however is an unforgiving range of white sash windows and simple brick. The center is pulled forward in a bowed projection which only slightly softens the regularity. Overall, the unrelenting red brick with large white sash windows and simple hipped roofs foreshadow the institutional, pared down 'Wrenaissance' designs of many of the halls of residence built in the first four decades of the twentieth century.

However, MacDonald created a slightly more welcoming and domestic street facade. This consists of twinned gables with Palladian windows within the gables and dormer windows between. The ground floor is elaborated by paired bay windows which light what was the dining room, each topped by curving crenellation and ball finials. These, plus the curving window aprons which the architect insisted upon,[55] are simple details borrowed from the 'Queen Anne' vocabulary, which ensured the 'good effect' despite the council's insistence on economy.

The floor-plan of the Maynard wing relies, like the other colleges discussed, on a

54. Roger Bowlder of English Heritage, "Westfield College, Kidderpore Ave., L. B. Camden," unpublished essay, 29 September 1989, 1.

55. Westfield College. Minutes of the Building Sub-Committee, 21 May 1890, Queen Mary and Westfield College, 52.

central corridor. This runs the length of the building and was lit at both ends by windows. On the ground floor a dining room extended in line with Kidderpore Hall. A large lecture room occupied the center of the range, opposite the entrance. The rest of the rooms along the corridor were allocated for students' bedrooms and sitting rooms. On the first floor a sick room and nurse's room were included at the far end of the building away from Kidderpore Avenue and another lecture room was found again in the center bow. Two floors above the dining hall were the servants' rooms, which could be accessed by a separate stair. Overall, the layout, with the students' rooms, corridors, front and back stairs, and infirmary, is much like the floor-plans of the other colleges discussed thus far, and was conditioned by the same concerns.

The details of the addition were worked out by both the building sub-committee and the household committee. During various meetings of the building sub-committee, it was decided to tile the floor of the corridor on the ground floor and use wood on the upper floors. All the bedrooms were to have red tile hearths and hanging closets. It was also decided that:

bells be fitted from each passage to the Servants' bed-room, from the Lecturers' room to the gyp-room, from the new Entrance to the passage, and an electric call-bell from the Ground floor passage to the basement of the old house.[56]

The household committee concerned itself with the smooth running of the house; the responsibilities of various servants, the ordering of carpets and wallpapers, and the basic assignments of rooms. It was decided at one meeting that the public rooms in Kidderpore Hall would be reassigned. The two smaller drawing rooms would be used as lecture rooms, the small sitting room would be for the committee and the large drawing room would be used as a common room. The library was placed in one of the large rooms on the first floor, as there was plenty of space and good light from the windows.

With the new house and its addition, life at Westfield continued in more spacious surroundings. While the numbers were seldom large enough to fill MacDonald's building, the students who did attend did well academically.[57] There were several changes to the staff during these years, with some of the lecturers leaving for other posts as lecturers and head mistresses. But overall, those who remained and those who arrived were praised for their teaching abilities. It should be remembered, however, that at this time Westfield would accept women of various degrees of academic competence. While some had passed the Matriculation exam and sought Honors or Firsts after a full three years, others arrived for a shorter time who had not passed the Matriculation exam, but wanted further training in certain subjects. This made the task of the lecturers more difficult as they had to cater to the needs of a more unevenly trained student body than their counterparts at Girton or Newnham.

It was also during this time that the University of London was undergoing reorganization. For many years the University had been criticized for being merely an examining board without proper standards of assessment. Over a period of several years, the issues of standardization and improved organization were addressed. In 1898, the University of London Act was passed, which established Statutes drawn up by seven Statutory Commissioners. Part of their work included preparing a list of

56. Westfield College, Minutes of the Building Sub-Committee, 20 March 1890.
57. Sondheimer, *Castle Adamant*, 53–54.

82. Skeel Library, Hampstead (by MacDonald, 1902).

which institutions were adequately qualified to prepare students for the University degree.[58] When the report was published in 1900, the Council of Westfield was dismayed not to find its name on the list. It applied to the Senate but was rejected on two points. The first was that some subjects were taught by teachers who were not recognized by the University and the second was that the library and laboratory were not up to the accepted standard.[59]

This problem sparked the decision in 1902 to recall MacDonald to build a proper library and more lecture rooms. The Skeel Library was opened in 1903. This purpose built library was a formal assertion of Westfield's collegiate status. As such it makes a more dramatic and impressive statement than the domestic Maynard wing. The building continues the facade along Kidderpore Avenue. The ground floor is of the same warm brick MacDonald had used in 1890, with large white sash windows and brick apron curtains. The main architectural interest of the building is on the first floor. Here grey stone surrounds the full-length windows. Semi-attached Ionic columns frame the large projecting bay. The building is crowned with a small cupola atop a large sheltering hipped roof. Though formal, the composition works well within its largely domestic environment. While the red-brick and large roof continue a domestic vocabulary, the use of stone and the Ionic order add a formality to the facade which proclaims a different function for this wing.

58. Ibid., 57.
59. Ibid., 58.

83. Dudin-Brown Wing, Hampstead (by MacDonald, 1905).

MacDonald's last work for the college was a small extension called the Dudin-Brown wing, added to the Skeel Library in 1905. It included sixteen more sets of students' rooms as well as rooms for a resident lecturer. The style was simply a continuation of the Maynard wing, with dominant gables, white sash windows and apron curtains. At the request of the committee, the casement dormers were replaced with sash windows. For safety, an iron spiral staircase was included which led to exit doors that could only be opened from the inside.[60] The use of iron bars on the ground floor windows was also considered, for reasons of protection. It was decided to reject them on the grounds of appearance and to seek other alternatives.[61] The alternatives decided on were probably the bolts which were fixed onto all the ground floor windows when the Maynard wing was built.[62] These precautions are all part of the overall concern for women's health and safety which conditioned so many of the decisions regarding the building of the women's colleges.

No more was built at Westfield until the 1920s. In 1927, Arthur Thompson and William Walford, a team of architects based in London who also worked with G. H. Fielder, were brought in to design another residential hall. This was called the Chapman Wing named after Lady Chapman, a faithful and long-standing member of the Council. This continued the red brick, white sash windows and dominant gables with Palladian windows which MacDonald had used previously. In 1929, Morley Horder and Verner Rees built a small and simple chapel in a secluded corner of the garden. Horder had done considerable work for other universities such as Nottingham, and at this point he and Rees were working on the London School of Hygiene and Tropical Medicine in London. Rees was again hired by Westfield in 1935 to build the Orchard Wing, another residence, and to remodel and enlarge the dining room. The Orchard Wing, a simple, streamlined, red brick block, together with a laboratory of 1921, served to enclose a loose quadrangle. The addition of the Orchard Wing brought the numbers of students up to 150, the maximum desired by the council at this time.

Discussions of the social life in women's colleges in their early years have been based thus far, on diaries, journal articles and novels which all endeavored to paint a

60. Westfield College, Minutes of the Building Committee, 28 April 1904.
61. Westfield College, Minutes of the Council, 9 November 1904, 277.
62. Westfield College, Minutes of the Building Committee, 18 March 1891.

rosy picture of the happy domestic life led by students away from home. In most cases, problems were minimized or ignored altogether for fear that they would result in bad publicity, and jeopardize the college's hopes of success. Westfield in its turn publicized a contented family life and laid great stress on the Christian virtues taught and encouraged above all else. But in the diaries of Louisa Maynard, which she kept on and off throughout her life, early college life was more honestly recorded and the troubles and fears of one of the early pioneers in women's education plainly voiced.

Maynard's behavior and attitudes were conditioned by her very strict, evangelical family background. Her desire to attend Girton when it first opened, and then to continue in women's education, was justified as a call from God and therefore a duty, while the pleasures of independence and scholarship were played down. She rejected an early proposal of marriage which she considered unequal in terms of both affection and values. This saddened her family who would have preferred her to marry and have children. Indeed, just prior to the opening of Westfield, her sister Nora expressed her disappointment at Maynard's career choice. Apparently, Nora lamented that Maynard had refused marriage to Christopher Roberts who "might have saved you [*Maynard*] from this solitary, hard, repressing life, that will spoil your face and your spirits and your pretty ways."[63] Not only does this illustrate the lack of support promised to Maynard as she began the career that would occupy her for the rest of her life, but it points out predicted repercussions that would result from such a career. Thus Maynard began her project without family encouragement or understanding, and with the decline of her femininity bleakly forecast. Such a quote gives an insight into the personal challenges confronted by women who were committed to careers outside marriage, and gives an indication of the problems which they faced not only from anonymous critics, but from family and friends as well.

The college venture was never easy for Maynard. She had moments of great joy and triumph, but these were less common than the times when she anxiously doubted herself, and was tormented by loneliness. Where Emily Davies was ambitious but distant, and Miss Clough was so obviously maternal, Maynard appears caught in the middle. She set about to play the role of mistress professionally, yet in a way her work at Westfield served as an outlet for her emotional feelings. She called the students her children, and was affectionate and loving. While she wanted to be responsible and caring, she herself longed to be supported and loved and at times her own and her students' needs became confused.

The affection she lavished on her early students was sometimes misconstrued, as one unfortunate incident illustrates. In January of 1883, one of her students, a Miss E. S. Maunder, had an attack of insanity, brought on by the tangle of her emotions, desires and society's expectations. Maynard recorded how Miss Maunder began to insist upon sleeping with Maynard every night, and reacted violently when Maynard called their relationship a friendship, insisting that it was a marriage. Maynard wrote of her attempts to soothe her student:

> *we talked in snatches on incoherent subjects. Some were very touching, giving glimpses of her past life, and of the problems of the hopeless perfectly self-controlled love that had evidently brought her to this state, and again she would talk of right and wrong and duty as if bracing herself to meet the whole world.*[64]

63. Maynard, Green Book 18, 17 September 1882, Queen Mary and Westfield College Archives, 144.
64. Maynard, Green Book 19, 14 January 1883, 45.

Maynard met this situation responsibly and did her best to counsel and console the woman before she was withdrawn from Westfield. Care was taken that the incident was not publicized, as such a nervous breakdown would obviously be blamed on the "unhealthy" conditions of a house full of women and the mental strain of academic life.

Although Maynard never collapsed so completely, she too was torn by doubts and confused by her feelings for her students and friends. Of one friendship she had with an early student, Margaret Brooke, Maynard wrote of their love as pure, but was not quite certain if her feelings were "kept in the right place." She assured her diary that "all these three months I have not only kept myself a little under control, but have scarcely dared to let myself accept the sweetness of her passionate endearments."[65]

Her diaries express a conscious attempt to repress her feelings for others. The love and support which she found from her students or the other lecturers was snatched as an illicit pleasure which she tried to deny herself. She fully condoned conventional relationships while with a martyred tone rejecting them for herself. One entry praises the heterosexual relationship and its "intoxicating"[66] effects, stating that she knows this well for never having indulged in the feelings. Maynard's emotional life suffered as she tried to appear conventional while rejecting its structures; tried to be maternal and supportive to those whose support she needed; and tried to appear cheerful and content when she was wracked with loneliness and despair. Maynard wanted to work as professionally as possible, while nurturing a familial environment within the close quarters of the house. But the intimacy of the situation in which work was designed to mirror family life, put a tremendous emotional strain on Maynard. She was torn by the strong desire to fulfill what she saw as her Christian and professional duty and her own, sometimes rebellious, emotions.

Maynard's life was fraught with dilemmas which made happiness and satisfaction difficult to achieve. On one of her depressed days she wrote:

> *college life so bright, so full of happy work here-to-fore, is shaded so that when I look at the animated faces around my table with a sort of longing pity, and when alone can scarcely get through a day without the bitter tears of blank loneliness. Work is good, but it is not one's whole being, Love is sweet but it leaves a sad craving, an aim is a comfort yet one sinks down before it wearied and dispirited.*[67]

Maynard was plagued by these fits of depression, as she struggled for what she believed against the tide of criticism from the very society to which she belonged. While she may have been moodier and more prone to depression than other women in similar situations, many of the issues that drained her, put a strain on those women as well, as they struggled to carve out an alternative to the narrow confines of the traditional female sphere.

It was not only her emotional life which confused her. Ever since her years at Girton, she had heard strong arguments in favor of secular education. While she listened with dismay and sometimes agreement to these petitions, she could not relinquish her determined faith. But her ardent belief in Christian education deprived her of the support of others involved in women's education, and served to further undermine her confidence and confuse her. Maynard's diaries provide an honest portrayal of one woman's dilemmas and struggles during this time of social

65. Maynard Green Book 19, 19 February 1883, 58.
66. Maynard Green Book 19, 1 April 1883, 76.
67. Maynard Green Book 19, 13 May 1883, 85.

upheaval. They illustrate some of the tensions which women faced when freed to live new independent lives, while plagued by feelings of guilt and repression due to the strict codes of behavior which society tried to enforce.

Everything in these women's lives had to be scrutinized before it was accepted or rejected. For example, when bicycles were becoming popular and students were requesting permission to ride them, Maynard and the council spent much time deliberating over the issue, trying to decide whether it would be seen as scandalous or acceptable by society. Similarly, Maynard and another resident lecturer and friend, Ralph Grey were very concerned about which books the library should keep. Since Westfield was such an evangelical institution their choices were small; they could only stock such books as would give the students a proper Christian message, and would in no way encourage radical or alternative thinking. What brought pleasure or pure entertainment was regarded first with suspicion.

Thus far women's colleges have been discussed within their architectural context and to see how the domestic house served as a model for the colleges for women. Both in architectural and social terms, domestic convention helped to alleviate fears about women away from their homes. Adherence to this convention meant that a familiar environment was created, thereby cushioning the drama of women's higher education. But Maynard's diaries give a glimpse of the stresses inherent within this domestic collegiate environment. At the women's colleges, proper social roles had to be followed more closely. Yet by their very nature, the women at these new institutions were rebelling against conformity by seeking alternatives to the private sphere. Inevitably, those women involved were torn by their desire for achievement, independence or their disregard for typical home-life, and their respect for decorum and propriety. These women, by leaving home, could not escape convention, indeed they were forced to cling to it more closely. It is not surprising then, to read of Maynard's conflicting desires, and her voice which spoke authoritatively of duty, right and wrong, while plaintively seeking a happiness which social convention could not offer.

Martha Vicinus wrote of this conflict that:

the public roles engendered a need for strong emotional support that was at odds with the characteristics that made for public success. In effect, single women established all-female families within their institutions, continuing the supportive, emotional ties of the traditional Victorian extended family, while attempting cool, professional ways of behaving and working on the job and in the world outside.[68]

Miss Wordsworth, Miss Shaw Lefevre and Miss Maynard all sought to recreate the home at college. They acted out of a shared conviction that a small intimate scale and domestic routine would protect both the students and the venture as a whole. What Miss Maynard's diaries clearly illustrate, is that this domestic environment, which so reassured parents and critics alike, and which provided opportunities for counsel and supervision, continued to inhibit and restrict the women involved. For this first generation, domesticity was both a positive part of the crusade for women's higher education, and the means of ensuring a static, at times stifling, code of social behavior.

68. Martha Vicinus, "'One Life to Stand Beside Me': Emotional Conflicts in First-Generation College Women in England" in *Feminist Studies* 8, no. 3 (Fall 1982): 604.

4 A PALATIAL RESIDENCE

Royal Holloway College

The Muses and the Graces, group'd in threes,
Enring'd a billowing fountain in the midst;
And here and there on lattice edges lay
Or book or lute; but hastily we past,
And up a flight of stairs into the hall.

Alfred Lord Tennyson, *The Princess*, 1847[1]

Of the six colleges for women considered here, Royal Holloway College was by far the most unusual. In terms of its history, patronage, and architecture it stands apart from the others as a palatial testimony of one wealthy man's beneficence. The vast building which houses the college was designed in the French Renaissance style and built in red brick with white stone dressings. It is ornate and exuberant and its lavish character added a glamour to women's higher education that the other colleges did not even attempt to achieve.

The college was founded by Thomas Holloway, a self-made millionaire who built up his fortune selling "Holloway's Pills and Ointments." These widely sold remedies were little more than panaceas for innumerable ailments, and Holloway's genius lay more in his skillful advertising than in his medical prowess. He advertised in papers around the world, from England to China to India, and by the 1850s had become a very wealthy entrepreneur.

His road to success did not begin smoothly. Holloway was born in Devon, the son of a sailor who later ventured into the grocery trade where he was modestly prosperous. Thomas Holloway was sent to school until the age of sixteen, when he began an apprenticeship with a chemist.[2] This was the extent of Holloway's medical training, which he put to use with great success in later years. After various jobs and tentative partnerships, Holloway began selling his ointment in 1837. His ambitious advertising led him to bankruptcy, and he served a sentence in Whitecross Street debtors' prison. But he was not easily defeated and was soon back at work, paying off his creditors and carrying on with his business. In spite of this set-back, the sale of Holloway's ointment and later his pills became extremely profitable.

In 1840, Holloway married Miss Jane Driver, to whom he was devoted all his life. There were no children from this marriage which may help to account for Holloway's philanthropy in later years. Jane's family played an important role in Holloway's life. His brothers-in-law, George Martin and Henry Driver, were trusted managers in Holloway's business affairs. In 1867, when Holloway bought his first house in the country, Tittenhurst Park, near Ascot, George Martin and his wife Sarah Ann, Jane's sister, all moved in together. This close alliance between family members was to continue up to Holloway's death in 1883.

It was in the 1860s that Holloway began to investigate philanthropic means of spending some of his vast fortune. His first interest appears to have been for the treatment of the insane. Holloway's concern for the suffering of the mentally ill was sparked by an address he heard given by Lord Shaftesbury in 1861. In this speech

1. Tennyson, *The Princess*, 23.
2. Caroline Bingham, *The History of Royal Holloway College 1886–1986* (London: Constable, 1987), 16.

Shaftesbury reported on the plight of the insane, and argued that, while the mentally-ill paupers were relatively well taken care of, those victims in the middle-classes were poorly cared for and mostly neglected by society. Three years after this speech, Holloway arranged a meeting with Shaftesbury to discuss founding an asylum for the insane from the middle classes. He decided to build a sanatorium which would be a temporary haven for the mentally ill, where, under proper care, they could regain their senses and return to the world and their professional lives.[3]

It seems that when Holloway had an idea for a building project, it took many years for the scheme to be realized in bricks and mortar. So it was with both his sanatorium and college. It was not until 1872 that a competition for an architect to design the sanatorium was held. There were three judging architects, Thomas Leverton Donaldson, emeritus Professor of Architecture at University College, London, and founder of the Royal Institute of British Architects, George Godwin, editor of *The Builder*, and T. H. Wyatt, who served the Lunacy Commission as a consulting architect.

The architect chosen by the panel was William Crossland. Crossland was a partner in "Crossland, Salomans and Jones" (Jones died shortly afterwards and by the time of construction, Salomans was no longer involved[4]) and a pupil of G. G. Scott. His first major commission was for a wealthy mill-owner, Edward Akroyd, from the Yorkshire town of Halifax. Akroyd showed an early interest in improving the lives of his mill workers, and had embarked on a housing scheme with his brother in 1852 to accommodate the workers in houses that were considered healthier than the average lower class dwelling. In 1855 he began another such scheme, this time employing G. G. Scott as the head architect. Crossland, working under Scott at the time, took over most of the responsibility for this project, and in 1860 plans were officially drawn up and presented to the public. Building was begun in 1861, in the "simple, yet bold" Gothic[5] requested by Mr. Akroyd.

In 1870, *The Architect* published two designs by Crossland. The first was for the Rochdale Town Hall, which was nearing completion in October 1870. The symmetrical plan was hidden by an ornate Gothic facade, with Flemish stepped gables, large traceried windows and a clock tower. Crossland's other work published in 1870 was for a New Corn Exchange in Mark Lane, London. In this great hall there is nothing left of the picturesque Gothic which Crossland used for Rochdale. The facade is decidedly French, with strong horizontal stringcourses defining the two floors, Classical sculptures relating to agriculture adorning the niches and roofline, and a glazed iron roof which covered a vast hall within. In addition to these commissions, Crossland had work designing churches and domestic houses, notably Langley, a house he built for Sir John Ramsden in Huddersfield.[6]

By 1873, when Crossland and his partners won the competition for Holloway's sanatorium, built in Virginia Water, Surrey, Crossland had proven himself master of different building types in various styles (see fig. 86). The winning design was published in *The Builder* in August 1872, and its interior arrangements carefully described. It was not until 1882 that the building neared completion and was discussed again in *The Builder*, which praised the architect's skillful manipulation of the Gothic vocabulary from the 13th, 14th and 15th centuries. It is said to have been inspired by the Cloth Hall at Ypres which Holloway had admired on his travels abroad.[7] The sanatorium was built on a magnificent scale, and its interiors were ornately decorated.

3. E. Hodder, *The Life and Work of the Seventh Earl of Shaftesbury, K.G.*, popular edition (London: Cassell, 1892), 572–73.
4. J. Mordaunt Crook, "Mr. Holloway's Architect and Mr. Holloway's Chateau," in *Royal Holloway and Bedford New College: Centenary Lectures 1886–1986*, ed. M. Moore (Egham, England: Royal Holloway and Bedford New College, 1988), 30.
5. "Akroydon, Improved Dwellings for the Working Classes," *The Builder* XXI, no. 1045 (14 February 1863): 110.
6. Crook, "Mr. Holloway's Architect and Mr. Holloway's Chateau," 29.
7. Bingham, *The History of Royal Holloway College*, 33.

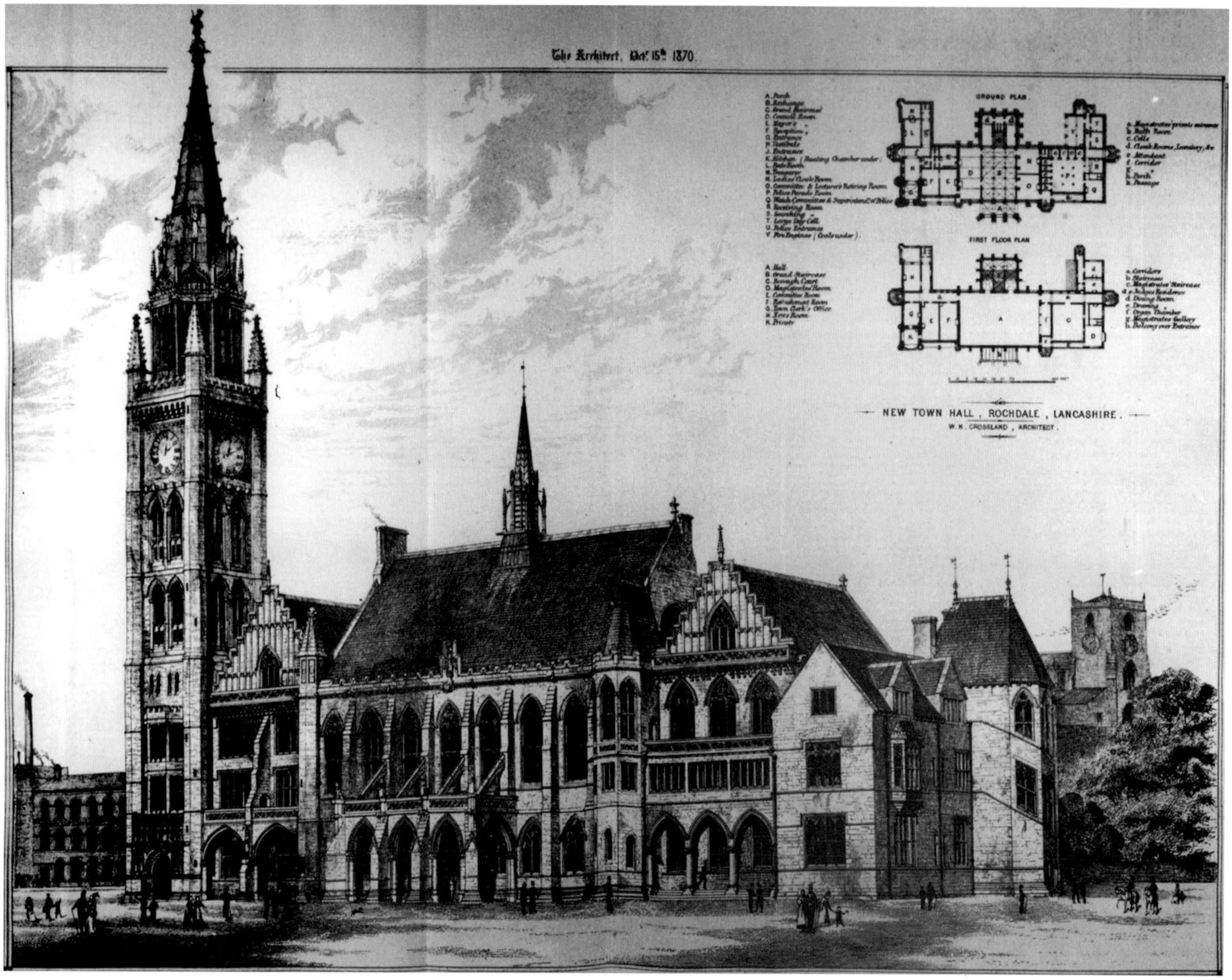

84. Rochdale Town Hall, Greater Manchester (by W. Crossland, 1870). From *The Architect* (15 October 1870), 217. *Reproduced courtesy of the Trustees of the Boston Public Library.*

When the work had begun on the sanatorium in 1873, Holloway was thinking of another philanthropic scheme on which to lavish his millions. Caroline Bingham points out that Holloway first wanted to build a hospital for incurables similar to the sanatorium.[8] He consulted Crossland about what style he would build in and Crossland recorded his response years later: "Now it appeared to me that a return either to the purer classical styles, or to the Renaissance of the sixteenth century, was certainly impending."[9] Holloway then went on to ask him how he would go about preparing for such a competition and Crossland replied that he would travel to the Loire for a period of careful sketching.[10] This was apparently the answer Holloway wanted to hear, for he gave up the idea of holding another competition, offered Crossland the commission, and sent him to the Loire valley in September 1873 where he joined him later. According to Crossland, it was after having seen Blois that Holloway decided upon brick instead of stone as the primary building material.[11]

There is some confusion as to the purpose of this intended building. The reasons

8. Ibid., 34.
9. W. H. Crossland, "The Royal Holloway College," *RIBA Transactions* III new series (1887): 142.
10. Ibid., 143.
11. Ibid.

85. Corn Exchange, London (by Crossland, 1870). From *The Architect* (5 November 1870), 261. *Reproduced courtesy of the Trustees of the Boston Public Library.*

86. Holloway Sanatorium, Virginia Water, Surrey (by Crossland, 1871–84). *Reproduced courtesy of the Victorian Society, London.*

for the change from a hospital for incurables to a college for women were never officially recorded. However, in an unpublished account of life at Royal Holloway by an early student, credit was given to Holloway's wife, Jane. Apparently, she encouraged Holloway to do something for women, "'because they are the greatest sufferers.'"[12] Furthermore, at his death, Holloway credited the decision to Jane.[13] Little is known about Jane Holloway. That she was a kindly woman and faithful to her husband and his work is clear from the existing accounts. But she was not involved in the organized movement for women's education. Indeed, it is not certain that she considered education to be the most urgent solution to women's suffering. In comparison with the other movements in women's education, which were driven by determined advocates of women's education, Holloway's involvement seems almost casual.

In 1874, Girton was quietly nestled outside of Cambridge, avoiding co-operation with Newnham, which was at the point of deciding whether or not to build a house. Oxford had made no moves in the direction of women's education, nor had the University of London yet agreed to admit women to degrees. Bedford and Queen's had offered classes to women for over twenty years, but as we have said before, in the 1860s and early 1870s their efforts were modest. In all these cases, the founders devoted their lives to the cause of women's education, out of their own frustrated ambitions or deeply held sympathy for women whose options were so limited.

In the case of Thomas Holloway and his wife Jane, there is no evidence of such

12. Marion Pick, "Social Life at Royal Holloway College 1887–1939," unpublished manuscript RF 131/7 Royal Holloway and Bedford New College Archives, 6.
13. Deed of Foundation of Holloway College, Mount Lee, Egham, Surrey, 11 October 1883, and Amended Deed, April 1906, Royal Holloway and Bedford New College Archives, 6.

87. Wellington College, Berkshire (by J. Shaw Jr. 1856–59). *Reproduced courtesy of W. G. Stewart.*

commitment. It is more likely that Holloway regarded the venture of founding a college for women as a unique opportunity, filling a void that was barely recognized in 1874, but which, in the eyes of a good businessman, might grow and take off like a worthwhile stock venture. This businesslike approach should in no way overshadow the fact of Holloway's munificence, but as will become clear, Holloway knew very little about women's education, and his interest in the cause did not seem to grow in conjunction with the building scheme.

In the early stages of planning, however, Holloway was an enthusiastic and supportive patron. As early as October 1874 he wrote that he was intending to found a college for women on the Mount Lee Estate in Egham, Surrey. He intended that this would be larger than Wellington College and "will have a palatial appearance and of its kind be superior to anything in this country."[14] In these early letters he compared his venture with Wellington several times. Wellington College was designed by John Shaw Jr. between 1856–59. It was founded as a school for the orphans of officers. The college was built in red brick with white stone window dressing and quoins. Many of its Baroque classical elements were borrowed from Wren's work.[15] It is a large, unified building that must have impressed Holloway and inspired him to build an even greater building for his college.

In his correspondence with Crossland, Holloway asked that the college be designed so that "there shall be nothing like it in Europe."[16] He requested Crossland to draw up the elevations so that "it may be as near Chambord in every respect as can

14. Thomas Holloway, Private Letter Book, 17 October 1874 – 8 February 1877, GB/130/1 Royal Holloway and Bedford New College Archives, 10.

15. Nikolaus Pevsner, *The Best Buildings of England*, comp. by Bridget Cherry and John Newman (Harmondsworth: Viking Penguin, 1986), 190.

16. Holloway, Private Letterbook, 19.

be."[17] Furthermore, Holloway had decided by early 1875, that while he would supply the land and the building, he would not endow the college; it should be self-supporting. The women students were to come from families that could afford to send their daughters to what Holloway envisioned as the sister university to Oxford and Cambridge.

In January and February of 1875, he set about trying to familiarize himself with the movement for women's higher education, its existing status and needs. He depended on Mr. James Beal, a friend and estate agent, and David Chadwick, M.P., to help him garner information and put him in touch with important figures in women's education. Many such figures were keenly interested in Holloway's scheme. Mrs. Maria Grey (see appendix) wrote to Holloway inquiring about his plans. Holloway, however, was not interested in working closely with many of the women involved in the movement. He wrote to Beal requesting him call on Mrs. Grey at some point because, in Holloway's words:

I really have no time to run about to see a parcel of Ladies—but I agree with you in believing, that it is in my best interest, to be on the best of terms with all such people, but as you are such a lady's man, I will ask you . . . to oblige me at your leisure, by seeing any lady who may desire to converse with me on any subject.[18]

Holloway's discomfort at the thought of long meetings with women such as Mrs. Grey, gives an indication of his feelings toward the college in general. In the early part of 1875, he showed great enthusiasm for the scheme, and obviously enjoyed envisioning a college that would rival the splendors of Europe. But his interest was limited and short-lived. After his wife died in September 1875, though the scheme went ahead slowly, Holloway himself had very little involvement.

However, at the start he spent a good deal of time working out the logistics and curriculum of the college. In spite of his earlier attempts to avoid meeting with large groups of women, in February 1875 he invited some of the leaders in educational reform, including a "bevy of Ladies,"[19] to a meeting in his offices on Oxford Street. The likes of Emily Davies, Millicent Fawcett, Maria Grey, and Dr. Elizabeth Garret Anderson were invited, as were Sir James Kay-Shuttleworth (famous for his work with teachers' training colleges), James Fitch, who played an important role in Girton's beginnings, and two MPs, Samuel Morley and David Chadwick. Significantly, David Chadwick brought along the Reverend William Hague, an American who sat on the Board of Trustees at Vassar College. Vassar was opened in 1865. It was one of America's first colleges for women, and it was to prove very influential for Holloway.

To this collection of notables, Holloway laid out his reasons for building a college for women, and what form he envisioned it taking. He prefaced his address with an apology for his ignorance about the needs of a women's college, and welcomed any advice which his guests could offer. In presenting his goals for the college he said:

I believe it can be brought about to benefit future generations . . . for how much do we not owe to our dear Mother's early training, and as she has been trained she will in most cases instill the same training into the minds of her children to benefit this commercial country.[20]

17. Ibid., 69.
18. Ibid., 120–21.
19. Ibid., 180.
20. Holloway, *Some Small Memories as to the Origin of Holloway College for Women* (London: G. Stahl Printer, n.d.), RF 103, Royal Holloway and Bedford New College Archives, 4.

He wanted to dedicate his ladies' college to the public, and hoped that it might "serve as a starting point for someone else to do a great deal better."[21] The college was to be a degree granting university, ultimately offering an M.A., or Double First to the women students.

As one might imagine, various opinions were put forward at this meeting as to how Holloway could best spend his millions. Sir Kay Shuttleworth hoped that Holloway might invest his money in a teachers' training college and a high school, but Holloway rejected this idea and insisted on a "Ladies' University." At the meeting, Holloway presented some early designs by Crossland, and announced that "The style of the building I propose shall be the Renaissance of which we see many examples in France. This may be somewhat expensive but for a public building I do not regret it."[22] It is not clear from the evidence what these preliminary designs looked like. The most we can know is that Holloway instructed Crossland to bring to the meeting drawings which were inspired by his study of Chambord and other French chateaux.

In 1887 William Crossland wrote about the meeting in his article on the building of Royal Holloway. He complained that Holloway:

came under the influence of certain highly-educated ladies, who had been interesting themselves in the scheme, and who persuaded him that the proper style of architecture to adopt was not the Renaissance, but 'the style in which most of the colleges at Oxford and Cambridge had been built'.[23]

One can imagine that Emily Davies was one of these "highly educated ladies" to whom he refers and that she was not a little envious of the ease with which Holloway could have purchased the grandeur and tradition which she so passionately wanted for her own college.

It appears that Holloway was influenced by their advice, and in spite of Crossland's misgivings, he took himself and his architect to Cambridge for an intensive study of the traditional men's colleges, such as Trinity and St. John's. At the meeting several practical points must have been raised. For instance, before leaving for Cambridge, Holloway wrote to Crossland that more space would be needed for the college, in order to provide education in all areas of scholarship. He reminded Crossland that "there must be a splendid library or a place for that purpose."[24] While at Cambridge, Holloway and his architect carefully studied the various colleges and had two assistants sketch those parts which Holloway liked best.

In a letter to Professor Henry Fawcett after the trip, Holloway described his reaction to Cambridge. It was not what he expected and he "was sorry to find that all the Colleges had been restored at various periods and with different styles of architecture."[25] Of all the colleges, Holloway preferred Trinity, although there was still much that he didn't like. But the trip to the University did resolve several issues for Holloway which he recorded in the following:

I am inclined to believe that the Ladies' College will surpass anything of the kind at Cambridge. It will be all one style of architecture. We cannot boast of Libraries such as you have, nor chapels, nor some of the other things, but otherwise it will I think be unique of its kind.

21. Ibid., 3.
22. Ibid.
23. Crossland, "The Royal Holloway College," 143–44.
24. Holloway, Private Letterbook, 189.
25. Ibid., 229.

It will consist of a double quadrangle, the length will be about 575 feet and width 350. Each student will have two rooms as suggested by Mrs. Fawcett.[26]

This letter gives the first indication of what the actual plan of the college was to be. The double quadrangle, once decided upon, was maintained, although the elevations went through various changes, the Gothic of Trinity and St. John's being discarded first. Crossland reported in his article of 1887 that soon after their adventure into the Gothic of academia, Holloway came down with a slight fever, during which time Crossland was again able to convince him of the greater merits of the French Renaissance, and the Gothic style was abandoned.

Holloway's meeting proved influential in other ways as well. Prior to the gathering, David Chadwick had lent Holloway a small booklet about Vassar College in America. Holloway had only glanced through it when he met the Reverend William Hague in mid-February.[27] After listening to Rev. Hague, Holloway was inspired by the example of Vassar which was founded by a self-made millionaire, whose marriage was also childless, and who subsequently devoted the bulk of his fortune to the founding of a ladies' college. Holloway found a kindred spirit in Matthew Vassar and many of the elements integral to the founding of Royal Holloway can be traced to Vassar's example.

In June 1875, Holloway wrote to Emily Davies and mentioned that his brother-in-law, George Martin, had been in New York on business, had visited Vassar and had described some of the workings of the college.[28] Through David Chadwick and Rev. Hague, Holloway collected more information about Vassar, which he used in organizing and planning his own college. The archives of what is now Royal Holloway and Bedford New College contain several pamphlets on Vassar, one written by Vassar himself outlining his aims for a ladies' college, and two written by the then President, John H. Raymond. Most are signed and annotated by Holloway; the annotations are a guide to those aspects of Vassar that particularly interested Holloway.

In Matthew Vassar's *Communications to the Board of Trustees of Vassar College* Holloway crossed out Vassar's stated belief that woman: "having received from her Creator the same intellectual constitution as man, has the same right as man to intellectual culture and development."[29] He left the paragraphs in which Vassar considered the importance of women as mothers and teachers and the value of education in successfully fulfilling those roles. Holloway also appeared interested in Vassar's discussion of the specifics of the curriculum; the modest sum charged to students; and the non-sectarian nature of the college, an issue that was very important to Holloway. Equally interesting to Holloway was Vassar's desire "that the College may be provided with commodious buildings, containing ample apartments for public instruction, and at the same time affording to the inmates the safety, quiet, privacy, and purity of the family."[30] Other aspects of the college that Vassar considered important included the careful upkeep of the grounds, a fine faculty and library and a picture gallery.

Holloway had two copies of a pamphlet entitled *Vassar College. A College for Women in Poughkeepsie N.Y. A Sketch*, which was written by the President, John Raymond. One of these was given to Holloway by David Chadwick and the other was signed by Mr. Raymond himself. This booklet outlines the domestic and academic organization of Vassar College and was presumably read by Holloway, as one of the copies is anno-

26. Ibid.
27. Ibid., 179.
28. Ibid., 267–68.
29. Matthew Vassar, *Communications to the Board of Trustees of Vassar College* (New York: John A. Gray & Green, Printers, 1869), GB/130/5-21, Royal Holloway and Bedford New College Archives, 5.
30. Ibid., 7

tated. Raymond pointed out that careful attention had been paid to the domestic arrangements of the college, the Trustees agreeing that:

students should be members of the college family; that they should live together under one roof; that the security and comforts of a well-ordered home should be assured them; and that the sanitary and social regulation of their life, as well as their intellectual training, should be taken under the responsible direction of the college authorities. Hence the erection of a large and costly edifice, with its suites of furnished private apartments, its thoroughly equipped kitchen and laundry . . . And hence a complete system of house regulations, matured by the Faculty, and intended to harmonize the personal with the student life of its members.[31]

The structure of the college, and the degree of control to be exerted over the women students, are thus likened to the structure of a family. Furthermore, the article assures the reader that whilst an opportunity for higher education is provided by the college, accepted standards of "womanly refinement and grace"[32] will not be abandoned. The domestic environment nurtured within one large building at Vassar was typical of other women's colleges in America such as Wellesley College, and is evidence that the concerns which conditioned women's colleges in England were shared across the Atlantic.[33]

Holloway took special notice of the provision made at Vassar to have a resident physician to take special care of the students' health. He also underlined the reference to the government of the college which specified that a board of gentlemen should ultimately be in charge of the college affairs, a point which he adopted for his college. Vassar stipulated that his college would be non-denominational and that the students were free to attend a church of their choice. Included in the building scheme at Vassar was a picture gallery to house Matthew Vassar's large collection of paintings by American artists. All of these elements eventually found their way into Holloway's college.

One of the most striking similarities between the two men and their plans was their shared ambition to make a dramatic and easily recognized statement regarding their wealth and benevolence. Vassar's interest in the scheme for a women's college was recorded in the following: "The novelty, grandeur and benignity of the idea arrested my attention."[34] This is not at all unlike what Holloway wrote to Professor Fawcett: "I propose that the 'Ladies University' at Egham, should be of its kind a grand imposing building that it may not by an insignificant style dishonour its name. You are aware I am sure that nowadays, it is necessary to fill the eye."[35] Each man wanted his college to succeed, but for both, success depended as much on the visual impression made by the buildings, their grounds and their pretty inhabitants, as the education and progress of women, if not more so. Indeed, after Holloway had carefully studied Vassar College he added to his ambitious plans his goal to "beat Vassar into fits."[36]

Vassar was not the only institution which Holloway studied while planning his college. In the archives of Royal Holloway and Bedford New College are pamphlets from other educational establishments, several of which were also founded through the beneficence of wealthy patrons. Some are signed and dated by Holloway proving that he read them in the spring months of 1876. The pamphlets he studied include those for the Owens College, founded in Manchester in 1851; the Girard College for Orphans; the "Scheme for the Establishment of a School or College for the Daughters

31. John H. Raymond, *Vassar College: A College for Women in Poughkeepsie N.Y. A Sketch.* (New York: S. W. Green, Printer, 1873), GB/130/9 Royal Holloway and Bedford New College Archives, 18–19.
32. Ibid., 21.
33. Paul V. Turner, *Campus: An American Planning Tradition*, revised ed. (Cambridge, Mass.: MIT Press, 1990), 133.
34. Raymond, *Biographical Sketch of Matthew Vassar, the founder of Vassar College* (1868), GB/130/6, Royal Holloway and Bedford College Archives, 790.
35. Holloway, Private Letterbook, 187.
36. Ibid., 330.

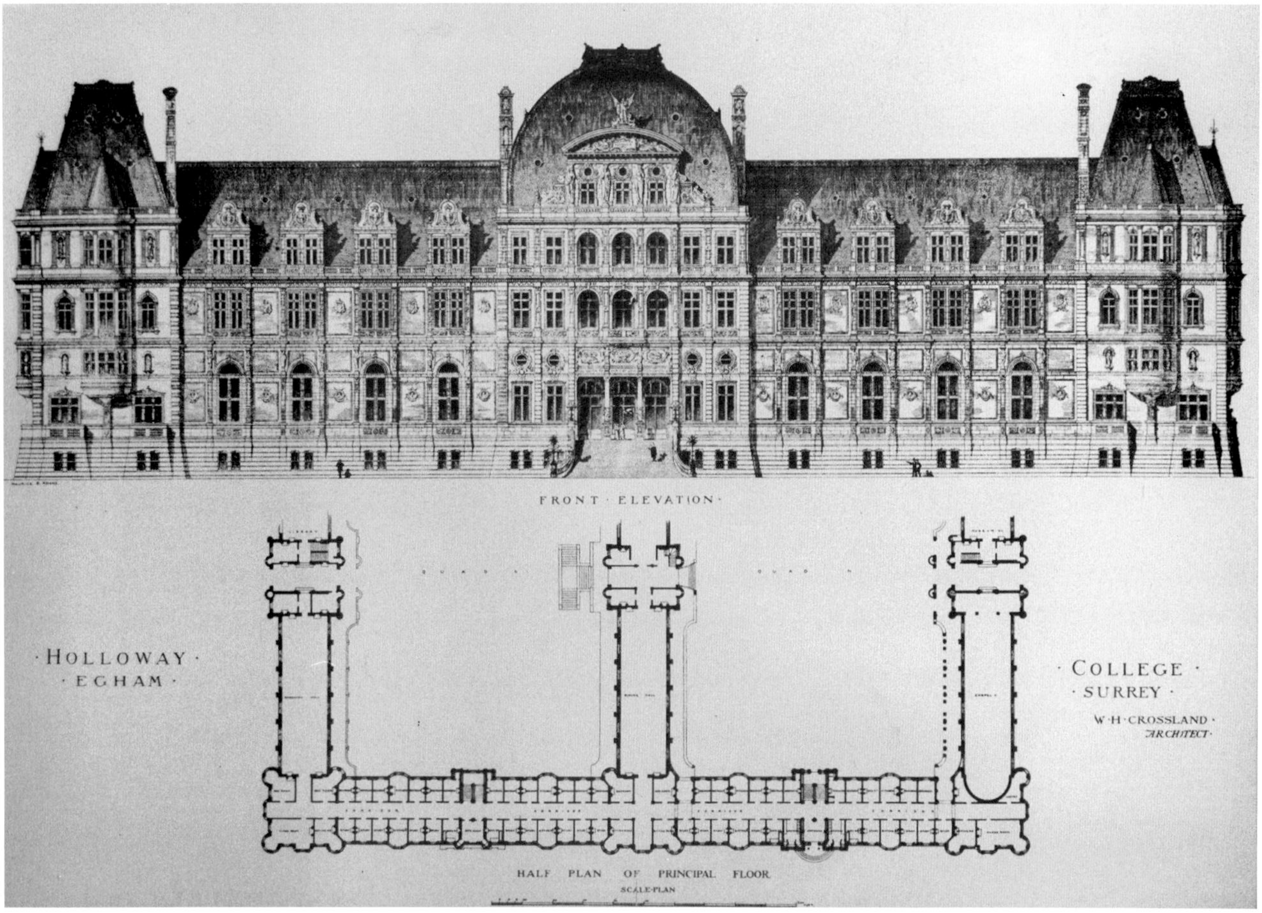

88. Early Elevation for Royal Holloway College, Egham, Surrey (by Crossland, 1877). From *Building News* (21 December 1877), 616. *Reproduced courtesy of the Archives, Royal Holloway, University of London.*

of Congregational Ministers," (what became Milton Mount College) and a pamphlet entitled "Girton College–Memorandum and Articles of Association and Bye Laws" on the cover of which was written simply "Imperfect," suggesting that what Davies and others had shaped into Girton College was not what Holloway envisioned for his own women's college.

Although certain aspects of Girton may not have interested Holloway, his encounter with Emily Davies proved fruitful. Where he seemed put off by the other women's ideas, he found Davies very helpful and turned to her for advice on logistical matters. She commented on the draft of his deed for the college and suggested ideas for the management of students, their age requirements and what examinations they should pass. He was very impressed with her expertise:

There is hardly anyone in the land whose experience and ability to advise me is equal to yours, and I am sure that the interest you take in this laudable work, encourages me to hope that I may venture to trouble you from time to time in asking you your opinion on various subjects as it is my desire to follow the course of teaching that is so admirably conducted at Girton College.[37]

37. Ibid., 267–68.

1. Old Hall (by Alfred Waterhouse, 1872).

2. Stanley Library, drawing with women studying. *From E. E. Constance Jones,* Girton College *(London: A. & C. Black, 1913), 16.*

3. Stanley Library (by Waterhouse, 1882).

4. Tower Wing, Girton College (by Waterhouse, 1886).

7. Clough Hall, Newnham College (by Champneys, 1886).

8. Clough Assembly Hall, interior (by Champneys, 1886).

5. Yattendon, Berkshire (by Waterhouse, 1876). *British Architectural Library, RIBA, London.*

6. Sidgwick Hall, Newnham College (by Basil Champneys, 1878).

9. Wordsworth Hall, Lady Margaret Hall (by Reginald Blomfield, 1895).

10. Wittington, Medmenham, Buckinghamshire (by Blomfield, 1897).

11. Talbot Hall, Lady Margaret Hall (by Blomfield, 1905).

12. Eleanor Smith Cottages, Somerville College (by Walter Cave, 1897–98). *Reproduced courtesy of Principal and Fellows, Somerville College, Oxford.*

13. Pfeiffer Library, Somerville College (by Champneys, 1903).

14. Maynard Hall, entrance front, Hampstead (by R. F. MacDonald, 1889–90).

15. Royal Holloway College, view in south courtyard (by W. Crossland, 1886).

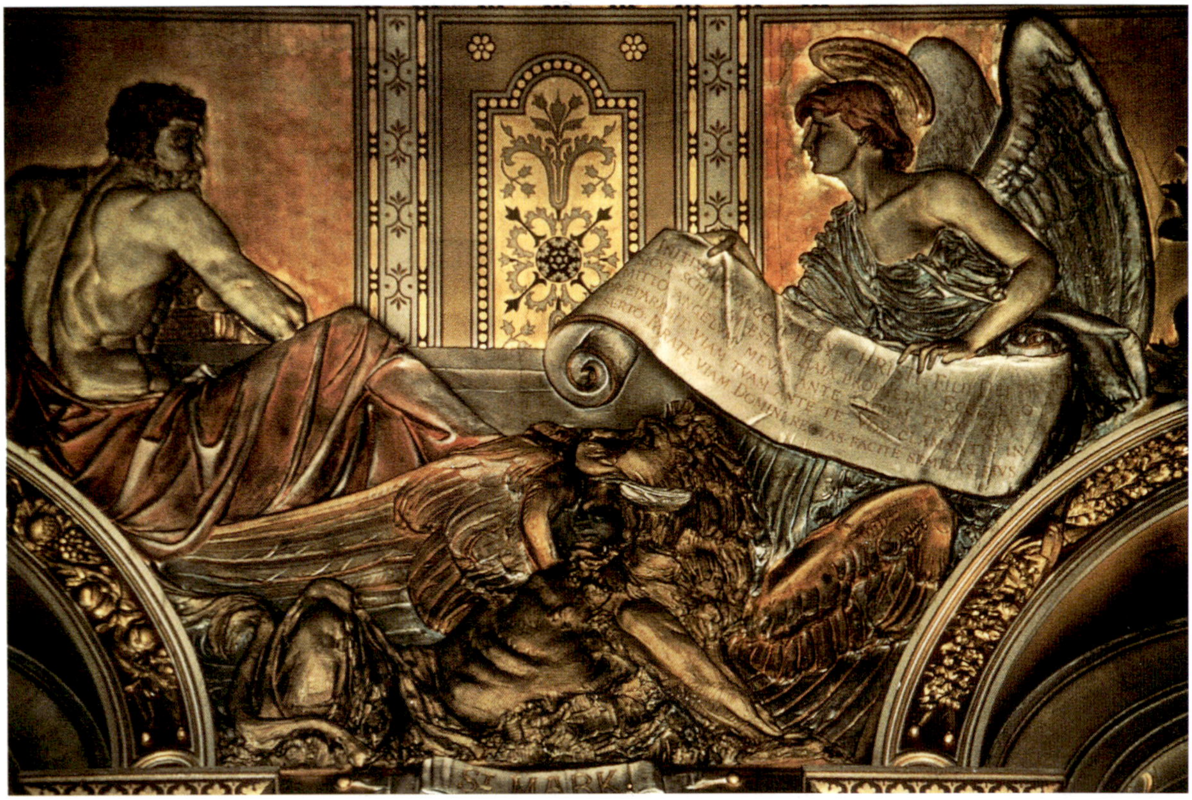

16. Chapel, detail, Royal Holloway College.

17. *The Babylonian Marriage Market* by Edwin Long (1829–91). *Royal Holloway and Bedford New College, Surrey/Bridgeman Art Library, London/New York*

89. The New Louvre, Paris (by L. T. J. Visconti and H. M. Lefuel, 1852–57). *Photo by Dr. Geoffrey Tyack.*

He even went so far as to ask Davies if she might be willing to leave Girton and become the principal of Holloway, an offer which she declined.

But Vassar proved to be the most significant architectural example for Holloway. The earliest existing elevation available for the college, which was published in the *Building News* in 1877, was a grand building in the French style, but with no quotations from Chambord. Rather, the design is much like the New Louvre which was built for Napoleon III by Visconti and Lefuel between 1852 and 1857 and widely publicized in the architectural press in the 1850s and 1860s. Both Vassar's college and this early design for Holloway College resemble Parisian examples.

Vassar employed the architect James Renwick Jr. to design a vast building in the style of the Tuileries Palace in Paris. The huge block had two extending wings and a grand central entrance. The mansard roofs, domed center block and Classical details all suggest the French inspiration. Crossland's first design is strikingly similar to the New Louvre and to Vassar College. In his elevation, there was a symmetrical building which consisted of one massive block with a pavilion wing projecting forward at each end. The pavilions are dominated by large French pitched roofs and three-storey oriel windows. Six bays in the center of the block are pulled forward to emphasize the entrance, their edges defined by quoins and the center three bays consisting of a trabeated loggia on the ground floor and arched loggias on the first and second. This center block was then dramatized by a large domed roof, much like that seen at Vassar, which was bracketed by two chimney stacks and embellished by a curving pediment and swirling volutes. Overall, the scheme is rich in carved details yet with a certain staid formality.

While Crossland recorded in his article that Holloway changed his mind about the traditional Gothic style of the Cambridge colleges, he does not indicate exactly when this happened or in which style the next set of plans were drawn. The evidence

90. Vassar College, Poughkeepsie, N.Y. (by J. Renwick Jr. 1865). *Photo of John A. Lowell engraving of Main Building, c. 1860s, Special Collections, Vassar College Libraries, Poughkeepsie N.Y.*

suggests that though Holloway wanted a return to French examples for his college, it was not the chateaux of Chambord and Blois that Holloway wanted imitated and out-done, but rather the French classicism of Matthew Vassar's college for women. By 1877, Holloway and Crossland were working with two precedents. Stylistically, they looked to the New Palace of the Louvre and Renwick's example. But the plan published beneath the elevation remained as Holloway had described it to Professor Fawcett in 1875, with two quadrangles and very long corridors. But the plan could in no way match the elevation and indicates that important decisions were yet to be made regarding the external appearance of Holloway's college.

In May 1874 Holloway had bought the ninety-four acres of land that comprised the Mount Lee Estate, in Egham, Surrey, about twenty miles outside London, and, like the sanatorium, easily accessible by rail. The site chosen was on the crown of a great hill, so the building could be seen from miles away. The site was:

situated at convenient distance from London, it is yet sufficiently removed to ensure a long continuance of that quiet seclusion in search of which many anciently-endowed institutions are now finding it necessary to move countrywards. At Mount Lee, it may be hoped, for generations to come, the students' pursuits will be followed under exceptionally pleasant and tranquilizing influences.[38]

A large brick wall was built around the edge of the estate to keep unwanted visitors out and to ensure the women's safety as they strolled through the extensive and very beautiful grounds.

The double quadrangle plan, published in 1877, was basically the same as built. In this, one huge rectangle was divided down the middle by a block containing the kitchen and dining hall. At the north end is an arched entrance with access to a recreation hall to the west and the chapel to the east. Down the length of the building

38. *The Royal Holloway College* (London: J. S. Virtue, 1886), Royal Holloway and Bedford New College Archives, 7.

91. Royal Holloway College, ground plan (by Crossland, c. 1880).

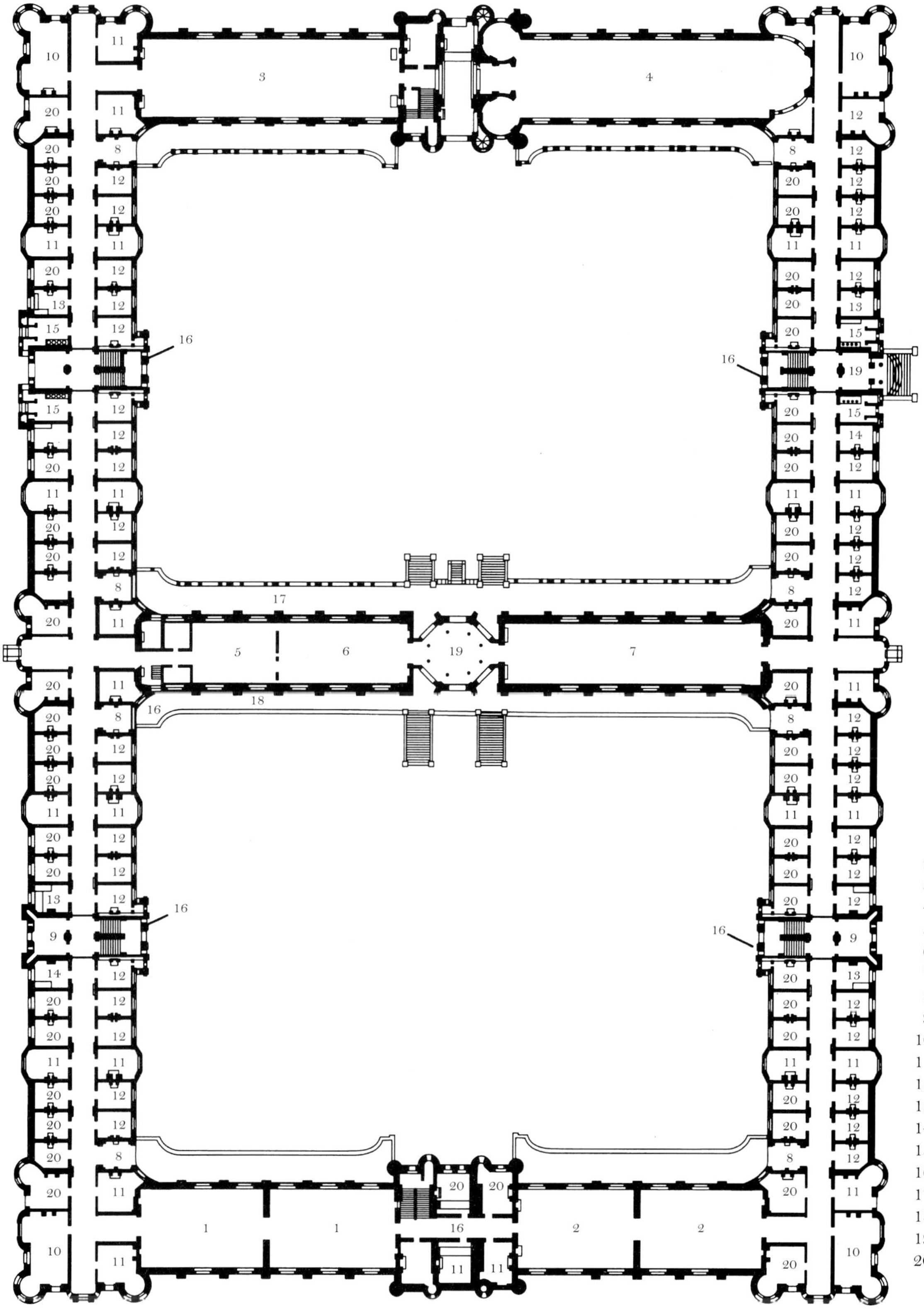

1. library
2. museum
3. recreation hall
4. chapel
5. scullery
6. kitchen
7. dining hall
8. lobby
9. ante-room
10. classroom
11. sitting room
12. study
13. servants' pantry
14. bathroom
15. lavatory
16. stairs
17. cloisters
18. balcony
19. entrance
20. bedroom

stretch vast corridors (estimated to be approximately a tenth of a mile long on each side!). Along these are the three hundred sets of bedrooms and studies for the students, each woman being given two rooms in the tradition of the Oxbridge colleges and of Girton. The bedrooms were placed on the west side of the corridors and the individual studies had the benefit of the morning sunshine from the east. Every six students were allocated a communal sitting room, and there were also provisions made for maids and pantries. At the southern end was a library on the west, and a museum was planned on the eastern half of the block. In the four corners, elaborated by round turrets, were classrooms, a lecture theater and suites for the resident lecturers.

Despite the simplicity of the plan, there are certain awkward elements which make circulation far more complicated than it first appears. For instance, it is impossible to pass from the upper courtyard to the lower without going into the longitudinal blocks. Moreover, Crossland did little to facilitate crossing from east to west. Students could only pass from a western corridor to an eastern one through the southern block; this meant walking through the museum and library, a solution that became impracticable when numbers increased and the traffic became disruptive. The only other routes were along the open cloisters which lined the connecting blocks. This was not ideal, as it meant that the women were subjected to the elements, and the cloister along the southern side of the upper quadrangle has since been glassed-in to remedy the situation. Protection from the elements is a very curious omission on the part of Crossland and his patron. While no expense was spared in creating a grandiose monument that would "fill the eye," less concern was given to the practical aspects of a functioning college for women, which so concerned the founders of the other colleges.

It is fitting to point out here that Holloway and his architect were not under the same constraints as the founders of Girton, Newnham and the other colleges. Money was not a problem in this case. But the situation goes deeper than just financial worries. The founders of the women's colleges discussed in previous chapters were speaking in a small voice for a controversial cause. The women themselves had little power in society, courting allies in prestigious positions to support their work. It was necessary, therefore, that they take whatever precautions were deemed necessary to defend their schemes against their critics while maintaining the good will of their patrons. The founders were, in a sense, the under-dogs and were forced to work doubly hard in defense of their colleges. Thomas Holloway was in no way an under-dog fighting against the odds for his cause. For him the means of success were money, advertising and a glorious building which offered a palatial residence for young ladies. He did not apologetically defend his venture with public assurances, but rather let the flamboyant monument speak for itself. Architecturally, the primary purpose of Royal Holloway was to impress, and those considerations, such as protection which so concerned the other colleges, came second or third on Holloway's list of priorities.

The college was built in four storeys, with an attic floor where the students' maids were to sleep. Each corridor wing has two stairwells, with massive stone stairs and heavy carved balustrades. The size of the rooms is quite regular, except where bay windows mark the communal sitting rooms and afford more space. Each student's study was warmed by an open fire, but the bedrooms were unheated. Because of the awkward plan the main entrance on the north, which basically leads nowhere, is

92. Chateau of Chambord, Loire Valley, 16th century. *Photo by Dr. Geoffrey Tyack.*

seldom used. Instead, access to the building has generally been from the smaller entrances on the east and west sides of the building.

In keeping with the intent to spare no expense in creating an elegant and palatial residence, and in accordance with the highest standards of Victorian efficiency and segregation, the services such as laundry and coal storage, were built about three hundred yards away to the east and connected with the college through an underground passage. Thus the magnificence of the building was in no way marred by the practical realities involved in running an institution so vast.

By the early 1880s the influence of the New Louvre designs and Vassar college had waned and new elevations showed a return to the French Renaissance chateaux. Although it is not clear from the existing evidence when or why the change was made, Crossland returned to his diligent sketches of the French chateaux for inspiration. As built, the college owes much of its detailing to Chambord, with small quotations from other chateaux along the Loire, as well as some borrowings from Hampton Court.

Holloway chose to build his college in red brick with white Portland stone dressings. A view down the west side of the building shows a regular if very busy rhythm beginning with attached turrets, then flat walls leading to curving bays, to an entrance pavilion and on to another bay at which point the pattern repeats itself. Each floor is divided by stone stringcourses and the regularly-spaced windows are dressed in stone with small rectangular carved panels above. The windows on the curving bays are elaborated by small oeil-de-boeuf windows above them. The area of greatest activity starts at the third storey, where a balustrade follows the wall surface. Above this sprouts an exuberant array of conical turret roofs, elaborately curved gables, chimney stacks crowned with half-shell motifs, and curving dormer windows. Finials add a delicate finish to the skyline. The entrances on the sides of the building are pulled forward slightly from the walls with corners defined by quoins. The doorways are marked by inset columns with more oeil-de-boeuf windows on either side. In the courtyards the stairway pavilions are highlighted with paired

93. Royal Holloway College (by Crossland, 1886). *Reproduced courtesy of the Archives, Royal Holloway, University of London, ref. PH100/1.*

pilasters bracketed by the three large arched windows which light each floor. These pavilions are topped by a balustrade and large curving pediments.

In spite of the exuberant carving and energetic skyline, there is a certain repetitious quality to the long corridor wings. The greatest variety is to be found in the crossings, which are crowned with large, elaborate towers. The north tower above the formal entrance rests on a huge square block, tiered like a wedding cake, with a small turret on each corner and beside the archway. The third tier houses a clock and the fourth is comprised of a monumental lantern elaborately carved. The middle block contains the kitchens and dining hall and its lower scale is emphasized by the strong horizontals of the cloister that runs in front of it on the north side and the cloister and balcony on the south side. It is divided into bays by blocked pilasters, each bay consisting of windows with alternating curved and triangular pediments. An elaborately carved water tower stands boldly in the center which, as Elizabeth Williams points out, is directly quoted from the lantern tower at Chambord.[39] Crossland's interpretation is more squat and heavier than its predecessor, and altogether more cumbersome. This is probably due in part to the requirement of Crossland's tower to hold water in large cisterns. The carvings that embellish the lantern all relate to the structure's aquatic function, and include swans, crocodiles, and storks.[40] The tower on the south closely resembles that on the north. The southern wing, containing the library and what was originally planned as the museum is striking for its quotation from Wren's work at Hampton Court Palace: its rhythmic bays are articulated by ocular windows and a loggia along the ground floor (see color illustration 15).

The interiors of the public rooms are grand, if somewhat cold. The huge library has carved mouldings, high stacks and a barrel-vaulted ceiling. The picture gallery is a similarly vast space, also barrel-vaulted, with a coffered ceiling. The chapel was

39. Elizabeth Williams, "An Architectural History of Royal Holloway College, Egham 1874–87," reprinted from *Surrey Archaeological Collections*, 77: 11.
40. Ibid., 113.

94. Library, Royal Holloway College, 1887–88: *Reproduced courtesy of the Archives, Royal Holloway, University of London, ref. PH100/2.*

95. Chapel, Royal Holloway College. *Reproduced courtesy of the Archives, Royal Holloway, University of London, ref. PH100/1.*

96. Dining Hall, Royal Holloway College. *Reproduced courtesy of the Archives, Royal Holloway, University of London, ref. PH100/2.*

97. Picture Gallery, Royal Holloway College. *Reproduced courtesy of the Archives, Royal Holloway, University of London, ref. PH100/1.*

laboriously decorated by the sculptor of all the carvings on the building, Ceccardo Fucigna (see color illustration 16). Fucigna had worked with Crossland under Gilbert Scott. The sculpture program on the interior of the chapel includes Pope Julius II, Muhammed, Confucius and Savonarola, an interesting choice of religious leaders, suggestive of the non-denominational character of the chapel. Decorations in painted relief include six Archangels and the Creation of Eve in the apse. Curiously, the sculptural program throughout the college includes very few famous women from history or the Bible, further evidence of the lack of interest on the part of Holloway and his architect in the actual scheme for women's education. Paved in black and white square tiles with the elaborate paintings above, the chapel is the most elaborate of all the public rooms. The dining hall is another grand room with a high coffered ceiling and severe pilasters which rise to the full height of the hall. This is also much like the picture gallery which was a vast space and held Holloway's large collection of paintings, mostly by contemporary British artists.

The process of design took place over many years, from the early inception of the idea in 1874, to the building's delayed opening in 1887. From the few comments made by Holloway about the building, it appears he wanted it to make a proclamation, not as much about women's higher education at the end of the nineteenth century, as about Holloway himself, his wealth and philanthropy. In the other colleges, the style of architecture chosen reflected the founders' wishes in as much as they made a quiet, modest statement about their enterprise with strong overtones of domesticity to reassure the public. Royal Holloway can hardly be called modest, and it is interesting to look at Holloway's and Crossland's choice of the French Renaissance within the larger architectural context, in order to understand better Holloway's motives and goals.

In the 1850s and 1860s, the designs for the New Louvre were widely published in the British architectural press. Elements of the French Renaissance were picked up and wielded within Classical designs, thus playing a part in the larger 'Battle of the Styles' which was raging at the time. In particular, the French mansard roof was employed as it was believed to accommodate the Classical orders nicely. Several large city hotels, such as the Langham of 1865, were built in the Second Empire style which was considered suitable for such grand, secular building types. Relations with France were considerably improved since the early years of the century, and there was an active exchange of culture going on in the Great Exhibitions in England and France in the 1850s and 1860s. Thus it is not surprising that a greater architectural correspondence had begun.

In Crossland's article about the building of Royal Holloway College, he credited T. H. Wyatt with suggesting to Holloway that the French Renaissance would be an appropriate style in which to build a large institution. Wyatt had showed him various prints of Chambord and was himself using the style in some of his domestic work. For example, in 1869 he remodeled Brockenhurst Park in Hampshire, borrowing elements from the smaller chateaux of the Loire. Crossland also believed that the style of the Renaissance was re-emerging.

In 1874, E. M. Barry delivered a "Lecture on Architecture" which was printed in *The Builder.* Here Barry outlined the reasons why a return to the Renaissance was a rational and logical choice. He assured those interested that:

98. Langham Hotel, London (by J. Giles, 1864–66).

They will find in them all that the 'Queen Anne' style gives them, and I think much more. To great boldness and variety of outline, these Renaissance buildings add an elegance of ornament which is based in some examples on Mediaeval, and in others on Classical precedents. . . . They are exceedingly rich in picturesque details, such as high roofs, turrets, chimney shafts, and dormer windows, and they adopt windows of various sizes and shapes, mullioned or otherwise, according to circumstances. The convenience of round arches and horizontal floor divisions is freely accepted and the great roofs, which are invariable, offer facilities for the provision of a number of secondary bedrooms, . . . without either meanness, on the one hand, or extravagance on the other.[41]

He goes on to praise the chateaux of the Loire, most particularly Blois and Amboise for their mediaeval details and Chambord and Chenonceaux for their Classical elements.

This interest in the French styles can be seen as a part of the growth of eclecticism that we have seen emerging in the 1870s in the work of Richard Norman Shaw, Basil Champneys and even on occasion, Alfred Waterhouse. But where Shaw and Champneys looked to rural England and its domestic traditions, Wyatt, Barry and Crossland, whose clientele was generally quite different, looked across the channel for inspiration.

Various styles of the French Renaissance were considered appropriate for various building types. While it was always used for secular buildings, the inspiration of the New Louvre was considered to be suitable for civic buildings on a grand scale. Indeed, when Crossland's 1877 scheme for the college was shown in the Royal Academy the reviewer noted the architect's careful study of the French example and criticized the design's "disproportionate central roof," but primarily found fault because "The whole is as unsuited for erection in a country place as anything

41. E. M. Barry, "Lectures on Architecture," *The Builder* (21 March 1847): 237.

99. Bowes Mansion and Museum, Barnard Castle, County Durham (by J. A. Pellechet, 1869–85). From *The Builder* (14 January 1871), 29.

architectural could possibly be. Buildings like this are essentially civic, and are entirely out of their element except in the streets of a great city."[42] This criticism may well have been one of the contributing factors in the decision to return to Chambord as the source of primary inspiration for the college.

The critic was several years too late to stop Mr. Bowes building the Bowes Mansion and Museum for his wife's painting collection. In 1871, *The Builder* published the plan and elevation for this building in Barnard Castle, County Durham, by the French architect J. A. Pellechet, and the builder J. E. Watson. The design bears a striking resemblance to Crossland's 1877 elevation, and Renwick's work at Vassar. In all three, a central domed pavilion marks the entrance, while the two projecting wings are capped by mansard roofs. The facades of Crossland and Pellechet are highly sculptural, with elaborate carvings around the windows and Classical details.

As the 1870s progressed, quotations from the chateaux of the Loire, which were considered to be more appropriate for lavish domestic commissions, proliferated. Donald Bassett points out:

The earlier Loire Chateaux . . . supplied the favorite motifs for use in the 1870s with their cone-roofed towers, sprocketed at the eaves to achieve a concave profile; heavy machiolation or cornice around the tops of these bastions; pronounced horizontal banding and vertical window-strips together creating a geometric grid upon the wall surface; and elegantly Classical interpretations of the essentially Gothic feature, the dormer window.[43]

Examples of such borrowings are common in houses from the 1870s and 1880s built for wealthy patrons. One good example is Wykehurst Park in Bolney, Sussex of 1871–74, designed by E. M. Barry. It was built for Henry Huth whose money came from banking. Set atop a hill commanding a splendid view, the reliance on French chateaux is evident. The solid rectangular block is dramatized by varied roof-lines,

42. "Architecture at the Royal Academy," *The Architect* (19 May 1877): 317.
43. Donald Bassett, "The French Renaissance Revival in British Architecture 1824–1914," (Ph.D. dissertation, University of Edinburgh, 1979), 294.

100. Wykehurst, Bolney, East Sussex (by E. M. Barry, 1871–74).

round and square towers and turrets and tall chimney stacks. Elaborately carved dormer windows look ahead to Crossland's work at Royal Holloway.

Another famous instance of the revival of French chateaux for a wealthy patron, was the house built for Ferdinand de Rothschild, Waddesdon Manor. In 1874 Rothschild bought land in Buckinghamshire, near Aylesbury, and hired a French architect, G. H. Destailleur, to build him a country seat. The result is a pastiche of the chateaux from the Loire that Rothschild admired, including the tower staircases from Blois, the chimneys from Chambord, and various other quotations from Anet and Maintenon. It was built in yellow stone with grey stone dressings. It is an altogether more sedate and gracious essay in the French Renaissance style than Crossland's work at Royal Holloway. Nevertheless, the great tower, the elaborate dormer windows and the tall chimney stacks with the shell motif are all elements which are found at Royal Holloway, and which were derived from the French example.

Before Waddesdon was even completed, the Rothschilds were building another French chateau at Halton, also in Buckinghamshire (see fig. 102). This is a smaller but equally elegant essay in the Loire style. Instances were common in which wealthy patrons commissioned houses in the chateaux style, either from French architects in the case of Destailleur, or English architects who had proven themselves well-versed in sixteenth century French architecture, such as Barry or Crossland.

The men who built such palaces tended to be successful industrialists. Bassett points out that many of them opted for the style in order to indulge "in unbridled romance and self-dramatisation—in flight from the ugly industrialisation in which so many had made their fortunes."[44] Such self-made men saw in the French Renaissance the best means available of advertising their wealth and success in the world. By the 1870s, these newly rich men had become more acceptable in society and more confident in choosing their own style in which to live:

44. Ibid., 14.

101. Waddesdon Manor, Buckinghamshire (by G. H. Destailleur, 1874–89). *Photo of North Front by Martin Charles. Reproduced courtesy of the National Trust, Waddesdon Manor.*

The resulting growth in prestige and self-confidence led to a specifically nouveau-riche style. It flourished in defiance of the Victorian doctrine that a gentleman's house should be marked by 'elegance and importance without ostentation'. It was imported from France, from the Second Empire world of new families and sometimes shady fortunes.[45]

The domestic house was, and still is, an expression of wealth. The lavish elegance of the French Renaissance style and its obvious associations with palace architecture, provided a popular means of expression for this growing sector of society. Additionally, the associations with a distant and foreign aristocracy could be seen to lend a certain regal flavor to the lifestyles of these families, without actually mimicking the established British aristocracy.

The residences of the nouveau-riche drew criticism from those who saw their

45. Mark Girouard, *The Victorian Country House* (New Haven: Yale University Press, 1979), 291.

102. Halton House, Halton, Buckinghamshire (by W. R. Rogers, 1884).

houses as gauche and ostentatious. For instance in 1897, H. Heathcote Statham roundly condemned such displays, although it is unclear whether his wrath was directed more at the French Renaissance style houses or the nouveau-riche who lived in them. While he praised Shaw's work at Cragside for its lack of pretension, he railed against the French Renaissance house which he considered "a rather typical specimen of the modern pretentious dwelling; a house which one would expect to find inhabited by a *nouveau riche*."[46] He went on to point out that by the end of the century, these new patrons had begun to mimic the older families and were building more sedate, less ostentatious houses for themselves.

But in the 1870s and 1880s, these wealthy men were happily building to impress, to "fill the eye." Thomas Holloway counted in the numbers of men who had risen from relative obscurity to become one of the richest men in Britain. As in the case of Matthew Vassar, Holloway needed a legacy on which to bestow his millions since he had no children of his own. In Royal Holloway College, Crossland built on such a scale as to guarantee that the college would "beat Vassar into fits" while at the same time, making the palatial home of the Rothschild's look puny in comparison. For his college for women, Holloway wanted a chateau, an ornate palace that would continue as a living monument to his name and achievements. The palaces of the Loire carried with them glamorous and opulent associations in which to cloak Holloway's college. What the college first lacked in academic organization, it made up for in its effusive and vibrant self-advertisement.

Holloway's choice of a palatial residence did not mean that he wholly neglected the academic side of the college. At least until his wife's death in 1875, he conscientiously looked into the running of a college for women, its curriculum and domestic arrangements. Once again he turned to Matthew Vassar's example, thoroughly

46. H. H. Statham, *Modern Architecture: A Book for Architects and the Public* (London: Chapman & Hall, 1897), 201.

reading the *Laws and Regulations of Vassar Female College, Poughkeepsie N.Y.* This outlined the role of the president and his responsibilities, giving him overriding powers within the college. Regarding the lady principal, Holloway made note of Vassar's proviso that:

She shall exercise over them a maternal supervision in their private apartments, in the dining-hall, in the corridors, in the public rooms and grounds of the College, and in their intercourse with the neighboring community; and she shall also use her best efforts to improve their personal habits, their social training, and their moral and religious culture.[47]

Such concerns for domestic discipline and supervision were shared by the colleges discussed previously.

Many of these issues reappear in Holloway's Deed for his college and in his will. The Deed was dated 1883 and laid out the "Nature and Principles of the College." It began by presenting the college as an institution for the middle and upper middle classes and for girls over seventeen who had passed either the Oxford or Cambridge Local Examinations. Furthermore, as with Vassar, there was to be no religious requirement, but the lady principal was granted permission to refuse anyone whom she deemed morally unsuitable. Holloway also stipulated that: "It is the Founder's desire that the domestic life of the College should be that of an orderly Christian household."[48] The Deed went on to discuss the duties of the lady principal, the need for the students to reside in college for the "companionship and discipline of collegiate life,"[49] requirements for dining and so on. The phraseology used here and in Vassar's Deed is important as it was intended to establish the tone of college life, and gives an indication of how the college was perceived to function. The ready comparisons with the domestic house, albeit a lavish one, clearly suggest that Holloway and the others involved in the scheme, deliberately relied on the private sphere for the internal arrangements of the college.

Much of the organization of the college was intended to preserve the womanliness of the students. For instance in 1886, before the college was opened, *The Times* reported that the huge kitchen facilities were intended not only to prepare the food for the students, but also to offer cooking classes.[50] Similarly, another unidentified article in the archives describes the fees and curriculum of the college. It lists the courses offered such as Classics, History and Mathematics. But it adds that "there are also yearly courses in hygiene, ambulance work, cookery and needlework, with classes for gymnastics, drawing and vocal music."[51] The "accomplishments" were not to be neglected during a woman's course of study at Royal Holloway College.

Other articles described the beauty of the site and praised the terraces around the building and the formal Italian garden laid out on the western side of the building. One author discussed the rooms on the ground floor, pointing out their function as rooms of business for the college, or ultimately as lecture rooms. The lecture theater was described as "built out, as an afterthought, below the ground-floor level, with low-pitched ceiling; which has a somewhat cold and gloomy effect."[52] Here again is evidence that the academic requirements of the college were met in a haphazard or makeshift way, taking second place in the list of priorities for the college.

After Holloway's death in 1883, the details of completion were taken on by his

47. *Laws and Regulations of Vassar Female College, Poughkeepsie N.Y.*, ed. by order of the Board of Trustees (New York: John A. Gray and Green, Printers, 1866), Royal Holloway and Bedford New College Archives, 7.
48. Deed of Foundation of Holloway College, Surrey, 11 October 1883, Amended Deed, April 1906, Royal Holloway and Bedford New College Archives, 8.
49. Ibid.
50. "The Royal Holloway College," *The Times* (1886), RF 125/2, Royal Holloway and Bedford New College Archives, 17.
51. Newspaper clipping in the Royal Holloway and Bedford New College Archives, RF 125/2, 21.
52. "The Last New College" (October 1887), RF 125/2, Royal Holloway and Bedford New College Archives, 24.

brother-in-law, George Martin, who had by then changed his name to George Martin-Holloway. Martin-Holloway shared the founder's ambition to create a grand and opulent women's college. In 1885, after the Prince and Princess of Wales had opened the Holloway Sanatorium, Martin-Holloway of requested of Queen Victoria's private secretary, Sir Henry Ponsonby, that the Queen herself open the Holloway College.[53] She agreed, and in June 1886 Queen Victoria officially inaugurated the Royal Holloway College. The royal blessing was a grand gesture in keeping with Holloway's ambitious early scheme for the college.

The college opened to students in 1887. With the exception of the chapel, museum and parts of the library, very little of the interior decor remains, and there is scant photographic evidence which gives a picture of what the corridors, common rooms and other private rooms looked like in the early days. Instead we must depend on the accounts of journalists who visited the college when it was first opened, or memories of the early students. In another unidentified clipping in the archives, the bedrooms and corridors are descriptively reviewed.

The walls of the room [the sitting room?] *are not yet papered, but distempered light lavender; the corridors are all colour-washed a salmon or pinkish tint. This somewhat relieves the impression of cold whiteness owing to the quantity of ornamental stucco, the ceilings, doors, etc., being adorned with designs in plaster panels . . .*[54]

This description is a far cry from the appearance of the corridors now which are stark and sadly institutionalized. But the ornate interiors described would certainly have been in keeping with the country houses such as Waddesdon.

Miss Marion Pick, an early student, wrote of her memories of the college in an unpublished manuscript in the college archives. Her descriptions of life in the fledgling college and of the environment in which she lived provide an invaluable insight into the college at its inception. At several points she equated her life at college with that of a country house:

our isolated site was perfect for the development of fresh ideals for a collegiate life. It is pleasant to visualise our Founder thinking of country-house life specially planned for those wishful to study, with a perfect library in constant use and delightful grounds in which to relax.[55]

She also related how Holloway had planned for each student to bring along her own personal maid who would sleep in the attic rooms and attend to the private needs of their mistresses. Although the provision for women's personal servants was in keeping with the grandeur of the college, in practice it turned out to be unnecessary. Most of the early students came from middle class backgrounds and were not able to live the upper class lifestyle which Holloway intended for them. The majority were daughters of clergymen, doctors, lawyers and some businessmen.[56] Scholarships, which were generous in the early years, were a crucial factor for many women applying to the college.

Miss Pick's descriptions of the dining hall and library offer valuable illustrations of life at Royal Holloway. The dining room was furnished with ordinary tables that were laid with elegant linens with the Royal Holloway monogram, and decorated

53. Bingham, *History of Royal Holloway College*, 61.
54. Newspaper clipping in the Royal Holloway and Bedford New College Archives, RF 125/2, 25.
55. Pick, "Social Life at Royal Holloway College 1887–1939," 13.
56. Bingham, *History of Royal Holloway College*, 77.

103. Sitting Room, Royal Holloway College. *Reproduced courtesy of the Archives, Royal Holloway, University of London, ref. PH100/2.*

with "good solid silver plate, always kept shining."[57] Of the library, she pointed out that the stacks partitioned the vast spaces into smaller, more intimate areas, each containing its own Turkish carpet. Once again she compared the room with libraries in private country houses. She confirmed reports that the lecture rooms were provided for as the need arose and were often makeshift and functional, although the lecturers tried to make them look "nicely feminine, yet learned."[58]

The bedrooms, studies and sitting rooms for the students were more carefully appointed. The furniture was often mahogany, and although the bedsteads were iron, the mattresses were comfortable. Apparently the "outstanding feature in each study was a large solid dresser with two long shelves and four small drawers above a flat open central portion for writing."[59] The rooms were laid with Turkish carpets and hung with damask curtains. Mirrors were required in each room at the request of the founder. As in the other colleges discussed, individual taste soon came to appear in each student's rooms as she decorated them with prints, fans, chairs and cushions.

57. Pick , "Social Life at Royal Holloway College 1887–1939," 26–27.
58. Ibid., 31.
59. Ibid., 50.

Marion Pick continued her analogy with a country house when describing the structure of their lives:

It seems to me that the pattern of life chosen was that of a country house, where the Staff were hostesses and the students guests who were to be introduced to a harmonious life of purposeful learning. The stateliness and orderliness of their lives were designed from the very beginning to match the grandeux [sic] *of the estate . . .*[60]

There are parallels to be drawn from this statement with the structure of life in the other women's colleges. For instance, Miss Wordsworth's writings made it clear that she insisted upon modest, humble and feminine behavior from her students. Somerville's first president forbade a student to go out wearing a hat of which she disapproved, fearing that it would not present the proper, middle class, modest image which the college wanted to foster. As we have seen, the buildings that grew up to house these women can be described in similar terms.

It is interesting to note therefore, that at Royal Holloway, life was structured to reflect the grandeur and elegance of the building. The service at meals and tea was always of a high and elegant standard. Perhaps the best example of this was the elaborate production of the evening meal. For this daily event great preparation was involved. Full evening dress was required, sometimes including long trains on dresses, and this meant a dramatic change from some women's otherwise drab or modest, daily costume. It was also stipulated that the students wear their hair up at all times. At the start of term, the student filled her diary with dinner partners so that every evening she would escort or be escorted by another student. The lecturers and lady principal would also select students as their escorts. Those privileged to take a member of staff to dinner would gather in the principal's drawing room before-hand. Similarly, if a student had a guest, she was required to bring her/him into the principal's drawing room for introductions. At 6:55 P.M. the students gathered, paired with their partners, in the library, arranged in order of seniority. The principal would formally lead the college through the corridors to the dining room at 7:00 P.M. They were then marshaled to their seats by head students. Grace was said and the women were waited on by the large staff of servants.[61] This ceremony bears little resemblance to the modest meals provided for the first five students at Girton, but one wonders if this was the "dignity and tradition" which Emily Davies so coveted.

Perhaps because of the great size of the college, or as a result of its paternal founder, the day to day routine for the early students was the most disciplined and ordered of the colleges discussed. The bulk of the day was carefully structured at Royal Holloway. Maids brought coal and water to the rooms each morning and took away the boots to be cleaned between 6:00 and 7:00 A.M. Chapel began at 8:00 A.M. Seats were assigned for both breakfast and lunch. Lectures were given between 9:00 A.M. and 1:00 P.M., and after lunch time was allotted for exercise. Tea took place at the expected hour of 4:00 P.M. and was remembered as the only informal time of the day. Once the college attendance had reached over one hundred and seventy, in the early years of the twentieth century, "College Families" were introduced. These consisted of small groups of women, between seven and ten in number, who came together to form a "Family." Members of a family would try and sit together at meals, and every

60. Ibid., 65.
61. Ibid., 110–11.

104. 'A College Family', Royal Holloway College. *Reproduced courtesy of the Archives, Royal Holloway, University of London, ref. PH271/3.*

day a different member would have tea in her room. Such a unit was like a formalized clique and ensured that every student belonged to a group. This was important as being alone was frowned upon except when studying. Tea was served on white linen and consisted of roll, jam and cakes and tea.

The students were then required to work from 4:45 to 6:45 P.M. when a bell rang indicating that it was time to dress for dinner. After dinner, small coffee parties were held by the resident lecturers for their guests and some students until 8:30 P.M. when the students were expected to be back at work till 10:00. A bell rang at 10:25 P.M. warning that it was almost time for bed and five minutes later silence was insisted upon. If a student broke this silence or disturbed the others who were working she was expected to write a formal apology the next day. A watchman patrolled the corridors at night, and if he discovered a woman's candle burning after hours, he would knock on her door and instruct her to go to bed. Such a practice ensured the safety of the students and protected the women from overwork, as only certain hours each day could be devoted to study. If the women did fall ill, a resident physician would take care of them.

The first principal, Miss Bishop, ran things very efficiently and took care to follow the Founder's will in most areas. Problems arose for her because she was fervently religious and discouraged alternative worship, contradicting Holloway's wishes for a non-sectarian college. The issue escalated to such a degree that Miss Bishop resigned in 1897. She was replaced by Miss Emily Penrose, who we know as principal of Somerville College, but who ran Royal Holloway from 1897 to 1907.

The atmosphere at the college was unusually quiet and was often considered to be more like a boarding school than a college. In her novel, *Dolores*, Ivy Compton-Burnett, herself an alumna of Royal Holloway, described her heroine's response to her collegiate surroundings:

> *As other days followed . . . she* [Dolores] *found herself with a place and purposes in a passionless, ardent little world — a world of women's friendships; where there lived in a strange harmony the spirits of the mediaeval convent and modern growth.*[62]

This "harmony" of two conflicting tendencies shows up time and again in the structure of Royal Holloway. Where there was the freedom of collegiate life, there was the rigid supervision of the students' lives. Where Holloway spent thousands on a grandiose college for women, lecture rooms were added as a haphazard afterthought. Where minute details were copied from Chambord and integrated into the design, there was no communication between quadrangles, and the women had to go outside to pass from one side of the building to the other. Great concern was paid to some issues of the planning and running of the college, while other, sometimes more important aspects of the organization of the college, were practically ignored.

Thomas Holloway's beneficence resulted in a luxurious college for women. But whether he himself was a committed pioneer in educational reform is doubtful. Certainly his millions and the hard work of the early principals and lecturers, resulted in a successful college for women. Royal Holloway was admitted as one of the schools in the Faculties of Arts and Science of the University of London in 1900, thereby granting degrees to women long before the Oxbridge universities offered similar benefits, and a couple of years ahead of Westfield.

The inconsistencies integral to the founding of the college are illustrated in one of the many paintings which Holloway purchased and hung in the college picture gallery. Amongst the English landscapes and Victorian genre scenes, is a painting by Edwin Long which Holloway bought in 1882. This work, entitled *The Babylonian Marriage Market*, depicts a group of young, helpless women being auctioned off for marriage to the highest bidder (see color illustration 17). Like cows or textiles, they are a commodity to be bought and sold. This was one of the first and most famous paintings bought by Holloway for his college for women. Such a purchase suggests that, while moved by the request of his wife to help women, he had little sympathy for or understanding of their plight. This is not intended so much as a criticism as a statement of fact. Royal Holloway College has been an important institution for women since its inception, offering quality education on a generous scale which the other colleges could not provide. Furthermore, its lavish and glamorous accoutrements may have lured many women to college, and probably did much to quell parents' fears about their daughters leaving home. That its founder was not keenly interested in women's education is far less important than the fact that, though not passionate about the cause, he built the college, thus providing generations of women with an opportunity for higher education.

62. Ivy Compton-Burnett, *Dolores* (Edinburgh and London: Blackwood and Sons, 1911), 110.

5 SOCIETY'S REACTION TO THE WOMEN'S COLLEGES

Their Architectural Influence

They formed a pretty, suggestive, pathetic sight, of whose pathos and beauty they were themselves unconscious, and would not discover till, amid the storms and strains of after-years, with their injustice, loneliness, child-bearing, and bereavement, their minds would revert to this experience as to something which had been allowed to slip past them insufficiently regarded.
Thomas Hardy, *Jude the Obscure*, 1895[1]

By the turn of the twentieth century the six women's colleges discussed above were firmly established and their graduates were moving on to work as teachers, social workers and doctors, as well as wives and mothers. English society had begun to accept more rigorous schooling for girls and some women, not as an anomaly but as a fact. However, with these positive strides in women's opportunities came a corresponding reaction of fear and mistrust of the "new woman" who was no longer being trained specifically for the private sphere. While more women were able to participate in higher education, arguments against women's emancipation from the home became more extreme. With theories such as Social Darwinism and eugenics, the strides within the women's movement were countered by threats of the physical and social breakdown of the English race if women continued to seek alternatives to their domestic roles. Such fears continued to influence women's educational opportunities and the social roles which were assigned to them.

Worries that women were abandoning the home and maternity for careers or were not being trained properly in the necessary domestic skills were re-expressed in scientific terms in the wake of Darwin's theory of evolution. Theorists such as Herbert Spencer and Patrick Geddes addressed the question of women and their education within the larger context of the healthy evolution of society. This ideology, referred to here as Social Darwinism, made it possible to justify and reinforce critics' concerns about women and their education, by positing women's different intellectual and physical capabilities within a new, authoritative scientific framework. Social Darwinists also stressed the need for individuals to work towards the collective good of the state, an idea which was shared with those involved in eugenics.

As early as 1874 Charles Kingsley had called on women to train themselves as good mothers in order to take on the important task of raising future generations and improving the English race.[2] In the 1860s and 1870s Herbert Spencer also wrote about the issue of women and the home, complaining in biological and sociological terms of the abnormal and unhealthy results that women's higher education or non-domestic duties might elicit.[3] But it was in the 1890s and the first decade of the twentieth century that arguments along these lines were heard most loudly. Interestingly, this was at about the same time as women began to call for degrees and suffrage in louder and more strident voices.

These new critics had the weight of scientific theory behind them. They posited that the roles of the sexes were biologically determined, thus to meddle with the

1. Thomas Hardy, *Jude the Obscure*, ed. Norman Page (1895; reprint, New York & London: W. W. Norton, 1978), 112–13.
2. Rev. Charles Kingsley, *Health and Education* (London: W. Isbister, 1874).
3. Carol Dyhouse, "Social Darwinistic ideas and the Development of women's education in England, 1880–1920," *History of Education*, 5, no. 1. (1976): 43–44. See also Jill Conway, "Stereotypes of Femininity in a Theory of Sexual Evolution" in *Suffer and Be Still*, ed. Martha Vicinus (London: Methuen, 1980), 140–154.

dictates of nature could only lead to social catastrophe. Critics of women's education continued to threaten that too much education would render a woman physically unfit for duties as a mother; that women would no longer want to perform their natural maternal roles; that all sorts of nervous and emotional disorders would result from their new, abnormal lifestyles;[4] and that the normal family structure, upon which so much was believed to depend, was crumbling as a result of women's new emancipation.

These arguments are relevant to our study because they illustrate that the evolution of women's rights was not a linear, straightforward progression. In spite of their successes at college women still found their options outside the home limited by society's mistrust of the "new woman." Consequently, most of the issues which conditioned the architecture of the earliest women's colleges continued to affect the designs of women's halls of residence well into the twentieth century, thus perpetuating stereotypical attitudes towards women and their education.

One of the most disturbing manifestations of this reactionary trend was the Report of the Inter-Departmental Committee of Physical Deterioration published in 1904. Carol Dyhouse described the Committee in the following:

This Committee had . . . been constituted in the period of acute concern over national welfare generated not least by the Imperialistic rivalries abroad in the early years of this century, and in particular after the revelation of the low standards of health prevailing among the recruits for the Boer War.[5]

In the report, much of the blame for the poor health of the English people was heaped onto women who, it was believed, were poorly trained in domestic hygiene and health, and who had left the home for work, thereby abandoning their proper duties. Eugenicists, doctors, government and education committee members wrote prolifically arguing that it was a woman's moral duty first and foremost to raise strong men and properly feminine women for the sake of the nation.[6]

Such ideas had the backing and support of some scientists and evolutionists who argued in Darwinistic terms for separate roles for the sexes. Two key figures in this group were Patrick Geddes and his student and partner Professor J. Arthur Thompson. Geddes was trained as a biologist under Thomas Henry Huxley, and his scientific achievements were considerable. But his interests and energies were wide and varied, ranging from educational reform and housing for the poor, to nationalistic issues and the science of evolution. His interest in these seemingly separate issues, was combined within a positivist belief in progress and social reform.

Geddes was also active in founding the first halls of residence for Edinburgh University. The earliest hall for men was begun in a pre-existing house and was run by the students themselves, who were to work together for the collective good of the house. The success of such halls eventually led to the present residences which sit on Castlehill overlooking the city of Edinburgh. A row of Georgian houses was remodeled largely by Sydney Mitchell between 1892 and 1894[7] in half-timber and white stucco, with 'Queen Anne' oriels and a varied roof-line of gables and chimneys. They conjure up associations of English domestic, rather than traditional collegiate, architecture. This was perhaps a reflection of Geddes' intention to make these halls

4. Dyhouse, "Social Darwinistic ideas," 44.
5. Ibid., 46.
6. Ibid., 47.
7. Gavin Stamp, "Architectural Notes," unpublished essay for the Victorian Society Summer Schools, 1992.

105. University of Edinburgh Halls of Residence, Castlehill, Edinburgh (remodelled by Sidney Mitchell, 1892–94).

autonomous, self-governing domiciles without the traditional, paternal figure of the master or warden of the Oxbridge college.

Geddes' work with university halls of residence and city planning earned him the support of feminists who were active in his schemes. As Helen Meller points out:

The administration of student halls was undertaken by women; the Edinburgh Social Union was largely run by women; women worked in the gardens and civic betterment schemes. The progressive young ladies who lived in the ladies' hostels . . . provided a fertile recruiting ground for voluntary social workers.[8]

Within these circles the debate over sex differences and men and women's natural, evolutionary roles flourished. Geddes believed that women were naturally fitted for nurturing roles and served as guardians of "tradition and moral values."[9] Education was necessary for women to help educate them for their important position in society; training the young both physically and emotionally in order to further advance the British race.

Such ideas were not new. The Christian Socialists held very similar views on the subject of women's education, hoping that more education would result in better wives and mothers, thereby enriching society. What is new here is that Geddes' arguments were based on biological determinism, the outgrowth of Darwin's highly acclaimed *Origin of the Species*, published in 1859. By the turn of the century, Geddes had developed his ideas further, in conjunction with Arthur Thompson, and had written several books on the subject.

In 1889 the two men published *The Evolution of Sex*. In their preface they discussed how the most fundamental principles of evolution and biology could be used as the basis for their study of human beings' social, psychological and ethical behavior and

8. Helen Meller, *Patrick Geddes: Social Evolutionist and City Planner* (London and New York: Routledge, 1990), 79.
9. Ibid., 82.

their subsequent educational needs.[10] Much of the book presents a careful study of cell behavior with a focus on the optimum conditions necessary for reproduction. The final chapter, entitled "Psychological and Ethical Aspects," extrapolated general, stereotyped emotional and intellectual differences between the sexes, based on the biological evidence of cell growth, development and reproduction. For Geddes and Thompson, this biological evidence was the fundamental key to explaining human behavior; it justified their views on women and their role in society. In their words: "What was decided among prehistoric Protozoa cannot be annulled by Act of Parliament."[11]

This sort of logic, based as it was on the elementary behavior and sex differentiation of cells, became the basis for numerous assertions by Geddes and Thompson about men and women and their respective roles. In discussing the women's movement, they criticized the politicization of women's opportunities and regretted that women were entering the work force. They foresaw "complexly ruinous results . . . [from] this inter-sexual competition."[12] Furthermore, they agreed with the basic sexual division of labor which they believed had been handed down through the centuries, finding evidence for these ideas in the understood sex differences between men and women. These they outlined in the following way: men were more intelligent and had bigger brains, they were stronger, more independent and more courageous. Women were more passive, altruistic, affectionate and sympathetic.

In 1911 these issues were discussed in a series of essays published together and entitled *The Position of Women: Actual and Ideal.* Arthur Thompson and his wife contributed the first essay. In this they stressed the biological differences between men and women and warned that women's infertility was the inevitable outcome of higher education and of "individuation generally." They went on to add that "It must be observed also, that part of the reduced fertility may be due to hypernutrition, and the like, to the frequent absence of love-marriages, to selfish celibacy and selfish non-maternity.[13] The bulk of the other essays, by both women and men, continue in this strain, citing women's selfish abandonment of their maternal duties as the root cause of many of society's ills. In the face of such arguments, grounded as they were in contemporary theories of biology and psychology, many of the leaders in women's education continued to temper their requests for greater opportunities with a reassuring emphasis on women's special nature.

Geddes' and Thompson's ideas became more extreme in their book *Problems of Sex: New Tracts for the Times* published in 1912. In this they discussed, again beginning with biology, the love between the sexes, pointing out that it exists even in the animal kingdom between males and females, but reaches its highest form in humans. With this "evidence" they could argue that the basic family structure was biologically determined. They used this argument in their criticisms of urban housing for the poor which was overcrowded and thus "provocative of abnormalities in sexual expression." Worse than this however was the:

More subtle, but yet more severe and disastrous, provocatives to sexual irregularities than those of family overcrowding alone are to be found in those social arrangements which leave large numbers of adults temporarily or permanently unmated.[14]

10. Patrick Geddes and A. J. Thompson, *The Evolution of Sex*, revised ed. (London: Walter Scott, 1901), vii.
11. Ibid., 286.
12. Ibid., 287.
13. J. A. Thompson, and Mrs. Thompson, "The Position of Women: Biologically Considered," in *The Position of Women: Actual and Ideal* (London: James Nisbet, 1911), 21.
14. J. A. Thompson and P. Geddes, *Problems of Sex: New Tracts for the Times* (London: Cassell, 1912), 33.

The authors focused on unmarried women to make their points clear. Using the analogy of queen and worker bees, they emphasized the unhealthiness of bees and women who did not mate. Furthermore, they saw evidence that this breed of female would, in all probability, die young.

They concluded their discussion with the warning that:

Irregularities in sexual behaviour or conduct have to be judged not merely by their effect on the individual, but by their influence on the race; and the latter influence may operate either organically through the channels of inheritance, or socially by affecting social institutions and social sentiment.[15]

This is evidence then, of the connection between biological determinism, Social Darwinism, and eugenics, which combined to assert the supremacy of the white English-speaking people and attempted to repress any deviation from what was considered the normal social structure.

The biological evidence, which Geddes and Thompson provided, gave fuel to the already existing fire of criticism of the women's movement. The fears that single women working or learning in competition with men would reject marriage and motherhood, or that such women would suffer ill-health and produce sickly children echo those which surrounded the genesis of the women's colleges. Such arguments suggest that, while considerable gains were made in women's education and rights, such progress could not be taken for granted. Indeed, the more sophisticated and scientific arguments of Geddes and others, together with the stress on collectivist principles which put the interests of the state before the individual, were a new, formidable hurdle for the women's movement by the turn of the century.

The ideas of Geddes and other Social Darwinists were assimilated by a wide variety of people. The government took their ideas seriously as they had important implications for the future of the country and the Empire. The impact was also felt in the schools, in both the social focus and in the curriculum. For example, Sara Burstall, who was the headmistress at Manchester High School for Girls, a lecturer in education at the University of Manchester and a sometime scholar at Girton, published a book in 1907 which incorporated many of the concepts discussed above. In her book *English High Schools for Girls,* she outlined the history of women's education, citing the work of Davies, Clough, Buss and Beale, as well as the larger movements in thought spurred on by Mill, Darwin and Herbert Spencer.

When discussing the present and future of girls' education Burstall cited conditioning factors, such as Darwin's ideas, collectivist principles and the emphasis of the state over the individual. The result of these influences on girl's education was that:

Greater emphasis is now placed on the special duties of women such as to the community, on the basic value to the social organism of the family and the home, on the reality and importance of biological and sociological differences between men and women.[16]

The consequence of these factors, she argued, was that education should be designed to accommodate women's and men's respective needs. Women, therefore, should be educated so as to be more womanly, to be better guardians of the future populace.

15. Ibid., 36.
16. Sara Burstall, *English High Schools for Girls* (London: Longmans, Green, 1907), 12–13.

Many of these concerns had been voiced fifty years earlier by the Christian Socialists and earlier reformers of women's education. After the progress that was made, and the enriched opportunities that were available to women by the 1880s and 1890s, the question is inevitably raised why these gains were then threatened and why further pressure was put on women to stay in or return to the home? This "backlash"[17] may be the result of the success of women in positions outside the home. For instance, as women became more confident of their position in the educational establishment and demanded Oxbridge degrees, the Oxbridge communities began at last to notice the women's colleges and react against them. When the women's colleges shed some of their modest humility, the supremacy of the male bastions was threatened. Some of the men and women who had supported the moves for better education for girls and women within chivalric terms, attempting to improve the plight of the unmarried woman, were not prepared for more rigorous intellectual arguments for degrees and equal governing power in the universities. In addition, there was a perception at the time (supported by the Committee of Physical Deterioration) that the stable social order based on the home and its healthy inhabitants was crumbling, with what Geddes and Thompson called "ruinous"[18] results. The response to this perceived decay was a call to re-establish the home with all its traditional values which would be the primary domain of women.

In his book *Jude the Obscure*, Thomas Hardy presented one of the most disturbing and yet sympathetic examples of this "new woman" and the issues which surrounded her. Sue Bridehead is an intelligent and well-educated woman. Jude, her cousin and her lover, calls her 'modern' for her liberal and non-conformist views on life, love and marriage. In much of the book, Hardy focused on the tension between an individual's independent will and society's pressure to conform along prescribed lines of behavior. Sue represents a modern woman in the sense that she attempts to reject society's traditional roles for the sexes, remain independent, and love Jude in a purely spiritual sense. But she lacks the courage of her convictions, makes a bad marriage and then runs away with Jude, with whom she eventually has children. Her radical lifestyle ultimately ends in tragedy with the death of her children and her return to her miserable marriage.

It is clear that Hardy has respect for Sue and sympathizes with her desire for nonconformity and independence. But it is equally obvious that her liberal aspirations yield tragic consequences for the home and family. In a sense, Hardy could not reconcile Sue's intellect and will with her sexuality and 'natural' role as mother. It was just this struggle to reconcile women's intellects with their sexuality that was seen as such a threat to society during the late nineteenth and early twentieth centuries.

As a consequence of these concerns about the emerging "new woman," steps were taken to secure proper domestic training for girls and women. The government took an active role in requiring that girls of the lower classes take courses in domestic economy and management from the 1880s on, and it was considered an important subject for the training of teachers.[19]

Sara Burstall also argued for proper domestic training to be included in the curriculum of girl's schools for the middle and upper classes. In her chapter "Direct Preparation for Practical Life, Especially in the Home" she reiterated the importance of domestic management in girls' education:

17. "Backlash" is a term used by Susan Faludi in her book *Backlash: The Undeclared War Against American Women* (New York: Anchor Books, Doubleday, 1991). In this she discusses the actions of the feminist movement and the reactions against it which historically follow. Although her concern is primarily with women in 1980s and 1990s America, the fears she cites attached to unmarried or highly educated women, such as infertility and nervous breakdown, are strikingly like those expressed by Geddes and others in the 1890s.
18. Geddes and Thompson, *The Evolution of Sex*, 287.
19. Dyhouse, "Social Darwinistic ideas," 48.

The teaching of cookery and the domestic arts to girls of every class is advocated on national grounds, as is the teaching of military drill and marksmanship to boys. The emergence of this view is of great interest philosophically. It has a scientific, biological basis, the idea that there are specialized functions in practical life for which the sexes should be separately prepared in the school—functions so basic in national existence that the State is not safe unless its young people are specially trained to fulfill them efficiently.[20]

The importance of domestic work for women had become not only an issue of social importance, but a vital state concern as well. Articles abound which cried for proper female training and which forecast the disastrous consequences which would result if girls grew up ignorant of the domestic arts.

These concerns were then integrated into the structure of girls' schools, teachers' training colleges and even some of the women's colleges. For example, in discussing the education of girls and women in Great Britain in 1897, C. S. Bremner praised Royal Holloway for its lavish "magnificence" and applauded Thomas Holloway for including several rooms which:

could easily be used for practical instruction in cookery what [sic] *time women choose to release themselves from the bondage of examination curricula laid down by men for men. Already courses of instruction have been given in cookery, ambulance work, sick nursing, wood carving, dressmaking.*[21]

It is interesting to note here, that this historian of women's education spoke against equality in education for men and women. While the gains for women were appreciated, Bremner did not call for more reform, but rather emphasized women's traditional roles.

Domestic science and economy courses were not included in the curricula of most of the women's colleges discussed here. It was a generally accepted principle that the subjects taught at the women's colleges were the same as those offered to men, although the timetable for examinations differed in some colleges. Indeed, when the question of whether domestic science could replace science as a discipline at Newnham was raised, the science tutor there, Ida Freund responded angrily, arguing that domestic science could in no way prepare a student to think and analyze in the proper scientific method.[22]

Outside these six women's colleges the domestic arts were given much attention in education circles. For instance, in London, King's College for women, which was affiliated with the University of London, had instituted a series of courses in domestic and social science in 1908. The lectures were organized for women

wishing to prepare themselves for the efficient management of their own homes, and for stimulating that interest which knowledge and thought can develop in those subjects with which all women are more or less concerned, whatever their other purposes may be.[23]

The syllabus included such courses as biology, chemistry, physiology, hygiene, household work, economics and psychology, all of which were to be applied to practical ends in the home. The new buildings that were erected to accommodate these

20. Burstall, *English High Schools for Girls*, 194.
21. C. S. Bremner, *Education of Girls and Women in Great Britain* (London: Swan Sonnenschein, 1897), 146.
22. Catherine Manthorpe, "Science or domestic science? The struggle to define an appropriate science for girls in early twentieth-century England," *History of Education* 15, no. 3 (1986): 200.
23. "King's College for Women: Current Architecture," *The Architectural Review* 40 (July 1916): 13.

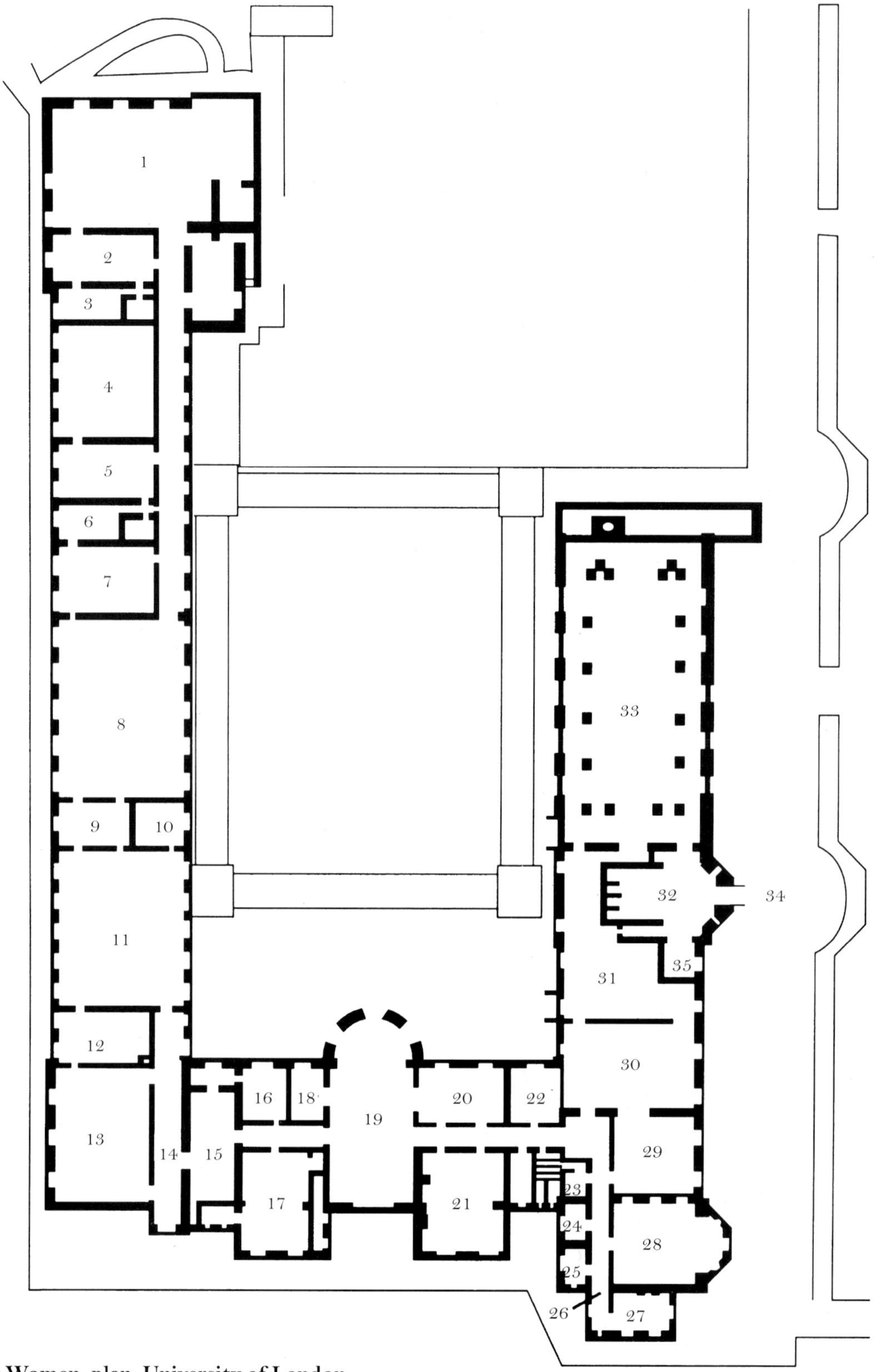

1. hygiene laboratory
2. preparation room
3. lecture room
4. meteorological laboratory
5. Professors' laboratory
6. lecture room
7. research room
8. physiology laboratory
9. optical room
10. lecture room
11. physics laboratory
12. preparation room
13. lecture room
14. corridor
15. staircase
16. teaching larder
17. teaching laundry
18. teaching office
19. teaching kitchen
20. teaching pantry
21. teaching scullery
22. Mrs. Keeper's store
23. store
24. larder
25. larder
26. teachers' entrance
27. housekeeper's office
28. servants' hall
29. scullery
30. kitchen
31. pantry
32. hall
33. refectory
34. entrance
35. porter

106. King's College for Women, plan, University of London, Campden Hill Road, London (by H. P. Adams and C. Holden, 1916).

107. King's College for Women, hostel (by Adams and Holden, 1914).

courses and the women enrolled were described in an article in the *Architectural Review* of 1916. The article stressed the importance of such an education system in terms of its relevance on a national level. The author argued that including domestic science in a university course would raise the status of this branch of education.[24]

The buildings themselves (now altered), designed by H. Percy Adams and Charles Holden, consisted of a central block and two wings, with one wing longer than the other, embracing an open courtyard, which was later closed by a library and classrooms. The three blocks included a hostel for the women students and a refectory. The longer wing was taken up with laboratories. On the ground floor of the women's hostel were a teaching kitchen, laundry, pantry, larder and so on, all fitted with the latest in domestic equipment. The refectory was a long room with a barrel-vaulted ceiling, severe Doric columns supporting a gallery and a platform at the end for the high table. The hostel included fifty-seven bed-sitting rooms, each with a dressing room attached and a common room with a fireplace and marble mantelpiece.

It will be recalled that one of the crucial features of the early women's colleges was the system of corridors which connected all parts of each building, and then connected separate buildings with each other. This enabled women to pass from their study-bedrooms to the dining hall or to the library without having to go outside if the weather was inclement, and was important for health and safety reasons. The scheme of King's College followed this precedent. In one U-shaped building, everything needed for study, relaxation, refreshment and rest was included. The women could gain access to their lectures, meals, and bedrooms by a series of corridors, only leaving the building for fresh air and exercise.

Of further interest is the architectural style chosen for the buildings. The same article in the *Architectural Review* described the stylistic treatment as evolved from the "Later Renaissance" and cited the refectory and entrance to the hostel as inspired by Wren's work at Hampton Court.[25] The buildings are of red brick with white stone

24. Ibid., 14.
25. Ibid., 16.

108. Toynbee Hall, Lady Margaret Hall, Oxford (by Blomfield, 1914).

trim. The hostel consists of five floors which are severe and regular in outline; a carved stringcourse separates the top floor from the first four. The flat roof and sharp angularity give hints of the modern trend in architecture that was developing in England at the time, in which reduced, functional forms replaced historical detailing, resulting in simplified, rectilinear buildings. But elements such as the stringcourses, blank niches, balustrades and overall crisp symmetry are characteristic of a style of "Stripped Classicism"[26] which was found in the work of architects such as Holden and Edwin Lutyens at this time.

Overall, there is a similarity in detail and general appearance with some of the buildings seen previously at Lady Margaret Hall, Somerville, and Champneys' last work at Newnham on the Peile building. What evolved at these colleges was a type of architecture based on red brick as the principal building material, with windows and doors outlined in white stone or painted trim, and simplified Classical details which lent a degree of refinement by alluding to the Renaissance. The origins of this can be seen most clearly in Blomfield's first building for Lady Margaret Hall, Wordsworth Hall. As mentioned earlier, Blomfield borrowed elements from his country-house style, which in turn looked back to the era of Wren. The terminology for this style is slightly controversial. The influence of the late Renaissance and Wren is generally agreed upon; however, in the *Buildings of England* series begun by Nikolaus Pevsner, these stylistic elements are grouped under the title "Neo-Georgian." But because of Wren's acknowledged importance, the term "Wrenaissance" will be used here.

The simple brickwork, pediments and cornices continued to appear in further buildings by Blomfield at Lady Margaret Hall, such as Toynbee Hall of 1914. For Maitland Hall at Somerville, Edmund Fisher also employed an elementary classicism which was both functional and attractive (see fig. 75 above). This style was affordable because of its simplicity, yet it was evocative of a significant architectural style. In contrast to the 'Queen Anne' which was by this time considered too busy and picturesque, the simplified 'Wrenaissance' offered a stable, often symmetrical style with

26. Alastair Service, *Edwardian Architecture: A handbook to Building Design in Britain 1890–1914* (New York & Toronto: Oxford University Press, 1977), 186.

109. Queen Alexandra's Court, Wimbledon, London (by Ernest George and A. Yeates, 1902–04). *Photo by Jennifer Ullman.*

elegant but subdued detailing. Instead of borrowing from eclectic sources, or recalling the vernacular village architecture of the late seventeenth and early eighteenth centuries, it had the advantage of drawing on the examples of an important period in English history and the work of England's greatest architect, Sir Christopher Wren. It was a style that continued to be popular for domestic houses well into the twentieth century, and was also adaptable for larger blocks of flats, such as Queen Alexandra's Court in Wimbledon, London of 1902–04, by Ernest George and A. Yeates. Thus, for reasons of economy, appearance and association, the 'Wrenaissance' style became popular for women's university residences during the first three decades of the twentieth century.

St. Hugh's College, Oxford, was founded in 1886 by Elizabeth Wordsworth. Her decision to found a sister to Lady Margaret Hall was made in response to what she saw as a void in the educational opportunities available for poorer students, especially daughters of the clergy, who, she felt, were not adequately supported by the Church.[27] Fees were fifteen and thirty pounds less per year than at Somerville and Lady Margaret Hall respectively. The venture began in a small house near Lady Margaret Hall on Norham Road. It was a private enterprise, overseen by Miss Wordsworth and run by Miss Anne Moberly, the first principal.

It should be noted that both St. Hugh's and St. Hilda's (discussion to follow) were not examined in detail in the previous chapters due to the fact that their earliest purpose-built buildings come after 1914 and were influenced by the pre-existing colleges. St. Hugh's remained in the house in Norham Road for many years. In 1892, a wing was added which provided accommodation for twelve more students, as well as a dining room and chapel. In 1912, plans were begun to buy the leasehold of The Mount, a house in North Oxford, demolish it, and replace it with a new, purpose-built building. Construction was begun in 1914 and completed by 1916, a year after Miss Moberly retired.

H. T. Buckland and W. Haywood, two Birmingham architects, produced designs for one large 'Wrenaissance' building, based on a symmetrical plan, with a central

27. Betty Kemp, "The Early History of St. Hugh's College" in *St. Hugh's: One Hundred Years of Women's Education in Oxford*, ed. Penny Griffin (Basingstoke & London: Macmillan, 1986), 16.

110. St. Hugh's College, Oxford, garden façade (by H. T. Buckland and W. Haywood, 1914–16).

entrance, two long arms extending from the center, and two short wings on either end. The street facade is highlighted by a dramatic entrance, but more interesting is the garden front. This is emphasized by a central pediment, broken by a large arched window. A cupola stands in the center of the roof. Bay windows enliven the range on either side of the entrance and boxy dormer windows punctuate the roof. The corners of the wings are articulated by brick quoins and a stone cornice runs the entire length of the building.

All these elements are common to the classicism seen at Lady Margaret Hall. The severity of the window treatment is reminiscent of Maitland Hall at Somerville which had just been completed when the work at St. Hugh's was begun. The plan is also similar. At St. Hugh's the formal entrance and staircase mark the center of the building, and corridors extend down each side. The corridor continues to the west into the addition of 1928, built in the same style. Thus in plan, style and materials St. Hugh's follows the precedents set by its sister colleges at Oxford.

Dorothea Beale, principal of Cheltenham Ladies College, founded St. Hilda's College, Oxford, as a modest venture. She wanted to offer the recently graduated students of her school a chance of attending lectures and absorbing the atmosphere of Oxford for a year before going out into the world. In 1893, she bought Cowley House, a Georgian house with recent, Victorian Gothic additions in which to house these students. The college grew slowly in stages. During the first half of the twentieth century its additions tended to be built in red brick in a simplified, what could easily be considered institutional, 'Wrenaissance' style.

This tradition of simplified Classical blocks continued in the building campaigns of the 1920s at Lady Margaret Hall, Somerville and Westfield. In 1926 Blomfield built his last block, Lodge Hall, for Lady Margaret Hall. This continued the tradition of red brick with white stone dressing. The stone rustication, quoins, columns and the lack of any softening features such as bow windows, create a formality not found at St. Hugh's. At Somerville, Penrose Hall of 1926 by Harold Rogers, is even more severe. Here the corners have brick quoins and the entrance is announced by a simple pediment over the door. It has a symmetrical, Classical simplicity characteristic of the twentieth-century 'Wrenaissance' style.

111. Lodge Hall, Lady Margaret Hall, Oxford (by Blomfield, 1926).

112. Penrose Hall, Somerville College, Oxford (by H. Rogers, 1926).

At Westfield, William Walford, an architect from the firm of Thompson, Walford and Fielder, built the Chapman wing in 1927. This is much like the Maynard building by MacDonald discussed in chapter three. The red brick, white sash windows and a large central gable, harmonize gracefully with the surrounding buildings. It is connected to Maynard Hall by a covered bridge. Once again, the details are kept to a minimum, but those that do exist share elements with the 'Wrenaissance' country houses of Blomfield and others, such as the Palladian window in the gable, the rusticated brick work on the ground floor and the abstracted, stretched pilasters that define the center. As in Maynard, a central corridor runs through each floor.

113. Chapman Wing, Westfield College (by W. Walford, 1927).

In the chapter on Newnham College, the new buildings for Bedford College were discussed briefly in reference to the evolution of Champneys' work. It is appropriate to return to them here, since the buildings in Regent's Park, dated 1913, share many of these 'Wrenaissance' attributes. Indeed, the classicism in the non-residential blocks, such as the science blocks or library, is more pronounced, with greater use of columns and pilasters, and carvings within the pediments. In the residential blocks, the only 'Queen Anne' elements remaining are the broken curving pediments in the gables. For Bedford, Champneys tempered his characteristic 'Queen Anne' exuberance with a more staid Classical vocabulary in keeping with the general trend in residential colleges for women.

The use of the 'Wrenaissance' style at these women's colleges influenced numerous university halls of residence built for women between 1900 and 1930 around the country. It was not a particularly exciting style, and may now be considered typical of much institutional architecture. But it served the women's colleges well. At the time, domestic architecture was generally built in the 'Wrenaissance' style of Blomfield and others, or in the more modest, vernacular-inspired houses of Lutyens, Voysey and other Arts and Crafts architects. The ideology underlying the houses of the Arts and Crafts Movement stressed the importance of site, the use of local materials, high standards of craftsmanship, and a holistic approach to design, where the architects designed not only the buildings themselves, but often the interiors and furnishings as well. Arts and Crafts houses were much too individualized, intimate and expensive to serve as collegiate examples, and the simple Classical work of the more formal school proved easily adaptable for larger residences for women.

This classicism, albeit often very reduced and severe, afforded the ideal solution to the problem of how to design a women's residence. The key ingredients deemed vital in planning a women's college, such as the corridor system and allusions to domesticity, could be easily incorporated. The simple blocks could be expanded without creating interminable corridors, thus maintaining the illusion of a smaller, more

114. Bedford College, hostel, Regent's Park, London (by Champneys, 1913).

personal home. The Classical references added an affordable elegance and dignity which the women's colleges sought, which did not vie with the male tradition of the Gothic quadrangle.

These Classical blocks were used in other plans for women's higher education in places such as Reading, Birmingham and Manchester. By the early twentieth century women's education was more accessible around England, largely due to the development of the "red-brick" universities that were becoming more firmly established in cities throughout the country. These universities were originally founded as alternatives to the Oxbridge colleges, which were, on the whole, expensive and elitist. For example, Owens College was founded in Manchester in 1851, in accordance with the will of John Owens, who made his fortune from manufacturing and shipping. Owens left money for a college which would offer education to men over fourteen years of age on a non-denominational, non-elitist basis. It was not residential as the students came from within the city or from the surrounding suburbs. This was true with most of the other red-brick universities which did not offer residential facilities until the turn of the century. The earliest of these halls of residence were to be found in pre-existing houses; the building of purpose-built halls was a slow and haphazard process.

When they did build, the authorities at the red-brick universities were concerned with the question of appropriate lodgings for both sexes. The ideological differences between residences for men and women attending these new institutions were discussed by the retired principal of Reading University, William McBride Childs, in his book on that university's history. He gives an account of how, in 1905, he had argued in favor of a system of quadrangles for men's lodgings in keeping with the Oxbridge tradition. For women, he

> *retained the opinion that appropriate buildings, each containing a cluster of students' rooms, grouped upon a garden site in harmonious subordination to central buildings of greater mass (dining hall, library, common rooms, and administrative headquarters) would make perhaps the best kind of hall of residence of women.*[28]

Much like the founders of the colleges discussed earlier, Childs wanted to encourage

28. William M. Childs, *Making a University: An Account of the University Movement at Reading* (London: J. M. Dent, 1933), 178.

115. University House, Edgbaston, University of Birmingham (by H. T. Buckland, 1907–09).

the life within these female halls of residence to have the character of a "'well-ordered home.'"[29]

The physical requirements mentioned by Childs reflect the earlier desire of such principals as Elizabeth Wordsworth, Miss Shaw Lefevre and Constance Maynard to preserve an intimate and home-like atmosphere within their colleges by maintaining small groups of students who could be easily looked after. Childs' ideals were realized in the buildings that made up Wessex Hall. With the exception of the dining-hall, these were pre-existing houses taken over by the university which enclosed a large garden. Furthermore, Miss Mary Bolam, the warden of another residence at Reading, St. Andrew's Hostel, had attended Somerville, and was an enthusiastic supporter of Miss Beale's ideas at Cheltenham. She brought high expectations of proper female behavior and decorum to her work at Reading.[30]

Birmingham University was begun in 1870 as Mason College. Its first premises were in the heart of the city, but in 1900 it moved to the nearby suburb of Edgbaston. Its principal administrative buildings were designed by Aston Webb and Ingress Bell between 1901 and 1909. The scheme begun was "a grandiose semi-circular plan . . . to meet Joseph Chamberlain's vision of a building to match the great cathedrals of the Middle Ages."[31] The style is eclectic, with much borrowed from Byzantine architecture, and with Gothic and Renaissance details added.

In contrast to the grand formality of the administrative buildings was the first hall of residence built for women. University House was built in the years between 1907–09 by H. T. Buckland, the same architect who, with his partner Haywood, designed the buildings for St. Hugh's five years later. For University House, Buckland drew on the simple 'Wrenaissance' style, although borrowings from Newnham's example are evident. It was built in Black Country brick, which gives a harsh appearance unlike the warm red of Newnham's bricks. It has been described as a "small country house, scaled up"[32] with its long range softened by bay windows and the dominant end gables. The segmental dormer windows are like those found at Newnham, as is the central pedimented dormer resting above a balustrade, which

29. Ibid., 180.
30. Ibid., 182–83.
31. Julian Orbach, *Blue Guide to Victorian Architecture in Britain* (London: A. & C. Black, 1987), 436.
32. Alan Crawford, "The Arts and Crafts Movement," *Victorian Society Conference Handbook*, University of Birmingham, 15–17 September 1978, 2.

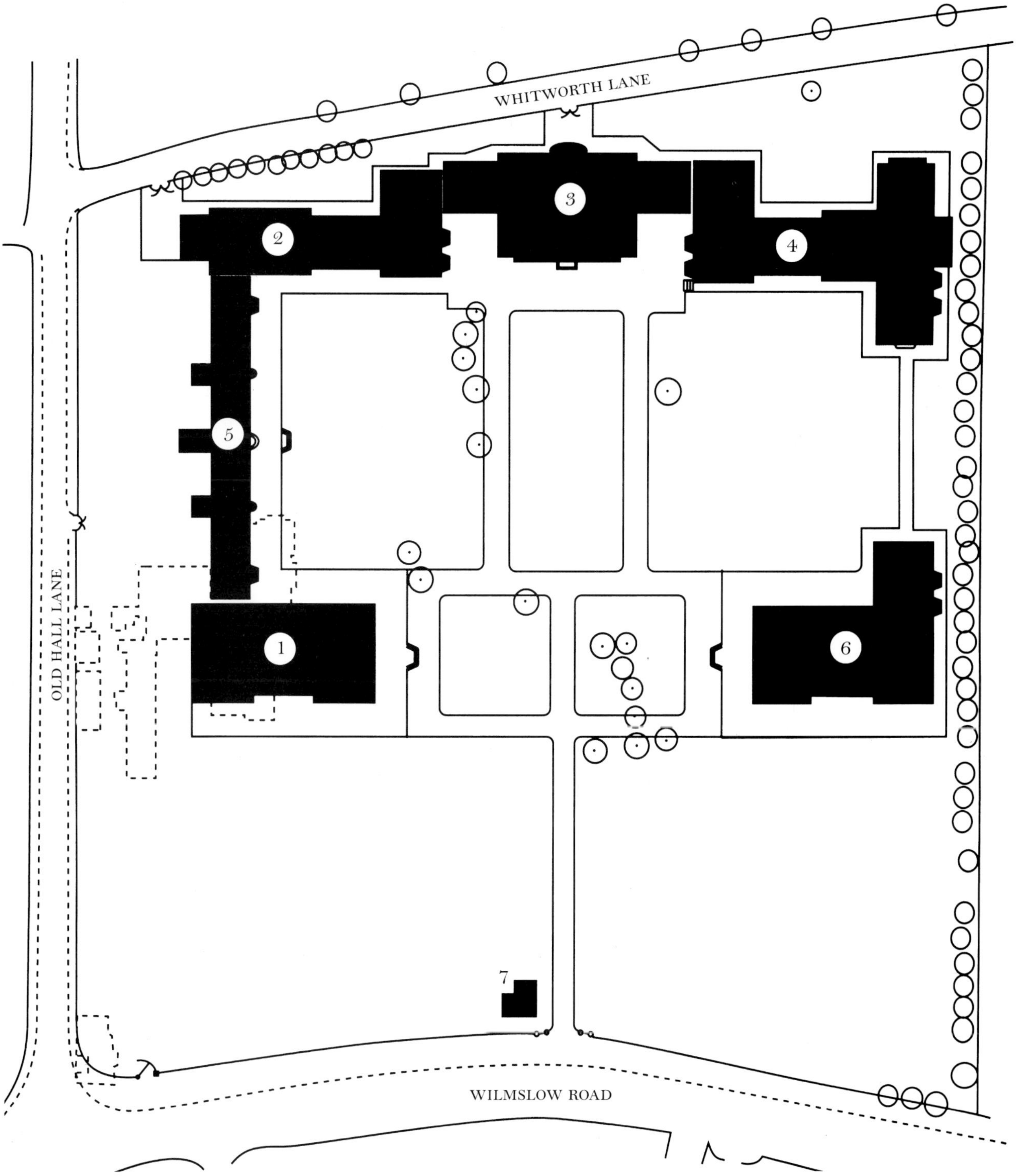

1. Original house, to be rebuilt later, with warden offices and accommodation for twenty students.
2. The Mary Worthington Wing – built in 1910, it was the first hostel for forty students.
3. Central block, built in 1925, comprising the hall, library and kitchen.
4. The Ward Wing – built in 1925 as a hostel for sixty students.
5. Future connecting wing.
6. Future hostel.
7. Future lodge.

116. Ashburne Hall, block plan, University of Manchester (by T. Worthington and Sons, 1910–25).

117. Ashburne Hall, center block (by Worthington and Sons, 1910–25).

118. Ashburne Hall, hostel (by Worthington and Sons, 1910–25).

adds a 'Queen Anne' touch. It is less formal than Buckland's subsequent work at St. Hugh's and is on a smaller scale, but it stands out as residential in character in keeping with the precedent set by the earlier women's colleges, such as Newnham.

Owens College became a part of Manchester's Victoria University in 1880. In 1908, the University bought The Oaks, a classical villa on the Fallowfield Estate, in the suburbs of Manchester, as a hall of residence for its female students. This soon proved inadequate and plans were drawn up by Percy Worthington to accommodate sixty more students; this became the Mary Worthington wing. Plans for another extension were drawn up in 1914 but these were delayed because of the War, and were taken up again in 1921. The overall scheme included a dining hall, library and another hostel grouped together in accordance with Childs' ideals at Reading. The scheme, called Ashburne Hall, was laid out in a loose, open quadrangle and included plans for future blocks, one of which would ultimately connect the old house with the newer buildings.

In 1925, when the library, dining-hall and new hostel were opened, the *Architectural Review* published a description of the buildings. The author praised the warmth of the red brick and the lovely setting. He noted that "The broad sheer brick simplicity of the central block, with its great shadowing cornice, and roof of Cotswold slates, has to my mind the character of Wren's work at Chelsea."[33] The overall massing of the central block is much like Maitland Hall at Somerville; it has the same simple outline and large windows drawing attention to the importance of the first floor. Here at Ashburne Hall, however, the great encompassing roof adds a further sense of comfort in contrast to the flat roof of Maitland.

The hostel wings were described in the *Architectural Review* as more "homely in treatment."[34] Certainly the large, deep roof and series of hipped dormers and chimneys lend a more domestic character. In addition, the low height of only three storeys and the intimate size of the Richardsonian arches which mark the entrance are on a domestic scale, common to many of the women's colleges and residences. The hipped dormer windows are much like those which Waterhouse used at Girton to soften the long ranges. The covered corridors connecting the hostels to the halls and lit with arched windows, are an obvious quotation from Champneys' work at Newnham. In keeping with the precedent set at the women's colleges, corridors connect the whole, with some being "delicately treated in plaster."[35]

Many of the red-brick universities were not able to build residences for their female students for many years and bought pre-existing villas to accommodate their students. But those that did have the funds for new buildings tended to build in the 'Wrenaissance' style, derived from the trend in country house building. The domestic aspects which were incorporated into the women's colleges in the 1870s and 1880s, such as corridors, privacy and efforts to create a more cozy, homelike atmosphere, continued to be drawn upon well into the twentieth century. Indeed there is evidence to suggest that the more personal and intimate character developed in the women's colleges ultimately had an impact on general attitudes towards residential living at these new universities.

In 1928, H. G. G. Herklots published *The New Universities: An External Examination*. In this report on the red-brick universities, Herklots discussed how halls of residence were becoming increasingly popular, especially in order to accommodate women students. He goes on to complain of the lack of purpose-built halls which would be more convenient and could house both men and women more appropriately. He argued against corridors for reasons of noise and praised the halls for men at Bristol and Reading which had been built on the staircase system.

The halls of residence built for the University of Bristol in the late 1920s and early 1930s were designed along different lines to accommodate men and women respectively. Charles Hanson was the early architect for Bristol and designed the first wing of a quadrangle in perpendicular Gothic in 1880, emulating the colleges at Oxford and Cambridge. The earliest purpose-built residence was not erected until 1929 when Wills Hall was opened. This was built for men, also in the Gothic Revival style and used the staircase system.

Three years later, Bristol University opened Manor Hall for women. In contrast

33. "Ashburne Hall, University of Manchester," *Architectural Review* 58 (October 1925): 138.
34. Ibid., 138.
35. Ibid., 141.

119. Mardon Hall, University of Exeter (by V. Harris, 1933).

to the men's hall, it was built in a stripped-down classicism, such as has been described above, with corridors connecting the individual study-bedrooms. Clearly Bristol University was looking back to the Oxbridge tradition for residential examples. What is significant is that no longer was this only a male example, but the women's colleges had also become a precedent to be followed.

In the 1930s, some experiments with these traditions were tried. At the University of Exeter, the ideas of the then principal Mr. Murray, were incorporated into Mardon Hall, the first purpose-built hall of residence, designed by Vincent Harris in 1933. This accommodated eighty male students, some in double rooms:

There were communal washrooms, and a large wooden hut served as a dining-room. These spartan features were off-set by lavish provision elsewhere: a large reception room; a common room, library, and music room. Built in what Murray termed a "country-house style," Mardon Hall was intended to provide in its public rooms at least something of the atmosphere of a gentlemen's residence.[36]

This is an interesting example of the desire on the part of university authorities to recreate a "home-like" atmosphere for their male undergraduates. Mardon Hall was built in a simple 'Wrenaissance' style similar to that seen in the women's residences at Manchester and Birmingham, and it relinquished the staircase system in favor of corridors.

This flirtation with the corridor system for men has its most interesting manifestation in the University of Sheffield's Oakholme Hall. Built in 1936 by the architect John Procter of Leeds, Oakholme Hall employs the corridor system on one wing of the open quadrangle and the staircase system on the other. The center block contains the dining hall and kitchens. The floorplan is a fascinating illustration of the debate between the two systems. The results of this experiment were recorded thus:

36. B. W. Clapp, *The University of Exeter: A History* (Exeter: University of Exeter, 1982), 130.

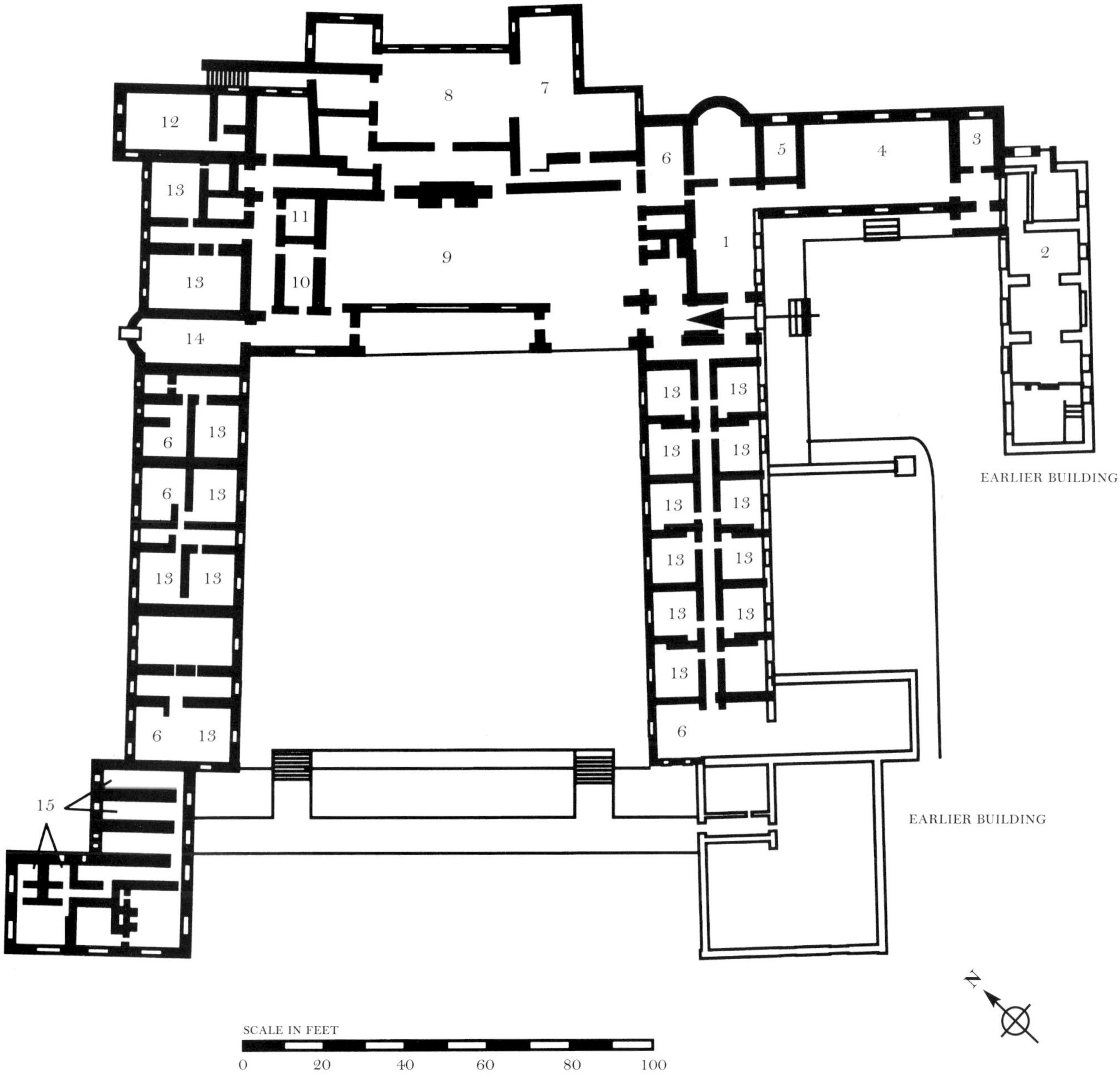

1. entrance hall
2. library
3. music
4. common room
5. guest room
6. lavatory
7. servants' hall
8. kitchen
9. dining hall
10. housekeeper
11. china
12. sick room
13. students' rooms
14. senior common room
15. cubicles

120. Oakholme Hall, floorplan, University of Sheffield (by J. Procter, 1936).

In the new Hall [Oakholme] one wing had been built on the corridor system, the other in staircases. It soon became evident, and experience abundantly confirmed, that the staircase plan was superior; the architects of the old collegiate buildings had known well what was best for housing vigorous young men.[37]

This is reminiscent of discussions from the early twentieth century when Butterfield's experiment with corridors for men at Keble College was condemned for encouraging cricket and bear-fighting.[38]

In 1948, a committee of vice-chancellors and principals from colleges and universities throughout Great Britain published a report on university halls of residence and their various advantages and vital requirements. The report first posited that halls of residence were preferable to the earlier system at red-brick universities where students lived at home or in hired lodgings. The committee cited a report from the University Grants Committee of 1936 which praised the hall of residence because

"It offers students exceptionally favourable opportunities for the stimulating interplay of mind with mind, for the formation of friendships, and for learning the art of understanding and living with others of outlook and temperament unlike their own. It can be, and it often is, a great humanizing force."[39]

The Committee's report goes into detailed analysis of the necessary components of halls of residences. Halls should be planned with study-bedrooms for each student. Suites were naturally preferable but were too expensive. The size and shape of the rooms should vary so as to avoid institutional regularity. Comfortable and pleasant common rooms were required, to afford spaces for social gathering and recreation; these should not be too close to the study-bedrooms, for reasons of noise. Three types of common rooms: the "music room, recreation room and library"[40] were recommended. In addition there should be rooms for storage, laundry, maids' rooms and pantries throughout.

Foyers and dining halls should be well appointed, so as to impress both the visitor and student with their dignified and elegant appearance. This, it was believed, would encourage the students to distinguish between mere eating and dining; the latter was endorsed, the former discouraged. Interestingly, the report also required that a sanatorium or sick bay be included in the building or in a nearby house. As noted above, infirmaries or sanatoriums were included in the women's colleges, sometimes just as individual rooms, or, in the case of Girton, in its own hospital wing. This special concern for the health of the students follows the example set at the women's colleges during the latter half of the nineteenth century.

The committee carefully studied the planning and layout of halls of residence for men and women. Quadrangles, though appreciated for their Oxbridge associations were considered stuffy, noisy and something of a fire hazard. Instead the report gave preference to a central block containing the dining hall, kitchens and common rooms, with residential wings. These wings were to be built along corridors for women and staircases for men.

The report outlined the advantages and disadvantages of corridors and stair-

37. A. W. Chapman, *The Story of a University: A History of the University of Sheffield* (London: Oxford University Press, 1955), 374–75.
38. Champneys' response to Edward Warren's "Collegiate Architecture," *The Royal Institute of British Architects Journal* 19 (19 February 1912): 292.
39. Committee of Vice-Chancellors and Principals of Great Britain and Ireland, *The Planning of University Halls of Residence* (Oxford: Clarendon Press, 1948), 3.
40. Ibid., 16

cases. Many of the points echo the concerns which conditioned the early women's colleges. For instance, corridors are described as healthier because they are less draughty than staircases and "Access can be obtained to more rooms without going outside, an advantage in bad weather."[41] On the other hand, the report also pointed out that corridors tended to be more communal, encouraging interaction which could disturb study. The advantage of the staircase system was "the privacy, quiet, and sense of independence which it undoubtedly provides."[42]

These two models were separately considered in relation to each sex. The report summarized its discussion of the planning of halls of residence by pointing out that male undergraduates preferred the staircases and women the corridors.[43] This assessment reflected the prevailing belief in the different needs and wants of men and women; a belief that had not changed dramatically since the 1870s when the first buildings at Girton and Newnham were built. Well into the twentieth century, indeed as late at the 1960s, women's needs were understood to be better accommodated in halls of residence which differed from men's.[44] Both the University of Nottingham and New Hall, Cambridge, founded for women in 1954, used corridors for their women's residences. The early buildings at New Hall, by Chamberlain, Powell and Bon of 1962–66, while designed in modernist concrete and white brick with no historical reference, still rely on the planning precedent established at neighboring Girton almost one hundred years earlier. Thus by the middle of the twentieth century, corridors were readily identified with female residences and staircases with male.

The first six purpose-built women's colleges were designed to accommodate women's special needs, to offer protection to their inmates and to encourage a closer, homelike community within their walls. Many elements in their planning came from the domestic house, the assigned female sphere. By the mid-twentieth century, although the intimate, domestic scale had been lost in the women's colleges and halls of residence, fundamental concerns such as health, safety, community and appearance remained crucial in the building of female residences. Indeed, some aspects such as the sick bay were adopted for men's halls as well, and, while corridors still provided too great a temptation for young men to resist playing indoor sports in them, there was a general belief that halls of residence should be "humanizing"[45] and somewhat refined. The roots of these concerns stem ultimately from the precedents set at the early women's colleges.

There are further examples of the influence of women's colleges on collegiate planning. In her dissertation on university architecture, Diane Chablo cited the Niblett Report of 1957, which, like the Report of the Vice-Chancellors of 1948, discussed the relative merits and demerits of the corridor system. Here the authors were critical of the impersonal, institutional effect of buildings based on extensive corridors. They advocated forming "'parlour groups' as a possible alternative to the impersonality of halls with long corridors."[46] Such groups would bring students together and increase intimacy, thereby reducing the sense of anonymity that could prevail in large institutions. This was precisely the solution created by William Crossland at Royal Holloway when he broke up the long corridors into units of six, with each small group sharing a common room, or 'parlour.' Thus, not only did some of the women's colleges establish a stylistic precedent based on domestic trends of the day which continued in women's halls of residences well into the following

41. Ibid., 58.
42. Ibid.
43. Ibid., 59.
44. Diane Chablo, "University Architecture in Britain 1950–1975," (Ph.D. dissertation, Wolfson College, Oxford University, 1987), 157–58. Chablo points out that staircases and quadrangles were used in men's residences while the corridor continued for women's halls.
45. Ibid., 3.
46. Ibid., 154.

121. Roedean School for Girls, Brighton (by J. W. Simpson, 1898).

century, but their solutions to problems of planning continued to provide viable examples for architects and administrators for decades.

The influence of these women's colleges was felt on the secondary school level as well. Many of the girl's schools that were founded towards the end of the nineteenth and early twentieth centuries accommodated their students in pre-existing houses. St. Leonard's and Wycombe Abbey School both took over buildings that could easily accommodate the schools, and in the case of St. Leonard's nearby houses were found for the girls, following a tradition established at Cheltenham Ladies College. For Wycombe Abbey School, W. D. Caroë built a series of boarding houses in the 'Queen Anne' style between the years of 1898 and 1903.

The Roedean School for Girls, founded by the Lawrence sisters in 1885, began much like its sister schools. But in 1898 the school moved to new, purpose-built premises in Brighton, designed by the architect J. W. Simpson. Roedean is therefore significant, because it provides an example of a building begun in accordance with the current ideas about residential schools and colleges. In 1898 Alice Zimmern described it thus:

The new premises consist of a convenient school-house and four separate boarding houses connected by covered passages with the central building. Something of college methods is to be brought into school by giving each girl a separate bedroom, while the eight seniors in each house are to have a study as well. Here they may give their Saturday tea-parties, entertain their friends and learn to take the responsibility of their own little domain.[47]

Roedean was, and continues to be, a school for the wealthy daughters of the upper classes. Set upon a hill overlooking the sea, its facade finished in grey stucco, Roedean presents a grim and institutional facade. It lacks the warm domesticity of Newnham or Lady Margaret Hall; nevertheless, it is significant that when ample funds were available, the model plans followed were the relatively new women's colleges.

47. Alice Zimmern, *The Renaissance of Girl's Education in England. A Record of Fifty Year's Progress.* (London: A. D. Innes, 1898), 159.

Other elements of planning which concerned the founders of the women's colleges affected high schools for girls in general ways. For instance, Sara Burstall, in her discussion of girl's schools, and particularly day schools, outlined the important logistics of high school education for girls, which included the optimum number of students, the buildings and equipment, discipline and curriculum. Ideally, she felt, schools should be kept small, with a maximum of one hundred and fifty pupils, so that the "general tone may be almost that of a family, so intimate, sympathetic, and united is it."[48]

As to the school building, she believed it should not be too lavish, but should be modest and dignified so as to train the girls in matters of taste without over-indulging them. She praised corridors "for ease in working, freedom of discipline, and general comfort."[49] Like Emily Davies thirty years earlier, Burstall wanted to see schools for girls set in pleasant sites away from the evils of the city such as factories, hotels, theaters, restaurants and pubs.

Such issues as intimacy, appearance, discipline and privacy, were first cogently and comprehensively explored by the founders of Girton and Newnham and the colleges which followed, and integrated into their plans. In subsequent years they became standard considerations in the building of residences for girls and women. By 1914, the fears which had conditioned the evolution of the women's colleges, such as the development of masculine women who would abandon the home for their careers or would be made infertile by study, were still prevalent and made more threatening with the scientific theories of Geddes and Social Darwinism.

The study of the six earliest, purpose-built colleges for women — Girton, Newnham, Lady Margaret Hall, Somerville, Westfield and Royal Holloway — chronicles the means by which social concerns were incorporated into the architecture of these new institutions. The built environment has been shown to reflect the prevailing attitudes towards the education of women and men in the nineteenth century. The stereotyped differences between the sexes continued to be built into the architecture of education well into the twentieth century and shaped the residences for men and women. Women's colleges, begun at times haphazardly and with a distinct domestic influence, set a precedent for women's schools and college residences throughout Great Britain. The attempt to re-create, at least in part, the home at college helped make it possible for the colleges to establish themselves. It was an idea that held sway for many years. By the late 1960s the idea of the home at college had become deeply ingrained in the ideology of collegiate residences. By this time student housing schemes were becoming much like general housing schemes with the "domestic 'Neo-vernacular' manner"[50] as a new architectural trend in college buildings for both sexes.

Much has changed since Emily Davies began her efforts in the small house in Hitchin in 1869 with five students. Coeducation is widely accepted, the spacious undergraduate's suites at the Oxbridge colleges have been divided up, the Morris paper is gone from most of the rooms at Newnham, Lady Margaret Hall and Somerville, and much of the old furniture has been replaced with cheaper, mass-produced items. Some of the cozy domesticity has gone from the interiors of these women's colleges. Of the six, only Newnham remains a single-sex college. Westfield's buildings were sold in 1992 to King's College, London, and the college has

48. Burstall, *English High Schools for Girls*, 22.
49. Ibid., 77.
50. Chablo, "University Architecture in Britain," 165.

merged with Queen Mary's in East London. Bedford has left its site in Regent's Park and moved to Egham as a part of Royal Holloway College.

Regardless of these changes, the buildings survive as testimonies of the struggles, worries and triumphs of the pioneers in women's education. In spite of their varied approaches to the higher education of women, the founders and architects created buildings which speak volumes about their age and the social conditions surrounding their erection. In the effort to offer new educational opportunities to women, the women's colleges physically manifested society's beliefs about women and their mental abilities. Their architecture continues to be relevant today, as the issues which it reflects continue to puzzle and plague society in the late twentieth century. The natural differences between men and women and their social ramifications are still hotly debated by psychologists, sociologists and the average man and woman. The aptitudes of the sexes for certain subjects over others is a rich and controversial area of study for educationalists. As women struggle to find a balance between their home-life and careers, these women's colleges stand as early symbols of women's emancipation from the strict confines of the home and of their venture into the broader world of higher education.

BIOGRAPHICAL APPENDIX

of some key figures involved with the 'Ladies of Langham Place' and the early efforts in women's education.

Key sources for these figures are: Olive Banks, Biographical Dictionary of British Feminists, vol. 1, 1800 – 1930 *(Brighton, Sussex: Wheatsheaf Books, distributed by Harvester Press, 1985); and Dale Spender, ed.,* The Education Papers: Women's Quest for Equality in Britain 1850–1912 *(New York and London: Routledge & Kegan Paul, 1987).*

Elizabeth Garrett Anderson 1836–1917

Anderson became the first British woman doctor. She had met Emily Davies in 1854 and through correspondence with her, became involved with the "Ladies of Langham Place" and their work for women's rights and education. Through their example and that of Elizabeth Blackwell, the first American woman doctor, she decided to become a physician in 1859. Together with the help of Davies, she petitioned to be allowed to sit the examinations for the Society of Apothecaries and was granted permission in 1865. In 1872 she opened a hospital run by women for women. She was married in 1870 to James Skelton Anderson and in spite of her career and marriage remained involved in feminist issues, helping to raise money for the opening of Girton College. During her career as a doctor, she was aloof from the suffrage campaign, but once she retired in 1902 and her husband died in 1907, she participated for several years.

See: Banks, *Biographical Dictionary*, 4–6; Jo Manton, *Elizabeth Garrett Anderson* (London: Methuen Press, 1965); Louisa Garrett Anderson, *Elizabeth Garrett Anderson 1836–1917* (London: Faber & Faber, 1939).

Dorothea Beale 1831–1906

Beale was one of the earliest students at Queen's College, attending in 1848, and later teaching mathematics there. After an unsuccessful stint as head teacher at Casterton School, she became principal of Cheltenham Ladies College in 1858, in which capacity she worked hard for girls' education and suffrage for women. However, she believed a woman's place was in the home, and modeled the students' living arrangements on the domestic example. In 1865 she testified with Emily Davies to the Schools Enquiry Commission on the poor education available to girls and young women. In the same year she gave a paper to the Social Science Congress, "On the Education of Girls." She was also involved in helping to improve the education of girls through organizations such as the Headmistresses' Association and The Teachers Guild. In 1899 she was given an honorary LLD from Edinburgh University.

See: Banks, *Biographical Dictionary*, 15–16; Spender, *The Education Papers*, 345; and Josephine Kamm, *How Different from Us: A Biography of Miss Buss and Miss Beale* (London: The Bodley Head, 1858).

Bessie Reyner Belloc *née Parkes* 1829–1825

In 1846 Belloc met Barbara Leigh Smith (later Bodichon) who was to be a key figure in her life. Throughout the 1850s she worked with Bodichon to improve women's political and marital lives. In 1856 she published, *Remarks on the Education of* Girls, and was one of the founding members of the "Ladies of Langham Place." She was editor of and contributor to the *Englishwoman's Journal* which was founded in 1858. Her concern for women who were forced for earn a living but had limited opportunity or training to do so prompted her to publish *Essays on Women's Work* in 1866. She went to France in 1867 where she met and married Louis Belloc, son of the painter Hillaire Belloc. After his death five years later she returned to England but never resumed her feminist work.

See: Banks, *Biographical Dictionary*, 19–21; and Lee Holcombe, *Victorian Ladies at Work: Middle-class Working Women in England and Wales 1850–1914* (Newton Abbot: David & Charles, 1973).

Barbara Leigh Smith Bodichon *née Smith* 1827–1891

Bodichon's father, a free-thinking Radical MP, encouraged her education and independence. In 1849 she attended Bedford College, and went on to play an active role in the movement for women's rights, suffrage and education. In 1857 she married Eugene Bodichon, a medical doctor who worked in Algeria. In keeping with her alternative lifestyle, she spent half the year in Algeria with him and the other half of the year in Britain on her own. In 1854 she published, *A Brief Summary in Plain Language of the Most Important Laws Concerning Women,* in which she complained of the complete legal submission to which a woman was subjected upon marriage and the resultant injustices that ensued. This was ultimately influential in the passing of the Married Women's Property Bill. Together with Elizabeth Whitehead (later Malleson), she opened the Portman Hall School which was a radical experiment, mixing classes and sexes in the classroom. On her honeymoon with her husband, she visited America where she was impressed with co-education and a more democratic approach to education. In 1857 she wrote "Women and Work" which argued for women's right to education and to work to earn a living. Also in 1857 Bodichon became involved with the "Ladies of Langham Place," whose members included, Bessie Parks, Jessie Boucherette and Emily Faithfull. They published the *English Women's Journal,* which was edited by Bessie Parkes. The group was concerned with many issues relating to women, including education, political rights, suffrage, prostitution, and emigration. Bodichon was an active supporter of John Stuart Mill and worked with him in the 1866 campaign for women's suffrage. She was very involved with the founding of Girton, but her efforts were not made public because of her many other Radical interests. She was also a talented watercolorist, and left many of her paintings to Girton College.

See: Banks, *Biographical Dictionary,* 27–30; Spender, *The Education Papers,* 346–47; Pam Hirsch, *Barbara Leigh Smith Bodichon, 1827–1891, Feminist, Artist and Rebel* (London: Pimlico, 1999); Jaquie Matthews, "Barbara Bodichon: Integrity in Diversity" in *Feminist Theorists: Three Centuries of Women's Intellectual Traditions,* edited by Dale Spender (London: Women's Press, 1983); and Shelia Herstein, *A Mid-Victorian Feminist, Barbara Leigh Smith Bodichon* (New Haven: Yale University Press, 1985).

Jessie Boucherett 1825–1905

Boucherett was a member of the "Ladies of Langham Place." Together with Adelaide Proctor she began the Society for Promoting the Employment of Women. By 1865 the *Englishwomen's Journal* was no longer being published and Boucherett revived it, changing its name to the *Englishwoman's Review* which she edited until 1871. She was involved with the training of women as clerks and bookeepers at a school in London and was a strong supporter of Girton College. She contributed an essay to Josephine Butler's work, *Woman's Work and Woman's Culture* in 1869, and an essay entitled "The Industrial Movement" to the book, *The Woman Question in Europe,* edited by Theodore Stanton and published in 1884. Together with Helen Blackburn she wrote, *The Conditions of Working Women and the Factory Acts* in 1896.

See: Banks, *Biographical Dictionary,* 32–33; and Spender, *The Education Papers,* 347.

Miss Frances Mary Buss 1827–1894

Buss was an evening student at Queen's College in 1849, after having taught school since the age of fourteen. She began the very successful North London Collegiate Day School for girls in Camden. This grew rapidly from 35 students to 115 in 1850. She turned the school from a private to an endowed school in 1871 so that she could offer education to girls who otherwise couldn't afford it. Buss was an active supporter of women's education, the anti-slavery campaign, women's suffrage and the temperance movement. She also testified to the Schools Inquiry Commission in 1865.

See: Banks, *Biographical Dictionary,* 40–41; Spender, *The Education Papers,* 347–48, Kamm, *How Different from Us;* and Annie E. Ridley, *Frances Mary Buss and her Work for Education* (London: Longmans, Green, 1895).

Josephine Butler 1826–1906

Upon moving from Oxford to Liverpool with her husband, Butler became active in the North of England Council for the Higher Education of Women, where she worked with Anne Clough. In 1867 she became president of the Council, and in 1868 she published a pamphlet, *The Education and Employment of Women* which argued for wider opportunities in women's education and employment. Like Clough she believed women were different from men and had different responsibilities and duties. When the Contagious Diseases Acts were passed in the 1860s, Butler withdrew from her other feminist causes to fight vigorously for its repeal and against the double standards which made prostitution prevalent.

See: Banks, *Biographical Dictionary*, 41–45; Spender, *The Education Papers*, 348–49; and E. Moberly Bell, *Josephine Butler, Flame of Fire* (London: Constable, 1962).

Frances Power Cobbe 1822–1904

Cobbe was a determined campaigner for women's higher education and ran in the feminist circles of the time. She was a journalist and published articles which highlighted the need for female education and greater opportunities for women outside the home. In 1862 she wrote "The Education of Women and how it would be Affected by University Examinations." In this she argued in chivalric terms for men to come to the aid of distressed women and allow them a greater education which would in turn, help them develop into healthier and more capable women, without changing the status quo radically. Her article, "The Little Health of Ladies," published in the *Contemporary Review* (vol. 31, January 1878) denounced the popular belief that women's health was so delicate that it precluded them from interests outside the home. In the 1870s she campaigned against violence to women by their husbands, publishing an article, "Wife Torture" in 1878. She worked hard for the Matrimonial Causes Act of 1878 which allowed a wife to leave an abusive husband. After the 1870s Cobbe became an active anti-vivisectionist and her role in the feminist issues declined.

See: Banks, *Biographical Dictionary*, 53–54; Spender, *The Education Papers*, 350–51; and Frances Power Cobbe, *The Life of Frances Power Cobbe by Herself* (London: Richard Bentley, 1894).

Emily Faithfull 1835–1895

Faithfull was involved with the "Ladies of Langham Place" and was particularly active in the founding of the Society for Promoting the Employment of Women along with Jessie Boucherette and Adelaide Proctor in 1859. In 1860 she founded the Victoria Press where women were responsible for all but the heavy labor of the printing process. For her work, Queen Victoria honored her as Printer and Publisher in Ordinary to her Majesty. To further publicize her belief that women needed better means of paid employment she began the *Victoria Magazine* in 1863. She also supported the campaign for women's suffrage and for women's education. Personal scandal in her life kept her from playing a prominent role in the founding of the women's colleges.

See: Banks, *Biographical Dictionary*, 74–75.

Maria Georgina Grey 1816–1906

Grey's early interest was in writing and together with her sister Emily Shirreff, she published several novels. In the 1870s after the death of her husband, she became active in the campaign for improved education for girls, and in 1871, she and her sister founded the National Union for the Improvement of the Education of Women of all Classes, or the Women's Education Union. This led to the Girl's Public Day School Company in 1873 and the Teacher's Training and Registration Society in 1876. The Maria Grey Training College for women was founded in her honor.

See: Banks, *Biographical Dictionary*, 89–90; and Edward W. Ellsworth, *Liberators of the Female Mind. The Shirreff Sisters. Educational Reform and the Woman's Movement* (London: Greenwood Press, 1979).

Elizabeth Malleson 1828–1916

In 1854 Malleson became a teacher in Barbara Leigh Smith's experimental school for children of all classes and both sexes. Ill health kept her from continuing in this capacity, but she remained involved with some of the "Ladies of Langham Place." After her marriage to Frank Malleson, the couple began working with the Reverend F. D. Maurice and the Working Men's College. Inspired by the work there, Malleson decided to start a similar venture for women in 1864, called the College for Working Women, with support from Barbara Bodichon, John Stuart Mill and George Eliot. In 1874 the sexes were mixed in the College for Men and Women. In the 1870s her interest was shifting to the repeal of the Contagious Diseases Acts, but by 1877 poor health forced her to retire from her active involvement in the campaign, though her interest in feminist issues remained strong.

See: Banks, *Biographical Dictionary,* 119–20.

Adelaide Proctor 1825–1864

Proctor died young so her involvement with the women's movement was limited. Through her friendship with Bessie Parkes, she became involved with the "Ladies of Langham Place" and in 1859 helped found the Society for Promoting the Employment of Women. In the same year the National Association for the Promotion of Social Science appointed her to investigate improved employment opportunities for women. She was a successful poetess, and her first book of poems, published in two volumes went through ten editions between the years 1858 and 1866.

See: Banks, *Biographical Dictionary,* 164–65; and Sir Leslie Stephen and Sir Sidney Lee, eds., *Dictionary of National Biography,* vol. XVI (London: Oxford University Press, 1986).

Emily Anne Elizabeth Shirreff 1814–1897

In the 1870s Emily Shirreff became very active in the campaign for women's higher education. She was even hired briefly as the Mistress of Girton College, though this venture was short lived. With her sister Maria Grey she founded the National Union for the Improvement of the Education of Women of all Classes, which came to be called the Women's Education Union, in 1871. She also founded the Girl's Public Day School Company in 1872. Her work in women's and girls' education waned as she became more and more involved in the Froebel movement from 1874 onwards.

See: Banks, *Biographical Dictionary,* 182–83; and Ellsworth, *Liberators of the Female Mind.*

BIBLIOGRAPHY

Archival Sources

Biographical File on Robert Falconer MacDonald, 1913, Royal Institute of British Architects, London.

Deed of Foundation of Holloway College, Mt. Lee Estate, Surrey, 11 October 1883; Amended Deed, April 1906. Royal Holloway and Bedford New College Archives, Royal Holloway and Bedford New College, Egham.

Fellows' Nomination Papers: Robert Falconer MacDonald, 1899, Royal Institute of British Architects, London.

Freehold Papers for Kidderpore Hall and Estate, 1892, Queen Mary and Westfield College Archives, Queen Mary and Westfield College, London.

"The Last New College" (October 1886), unidentified newspaper clipping in RF125/2, Royal Holloway and Bedford New College Archives, Royal Holloway and Bedford New College, Egham.

Laws and Regulations of Vassar Female College, Poughkeepsie N.Y. Edited by order of the Board of Trustees. New York: John A. Gray & Green, Printers, 1866, Royal Holloway and Bedford New College Archives, Royal Holloway and Bedford New College, Egham.

Newspaper clipping in the Royal Holloway and Bedford New College Archives, RF 125/2, 21. Royal Holloway and Bedford New College, Egham, Surrey.

Particulars and Valuation of a Dwelling House and Premises; #21 Norham Gardens, Oxford, 18 February 1879, Field and Castle, Oxford, Lady Margaret Hall Archives.

"The Royal Holloway College." *The Times* (1886): 17, RF 125/2, Royal Holloway and Bedford New College Archives, Royal Holloway and Bedford New College, Egham, Surrey.

The Royal Holloway College. London: J. S. Virtue, 1886, Royal Holloway and Bedford New College Archives, Royal Holloway and Bedford New College, Egham, Surrey.

Champneys, Basil. Letters to Miss Ewart, 9 and 27 March 1874, Buildings Box 1874–1910, Newnham College Archives, Newnham College Cambridge.

Clough, Miss A. J. Letters to Dr. George Reyner, 1873–77, Estate Papers, Newnham College, SB21.50. St. John's College Archives, St. John's College, Cambridge.

Davies, Emily. "Family Chronicle." 1866–68, unpublished manuscript, Girton College Archives, Girton College, Cambridge.

Davies, Emily. Letters to Barbara Bodichon, 1866–83, Girton College Archives, Girton College Cambridge.

Davies, Emily. *Women in the Universities of England and Scotland.* Cambridge: Macmillan and Bowes, 1896. Eleanor Sidgwick Correspondence Box 3, Newnham College Archives, Newnham College, Cambridge.

Delp, W. E. "Royal Holloway College 1908–1914." Paper presented at the Professor's Wives Club 1969, RF 131/1 Royal Holloway and Bedford New College Archives, Royal Holloway and Bedford New College, Egham.

Fisher, H. A. L., Vice Chancellor of Sheffield University. "Address from the President of the College," 1913, in the "Log Book, 1907–1914." Somerville College Archives, Somerville College, Oxford.

Harrison-Barbet, Anthony. "Thomas Holloway, Victorian Philanthropist; a Biographical Essay." 1986, unpublished manuscript, Royal Holloway and Bedford New College Archives, Royal Holloway and Bedford New College, Egham.

Holloway, Thomas. Private Letterbook, 1874–77, GB/130/1 Royal Holloway Holloway and Bedford New College Archives, Royal Holloway and Bedford New College, Egham.

———. *Some Small Memories as to the Origin of Holloway College for Women,* London: G. Stahl, Printer, n.d. RF 103, Royal Holloway and Bedford New College Archives, Royal Holloway and Bedford New College, Egham.

Jackson, Henry. "Memoir of Henry Sidgwick." 1900, unpublished manuscript, Add. Ms.c. 43 54–55, Wren Library Archives, Trinity College Cambridge.

Lady Margaret Hall. "The Brown Book, 1892–1907," Lady Margaret Hall, Oxford, Lady Margaret Hall Archives, Lady Margaret Hall, Oxford.

Lady Margaret Hall. "Minutes of the Hall Committee." 1878–79, Lady Margaret Hall Archives, Lady Margaret Hall, Oxford.

Maynard, Constance Louisa. Diaries, 1872–75, CLM/MSS/D, Queen Mary and Westfield College Archives, Queen Mary and Westfield College, London.

———. Green Books, 1871–75. CLM/MSS/GB 8–12, Queen Mary and Westfield College Archives, Queen Mary and Westfield College, London.

———. Green Books, 1881, CLM/MSS/GB 18, Queen Mary and Westfield College Archives, Queen Mary and Westfield College, London.

Newnham College. "Minutes of the Building Committee," 1874–1880. Newnham College Archives, Newnham College, Cambridge.

Newnham College. "Minutes of the Building Committee," 1886. Newnham College Archives, Newnham College, Cambridge.

Newnham College"Minutes of the Council Meetings and of the General Meetings of Newnham College," 1880–97. Newnham College Archives, Newnham College, Cambridge.

Newnham College. "Report from the Building Committee." 18 November 1893, Newnham College Archives, Newnham College, Cambridge.

Newnham College. "Report of the Building Committee." 17 November 1894, Newnham College Archives, Newnham College, Cambridge.

Omond, T. S. Letters to Basil Champneys, 1880. St. John's College Archives, St. John's College, Oxford.

Pick, Marion. "Social Life at Royal Holloway College, 1887–1939," unpublished manuscript. RF 131/7, Royal Holloway and Bedford New College Archives, Royal Holloway and Bedford New College, Egham.

Raymond, John H., *Biographical Sketch of Matthew Vassar, the Founder of Vassar College*, 1868. GB/130/9, Royal Holloway and Bedford New College Archives, Royal Holloway and Bedford New College, Egham.

———. *Vassar College: A College for Women in Poughkeepsie N.Y. A Sketch.* N.Y.: S. W. Green, Printer, 1873. GB/130/9, Royal Holloway and Bedford New College Archives, Royal Holloway and Bedford New College, Egham.

Reyner, Dr. George J. Letters to Miss A. J. Clough, 1873–77, Estate Papers, Newnham College, SB21.50. St. John's College Archives, St. John's College, Cambridge.

Shaw Lefevre, Emily. "Miss Madeline Shaw Lefevre, First Principal of Somerville College, Oxford, 1879–1889, died 1914." Shaw Lefevre File, Somerville College Archives, Somerville College, Oxford.

Sidgwick, Henry. Letters to Mrs. Mary Benson, 1867–81. Add.Ms.c. 100, 1-83, Trinity College Archives, Trinity College, Cambridge.

Sidgwick, Mrs. Henry. "The University Education of Women." Paper presented at the International Health Exhibition, 8 August 1884. London: William Clowes. Eleanor Sidgwick Correspondence Box 1, Newnham College Archives, Newnham College, Cambridge.

———. The Progress of the Women's Suffrage Movement. Paper presented at the Conservative and Unionist Women's Franchise Association, Cambridge Branch 1913. Eleanor Sidgwick Correspondence Box 5, Newnham College Archives, Newnham College, Cambridge.

Somerville College. "Log Book," 1879–1907. Somerville College Archives, Somerville College, Oxford.

Somerville College, "Somerville Hall, Oxford, 'General Report 1884–85'." In *The Report Book of 1879–99.* Oxford: Baxter Pointer. Somerville College Archives.

Taylor, Mr. Sedley. Letters to Barbara Bodichon, 1869–70. Bodichon 1, B401–459, Girton College Archives.
Vassar, Matthew. *Communications to the Board of Trustees of Vassar College.* New York: John A. Gray & Green, Printers, 1869. GB/130/5-21, Royal Holloway and Bedford New College Archives, Royal Holloway and Bedford New College, Egham.
Westfield College. "College for Ladies at Westfield: for the Preparation of Students for the Degrees of London University. Report of the First Year." 1883, Westfield and Queen Mary College Archives, Queen Mary and Westfield College, London.
Westfield College, "Minutes of the Building Committee 1904." Queen Mary and Westfield College Archives, Queen Mary and Westfield College, London.
Westfield College, "Minutes of the Building Sub-Committee 1890." Queen Mary and Westfield College Archives, Queen Mary and Westfield College, London.
Westfield College, "Minutes of the Council 1882–1887." Queen Mary and Westfield College Archives, Queen Mary and Westfield College, London.
Westfield College, "Minutes of the Council 1887–1889." Queen Mary and Westfield College Archives, Queen Mary and Westfield College, London.
Westfield College "Minutes of the Council 1889–1894." Queen Mary and Westfield College Archives, Queen Mary and Westfield College, London.

Primary Sources

Ackworth School 1779–1929. York: Illiam Sessions, the Ebor Press, 1929.
"Additions to Worcester College, Oxford." *The Builder* (19 September 1943): 260–62.
"Akroydon. Improved Dwellings for the Working Classes." *The Builder* XXI, no. 1045 (14 February 1863): 109–11.
"Architecture at the Royal Academy." *The Architect* (4 June 1887): 827–28.
"Architecture at the Royal Academy." *The Architect* (9 May 1874): 263–64.
"Architecture at the Royal Academy." *The Architect* (19 May 1877): 317.
"Architecture at the Royal Academy." *The Builder* (10 May 1873): 538–39.
"Architecture at the Royal Academy II." *The Builder* (11 May 1889): 350.
"Ashburne Hall, University of Manchester." *Architectural Review* 58 (October 1925): 138–147.
"Bedford Girl's High and Modern Schools." *Building News* (28 July 1882): 119.
"Clare College, Cambridge." *Architectural Review* 56 (December1924): 220–27.
"Concerning 'Queen Anne'." *American Architect and Building News* 1 (16 December 1876): 404–05.
"Contemporary Architects and Their Work: Mr. Basil Champneys." *The Builder* (28 June 1912): 751–57.
"Convalescent Home for Ladies." *The Builder* (28 September 1889): 226–27.
"Current Architecture: Gonville & Caius." *Architectural Review* 16 (August 1904): 74–80.
"Current Architecture: King's College for Women." *Architectural Review* 40 (July 1916): 13–17.
"Current Architecture; College Buildings, I." *Architectural Review* 90 (October 1941): 105–07.
"Edinburgh Architectural Association." *The Architect* (12 November 1870): 279–80.
"Exeter Grammar School." *The Builder* (19 March 1881): 351.
"A Few More Words About 'Queen Anne'." *American Architect and Building News* 2 (6 October 1877): 320–22.
"The Higher Education of Women—The Ladies Colleges at Cambridge." *Graphic* (16 June 1877): 565.
"Hints on the Modern Governess System." *Fraser's Magazine* 30 (1844): 571–83.
History of the Ackworth School. Ackworth: George F. Linney, 1853.
"The Holloway Sanatorium." *The Builder* (7 January 1882): 23–24.
"Keble College, Oxford." *The Architect* (2 July 1870): 12.

"A Lady 'Above the Senior Wrangler': The Triumph of Miss Fawcett." *Pall Mall Budget* (12 June 1890): n.p.
"The Liverpool Convalescent Hospital." *The Architect* (16 August 1873): 77.
"*Living in Birmingham.* Birmingham: University of Birmingham, 1979.
"Lodging Houses for Clare College, Cambridge." *Architectural Review* 125 (June 1959): 382–84.
"Lunatic Aslyums." *The Architect* (23 April 1870): 199.
"Miss Shaw Lefevre." *Journal of Education* (November 1914): 793–94.
The Mount School, York 1857–1957. York: William Session, 1957.
"New Work at Oxford." *Architectural Review* 72 (October 1932): 127–28.
"Oakholme Hall, University of Sheffield." *Architect and Building News* 148 (27 November 1936): 249–51.
Our Public Schools. London: C. Kegan Paul, 1881.
"Owen's College, Manchester." *The Architect* (9 April 1870): 177–78.
"Professor Ruskin's Lectures." *The Architect* (15 and 22 October 1870): 211–13, 225–27.
"The 'Queen Anne' Style." *American Architect and Building News* VII, no. 217 (21 February 1880): 73.
"The Question of Domestic Architectural Style as it now Prevails in England." *American Architect and Building News* IV, no. 137 (10 August 1878): 46.
"The Royal Holloway College at Egham." *The Architect* (2 July 1886): 1.
"Sin and Madness from a Physicians Point of View." *British Quarterly Review* 62, no. 1242 (1875): 114–26.
Some Account of St. Mary's Home for Penitents at Wantage, Berkshire, by the Chaplain. Oxford: John Henry Parker, 1851.
"Somerville Hall, Oxford." *Building News* (9 September 1887): 394.
St. Katharine's School, Wantage. Gloucester: British Publishing Co., 1920.
"Stanley's Life of Arnold: School Life at Rugby." In *Arnold of Rugby: His School Life and Contribution*, edited by J. J. Findlay. Cambridge: Cambridge University Press, 1897.
The Story of Thomas Holloway 1800–1883. Glasgow: Robert Maclehose, the University Press, 1933.
"Study Bedrooms, Corpus Christi, Oxford." *Building* 37 (12 September 1969): 103–06.
"A Talk About 'Queen Anne'." *American Architect and Building News* 2 (28 April 1877): 133.
"The Ultimate Type of London Board Schools." *The Building News* (27 November 1874): 631–32.
Armstrong, Walter. "Royal Holloway College." *Art Journal* (1885): 5–19.
Arnold, Thomas. *Thomas Arnold on Education.* Edited by T. W. Bamford. Cambridge: Cambridge University Press, 1970.
Bailey, Gemma. *Lady Margaret Hall: A Short History.* Oxford: Oxford University Press, 1923.
Barry, Edward M. "Lectures on Architecture." *The Builder* (21 March 1874): 234–37.
Beale, Dorthea. *On the Education of Girls.* Paper presented at the Social Science Congress. London: Bell & Daldy, 1865.
Bede, Cuthbert. *The Adventures of Mr. Verdant Green.* London: Nathaniel Cooke, 1853.
Besant, Walter. *All Sorts and Conditions of Men.* 3 vols. London: Chatto & Windus, 1882.
Blomfield, Sir Reginald. *Memoirs of an Architect.* London: MacMillan, 1932.
———. "Basil Champneys." *Journal of the Royal Institute of British Architects* 42, series 3 (1935): 737–38.
Bodichon, Barbara Leigh Smith. "An American School." In *The Education Papers: Women's Quest for Equality in Britain 1850–1912*, edited by Dale Spender, 34–36. New York & London: Routledge & Kegan Paul, 1987.
Bremner, C. S. *Education of Girls and Women in Great Britain.* London: Swan Sonnenschein, 1897.

Brontë, Charlotte. *Jane Eyre.* edited by Q. D. Leavis, 1847. Reprint, London: Penguin Books, 1987.

Brown, James Baldwin. *The Home Life: In the Light of Its Divine Idea.* London: Smith, Elder, 1866.

———. *Young Men and Maidens: A Pastoral for the Times.* London: Hodder & Stoughton, 1871.

———. *The Work of a Ladies College: an Address to Parents and Pupils, delivered in the ladies college, Bedford SQ on Friday, June 27, 1856.* London: Walton & Maberly, 1856.

Burges, William. " On Things in General." *The Builder* (25 December 1875): 1145–46.

Burstall, Sara A., M.A. *English High Schools for Girls.* London: Longmans, Green, 1907.

Butler, Josephine. "The Education and Employment of Women." In *The Education Papers: Women's Quest for Equality in Britain 1850–1912,* edited by Dale Spender. New York: Routledge & Kegan Paul, 1987, 69–90.

Byrne, Muriel St. Clare and Catherine Hope Mansfield. *Somerville College 1879–1921.* Oxford: Oxford University Press, 1921.

Champneys, Basil. " The Architecture of Queen Victoria's Reign." *Art Journal* 39 (June 1887): 203–09.

———. "A Comparison of the Claims of the Gothic and Renaissance Architects." *The Builder.* (12 February 1898): 158.

———. "The Planning of Collegiate Buildings." *Journal of the Royal Institute of British Architects* 10, 3rd series. (1903): 205–12

———. "Some Principles and Methods of Architectural Design." *The Builder* (14 March 1891): 207–09.

———. "Style." *British Architect* (11, 18, and 25 January 1889): 41–43, 61–62, 81.

The Chaplin. *Some Account of St. Mary's Home for Penitents at Wantage, Berkshire.* Oxford: John Henry Parker, 1851.

Childs, William M. *Making a University: An Account of the University at Reading.* London: J. M. Dent & Sons, 1933.

Clough, Blanche Athena. *A Memoir of Anne Jemima Clough.* London: Edward Arnold, 1897.

Clouston, T. S. "Psychologial Dangers to Women in Modern Social Developments." In *The Position of Women: Actual and Ideal.* London: James Nisbet, 1911.

Cobbe, F. P. "The Education of Women & How it Would be Affected by University Examinations." In *The Education Papers: Women's Quest for Equality in Britain 1850–1912,* edited by Dale Spender. New York: Routledge & Kegan Paul, 1987, 37–50.

———. "The Little Health of Ladies." *Contemporary Review* 31, no. 291 (January 1878): 276–96.

Colman, Edith M. "Newnham." *Laurel Leaves Edgbaston High School Magazine* (31 January 1900): 308.

Committee of Vice-Chancellors and Principals of Great Britain and Ireland. "University Grants Committee 1929–30 to 1934–35." In *The Planning of University Halls of Residence.* Oxford: Clarendon Press, 1948.

Compton-Burnett, Ivy. *Dolores.* Edinburgh and London: Blackwood, 1911.

Cooper, Thomas. "Alfred Waterhouse." *Journal of the Royal Institute of British Architects* XII, series 3 (1905): 609–18.

Coupland, W. C. "The Discipline of the Mind and The Formation of Habits." *The Governess* 1 (April–November 1882): 306–07, 337–39.

Cowell, H. "Sex in Mind and Education: A Commentary." *Blackwood's Magazine* 115 (June 1874): 736–749.

Crossland, W. H. "The Royal Holloway College." *RIBA Transactions III new series* (1887): 141–148.

Davies, Emily. *The Higher Education of Women.* London: Alexander Strahan, 1866.

———. "Home and the Higher Education." In *The Education Papers: Women's Quest for Equality in Britain 1850–1912*, edited by Dale Spender. New York: Routledge & Kegan Paul,1987, 111–22.

———. "Some Account of a Proposed New College for Women." *Contemporary Review* 9 (December, 1868): 540–57.

———. "Special Systems of Education for Women." In *The Education Papers: Women's Quest for Equality in Britain 1850–1912*, edited by Dale Spender, 99–110. New York: Routledge & Kegan Paul, 1987.

Davies, J. "Female Education." *Quarterly Review* 119 (April 1866): 499–515.

Downs, Brian W. *Cambridge, Past and Present.* London: Methuen, 1925.

E. T. M. "An Interior View of Girton College, Cambridge." In *The Education Papers: Women's Quest for Equality in Britain 1850–1912*, edited by Dale Spender. New York: Routledge & Kegan Paul, 1987.

Eastlake, Lady. "Vanity Fair, Jane Eyre, and the Governesses' Benevolent Institution." *Quarterly Review* 84 (1848): 153–85.

Eastlake, Sir Charles. *A History of The Gothic Revival.* London: Longmans, Green, 1872.

Engels, Frederick. *The Condition of the Working-Class in England in 1844.* Translated by Florence Kelly Wischnewetzky. London: Swan Sonnenschein, 1892.

Ferrey, Edmund B. "Modern Gothic Architecture." *The Architect* (27 September and 4 October 1873): 156–58, 169–70.

Fletcher, Banister F. and Phillip H. Fletcher. *The English House.* 2nd ed. London: Methuen, 1911.

Gardner, P. "The Women at Oxford and Cambridge." *Quarterly Review* 186 (1897): 529–51.

Gaskell, Elizabeth, ed. *Wives and Daughters.* Edited by Frank Glover Smith. 1864–66. Reprint, London: Penguin Books, 1969.

Geddes, Patrick and J. Arthur Thompson. *The Evolution of Sex.* revised ed. London: Walter Scott, 1901.

Hardy, Thomas. *Jude the Obscure.* Edited by Norman Page. 1895. Reprint, New York: W. W. Norton, 1978.

Herklots, H. G. G. *The New Universities: An External Examination.* London: Ernest Benn, 1928.

Hodder, Edwin. *The Life and Work of the Seventh Earl of Shaftesbury, KG*, popular edition. London: Cassell , 1892.

Hodgetts, E. A. Brayley. "Girton and Newnham Colleges." *Strand* (1893): 507–16.

Hughes, Tom. *Tom Brown at Oxford.* London: S. W. Partridge, 1921.

Jackson, Sir T. G. *Architecture.* London: Macmillan, 1925.

———. *Reason in Architecture.* N.Y.: E. P. Dutton, 1906.

James, John Angell. *Female Piety or the young Woman's Friend and Guide.* London: Hamilton Adams, 1864.

Jeune, Mrs. Mary. "Women of Today, Yesterday and Tomorrow." *National Review* XIV (1889–90): 547–61.

Johnson, Mrs. Bertha J. "University Degrees for Women: the Case Against." *The Humanitarian*, 8:4 (April 1896).

Jones, E. E. Constance. *As I Remember: An Autobiographical Ramble.* London: A. & C. Black, 1922.

———. *Girton College.* London: A. & C. Black, 1913.

Kerr, Robert. "Architectural Propects: The Queen Anne Style." *The Architect* (3 January 1874): 1–2.

———. *The Gentleman's House.* London: John Murray, 1865.

Kingsley, Rev. Charles. *Health and Education.* London: Isbister, 1874.

A Lady Undergraduate. "A Day in Her Life at Oxford." *Murray's Magazine*, vol. 3 (1888).

Lendrum, Mrs. "The Place of Women in the Family." In *The Position of Women: Actual and Ideal.* London: James Nisbet, 1911.

Lock, J. B. "On the Planning of Collegiate Buildings." *Journal of the Royal Institute of British Architects* xi, 3rd series, no. 14 (16 May 1904): 381–94.

Lodge, Eleanor. *Terms and Vacations.* Edited by Janet Spens. London: Oxford University Press, 1938.

Lodge, Richard, M.A., LL.D. "Closing Address." In *The Position of Women: Actual and Ideal.* London: James Nisbet, 1911.

Lumsden, Louisa Innes. "The Position of Women in History." In *The Position of Women: Actual and Ideal.* London: James Nisbet, 1911.

Lyte, Sir H.C. Maxwell. *A History of Eton College (1440–1910).* 4th ed. London: Macmillan, 1911.

Lyttelton, Hon. Alfred. "Eton College: As a School." In *Great Public Schools.* London: Edward Arnold, 1893.

Markby, Thomas. "On the Education of Women." *Contemporary Review* 7 (February 1868): 242–61.

Marshall, Mary Paley. *What I Remember.* Cambridge: Cambridge University Press, 1947.

Maurice, Rev. Frederick Denison. "Queen's College, London: Its Objects and Method." In *Introductory Lectures, Delivered at Queeen's College, London.* London: John W. Parker, 1849.

Maynard, Constance Louisa. *Between College Terms.* London: James Nisbet, 1910.

Meade, L. T. "English Girls and Their Colleges." *Lady's Pictorial* v (2 January 1892).

———. *A Sweet Girl Graduate.* London: Cassell, 1891.

———. *The Girls of Merton College.* London: W. R. Chambers, 1911.

Melville, Miss Frances. "The Education of Woman." In *The Position of Women: Actual and Ideal.* London: James Nisbet, 1911.

Mill, John Stuart. "On the Subjection of Women." In *On Liberty, with The Subjection of Women and Chapters on Socialism,* edited by Stefan Collini. 1868. Reprint, Cambridge: Cambridge University Press, 1989.

A Newnham Girl. "'Up' at the University." *The Student, the Journal of the Tyneside Students' Association* vol. I (1892): 252–55.

Osborn, Christabel. "Newnham and After." *Windsor Magazine* IV (July–November 1896): 301–08.

Parkin, George R. *Edward Thring. Headmaster of Uppingham School. Life, Diary and Letters.* 2 vols. London: Macmillan, 1898.

Patmore, Coventry. *Angel in the House.* 2 vols. London: George Bell, 1879.

Pearson, Miss Edith. "Spiritual Motherhood and Philanthropic Service." In *The Position of Women: Actual and Ideal.* London: James Nisbet, 1911.

Peile, Dr. "A Change of Front." In *A Newnham Anthology,* 2nd ed., edited by Ann Phillips, Cambridge: Newnham College, 1988.

Rathbone, K. M. "A College with Status." In *A Newnham Anthology,* 2nd ed., edited by Ann Phillips, Cambridge: Newnham College, 1988.

Rogers, Agnes L. "Newnham College Cambridge England." *The Journal of the Association of Collegiate Alumnae* XI, no. 2 (October 1917): 80–86.

Romanes, George J. "Mental Differences Between Men and Women." In *The Education Papers: Women's Quest for Equality in Britain 1850–1912,* edited by Dale Spender. New York: Routledge & Kegan Paul, 1987, 1–9.

Ruskin, John. *Lectures in Architecture and Painting.* 1853. Reprint, London: George Allen, 1907.

———. *Sesame and Lilies.* 1865. Reprint, London: George Allen, 1908.

Scott, G. G. *Remarks on Secular and Domestic Architecture: present and future.* 2nd ed. London: L. Murray, 1858.

Sewell, Elizabeth Missing. *Principles of Education drawn from Nature and Revelation and Applied to Female Education in the Upper Classes.* 2 vols. London: Longman, Green, Longman, Roberts & Green, 1865.

Sheavyn, Miss Phoebe. "Professional Women." In *The Position of Women: Actual and Ideal.* London: James Nisbet, 1911.

Shirreff, Emily. "College Education for Women." *Contemporary Review* 15 (August 1870): 55–66.

———. "The Work of the National Union." In *The Education Papers: Women's Quest for Equality in Britain 1850–1912*, edited by Dale Spender. New York: Routledge & Kegan Paul, 1987, 199–229.

Sidgwick, Ethel. *Mrs. Henry Sidgwick: A Memoir by her Niece.* London: Sidgwick & Jackson, 1938.

Sidgwick, Henry. *Miscellaneous Essays and Addresses.* Edited by Eleanor Mildred Sidgwick and Arthur Sidgwick. London: Macmillan, 1904.

Sidgwick, Mrs. Henry and Arthur Sidgwick. *Henry Sidgwick, A Memoir.* London: Macmillan, 1906.

Sidgwick, Mrs. Henry. *Health Statistics of Women Students of Cambridge and Oxford.* Cambridge: Cambridge University Press, 1890.

———. *University Education of Women: A Lecture Delivered at University College, Liverpool, May 1896.* Cambridge: Macmillan & Bowes, 1897.

———. *University Education of Women: A Paper Given to the International Health Exhibition Conference, 8 August 1884.* London: William Clowes, 1884.

Spiers, Phene. "Architectural Association: Dutch or Queen Anne Architecture." *The Builder* (26 March 1881): 387–88.

St. John Conway, Katharine. "Life at Newnham." *Young Woman* iii (October 1894–September1895): 99–103.

Stanley, H. M. of Alderley. "Personal Recollections of Women's Education." *Nineteenth Century* (6 August 1879): 308–21.

Stannus, Hugh H. "Queen Anne and the Gothic Revival." *The Builder* 33 (13 March 1875): 226–27.

———. "The Queen Anne Style." *The Builder* (27 March 1875): 285.

Statham, H. Heathcote. *Modern Architecture: A Book for Architects and the Public.* London: Chapman & Hall, 1897.

Stevenson, J. J. *House Architecture.* 2 vols. London: Macmillan, 1880.

———. "House Architecture." *American Architect and Building News* VII, no. 237 (10 July 1880): 15.

———. "On the Recent Reaction of Taste in English Architecture." *The Architect* 11 (20 June 1874) (supplement): 9–12.

———. "The Queen Anne and Other Forms of Free Classic Architecture." *The Builder* 33 (27 February 1875): 179–81.

Stronach, Alice. *A Newnham Friendship.* London: Blackie, 1901.

Tennyson, Alfred. *The Princess: A Medley.* 1847. Reprint, London: Macmillan, 1899.

Thompson, J. Arthur and Patrick Geddes. *Problems of Sex, New Tracts for the Times.* London: Cassell, 1912.

Thompson, Prof. J. Arthur & Mrs. Thompson. "The Position of Women: Biologically Considered." In *The Position of Women: Actual and Ideal.* London: James Nisbet, 1911.

Thring, Rev. Edward. *Education and School.* Cambridge & London: Macmillan, 1864.

Tod, Isabella M. S. "On the Education of Girls of the Middle Classes." In *The Education Papers: Women's Quest for Equality in Britain 1850–1912*, edited by Dale Spender, 230–47. New York: Routledge & Kegan Paul, 1987.

Undergraduate, An. "A Day in His Life at Oxford." *Murray's Magazine* 3 (1888).
Verall, Dr. A. W. "University Degrees for Women: The Case For." *The Humanitarian* (April 1896).
W. G. N. "Ashburne Hall, University of Manchester." *Architectural Review* 58 (October 1925): 138–47.
W. Y. "Lunatic Asylums." *The Architect* (12 March 1870): 123–24.
Ward, Mrs. Humphrey. *A Writer's Recollections.* London: W. Collins & Sons, 1918.
Warner, Joseph B. "Radcliffe College." *Harvard Graduate's Magazine*, (March 1894).
Warren, Edward. "Collegiate Architecture." *Journal of the Royal Institute of British Architects* 19 (19 February 1912): 264–96.
Waterhouse, Alfred. "Presidential Address to Students." *The Builder* (1 February 1889): 90–91.
Whilbey, Charles. "The Encroachment of Women." *The Nineteenth Century* (April 1897): 531–37.
White, William. "The Dolly Varden Rediviva." *The Architect* 10 (13 and 20 September 1873): 128–29, 142–44.
———. "The Present State of Thought Concerning Architecture." *The Architect* (31 January 1874): 63–66.
———. "Scenic Architecture III." *The Architect* (8 November 1873): 237–38.
Wightwick, George. "Principles and Practice of Architectural Design." In *Detached Essays of the Architectural Publication Society.* London: Architectural Publication Society, 1853.
Wilkinson, William. *English Country Houses.* 2nd ed. London: James Parker, 1875.
Willis, Robert, and John Willis Clark. *The Architectural History of the University of Cambridge and of the Colleges of Cambridge and Eton.* 5 vols. Cambridge: Cambridge University Press, 1886.
Wordsworth, Elizabeth. "First Principles in Women's Education." *Church Congress*, Exeter: James Parker, 1894.
Yonge, Charlotte. *The Daisy Chain or Aspirations, a Family Chronicle.* 1856. Reprint, London: Macmillan, 1899.
Zimmern, Alice. *The Renaissance of Girl's Education in England: A Record of Fifty Year's Progress.* London: A. D. Innes, 1898.
———. "Women at the Universities." *The Leisure Hour* (1897–98): 433–42.

Secondary Sources

Allan, Adrian. *Redbrick University: A Centenary Exhibition Held at Senate House, Abercromby SQ.* Liverpool: University of Liverpool, 1981.
Allchin, A. M. *The Silent Rebellion: Anglican Religious Communities 1845–1900.* London: SCM Press, 1958.
Anson, Peter F. *The Call of the Cloister.* London: SPCK, 1955.
Banks, Olive. *Biographical Dictionary of British Feminists, 1800–1930*, vol. 1. Brighton, Sussex: Wheatsheaf Books, distributed by Harvester Press, 1985.
Bassett, Donald J. D. "The French Renaissance Revival in British Architecture 1824–1914." Ph.D. dissertation, University of Edinburgh, 1979.
Battiscombe, Georgina. *Reluctant Pioneer, A Life of Elizabeth Wordsworth.* London: Constable, 1978.
Betjeman, John. "Palaces from Pills." *Weekend Telegraph*, new series 23 (January 1951): 46–52.
Binfield, Clyde. *Belmont's Portias: Victorian Non-comformists and Middle-class Education for Girls.* London: Dr. William's Trust Library, 1981.
Binfield, Clyde. "Holy Murder at Cheshunt College:The Formation of an English Architect P. R. Morley-Horder 1870–1944." *Journal of the United Reformed Church History Society* 4, no. 2 (May 1988): 119.

Bingham, Caroline. *The History of Royal Holloway College 1886–1986.* London: Constable, 1987.

Bowlder, Roger. "Westfield College, Kidderpore Ave. L.B. Camden." Unpublished essay (29 September 1989).

Boys, Jos. "Is There A Feminist Analysis of Architecture?" *Built Environment* 10, no. 1 (1984): 25–33.

Branca, Patricia. *Silent Sisterhood: Middle Class Women & the Victorian Home.* London: Croom Helm, 1975.

Braun, Hugh Stanley. *Elements of English Architecture.* Newton Abbot: David & Charles, 1973.

Briggs, Asa. *Victorian People.* London: Odhams Press, 1954.

Brooke, Christopher. *A History of Gonville and Caius College.* Suffolk: Boydell Press, 1985.

Brooke, Christopher & Roger Highfield. *Oxford and Cambridge.* Cambridge: Cambridge University Press, 1988.

Brown, Jane. *The Making of the Gardens; Newnham College.* Cambridge: Newnham College, 1988.

Burstyn, Joan N. *Victorian Education and the Ideal of Womanhood.* London: Croom Helm, 1980.

———. "Women's Education in England during the 19th Century: A review of the literature 1970–76." *History of Education* 6, no. 1 (1977): 11–19.

Byatt, A. S. *Still Life.* New York: Collier Books, 1985.

Calder, Jenni. *The Victorian Home.* London: Batsford, 1977.

Chablo, Diane. "University Architecture in Britain 1950–1975." Ph.D. dissertation, Oxford University, Wolfson College, 1987.

Chapman, Arthur W. *The Story of a University: A History of The University of Sheffield.* London: Oxford University Press, 1955.

Charlton, H. B. *Portrait of a University 1851–1951.* Manchester: Manchester University Press, 1951.

Christ, Carol. "Victorian Masculinity and the Angel in the House." In *A Widening Sphere,* edited by Martha Vicinus. London: Methuen, 1980.

Christie, O. F. *A History of Clifton College 1860–1934.* Bristol: J. W. Arrowsmith, 1935.

Clapp, B. W. *The University of Exeter: A History.* Exeter: University of Exeter, 1982.

Clark, Kenneth. *The Gothic Revival.* New York: Holt, Rinehart & Winston, 1962.

Clarke, A. K. *A History of Cheltenham Ladies College 1853–1979.* 3rd ed. Kettering: David Green Printers, 1979.

Coignard, Alain Jerome. "Basil Champneys, Architect, 1842–1935." Ph.D. dissertation, Sorbonne, Paris, 1984.

Conway, Jill. "Stereotypes of Femininity in a Theory of Sexual Evolution." In *Suffer and Be Still,* edited by Martha Vicinus. London: Methuen, 1980.

Cottle, Basil, and J. W. Sherborne. *The Life of a University.* Bristol: J. W. Arrowsmith, 1959.

Crawford, Alan. "The Arts and Crafts Movement." Paper presented to the Victorian Society Conference, University of Birmingham, 15–17 September 1978.

Crook, Alec C. *From the Foundation to Gilbert Scott: A History of the Buildings of St. John's College Cambridge 1511 to 1885.* Cambridge: Cambridge University Press, 1980.

Crook, Joe Mordaunt. *The Dilemma of Style; Architectural Ideas from the Picturesque to the Post Modern.* London: John Murray, 1989.

———. "Mr. Holloway's Architect and Mr. Holloway's Chateau." In *Royal Holloway and Bedford New College: Centenary Lectures 1886–1986,* edited by Moreton Moore. Egham: Royal Holloway and Bedford New College, 1988.

———. *William Burges and the High Victorian Dream.* Chicago: Chicago University Press, 1981.

Cunningham, Colin, and Prudence Waterhouse. *Alfred Waterhouse 1830–1905: Biography of a Practice.* Oxford: Clarendon Press, 1992.

Darley, Gillian. "Informality in a Formal Layout: Whitely Village, Surrey." *Country Life* 160 (November 18, 1976): 1484–85.

Davidoff, Leonore, and Catherine Hall. *Family Fortunes: Men and Women of the English Middle Class 1780–1850.* London: Hutchinson, 1987.

Delamont, Sara. "The Contradictions in Ladies Education." In *The Nineteenth Century Woman: Her Cultural and Physical World*, edited by Sara Delamont, 134–63. London: Croom Helm, 1978.

———. "The Domestic Ideology and Women's Education." In *The Nineteenth Century Woman: Her Cultural and Physical World*, edited by Sara Delamont, 164–87. London: Croom Helm, 1978.

Dent, H. C. *Universities in Transition.* London: Cohen & West, 1961.

Dixon, Anne Campbell. "Ruskin's Romantic Fancies." *Country Life* (27 April 1989): 130–33.

Dixon, Roger and Stefan Muthesius. *Victorian Architecture.* New York: Oxford University Press, 1978.

Dyhouse, Carol. *Girls Growing Up in Late Victorian and Edwardian England.* London: Routledge & Kegan Paul, 1981.

———. "Social Darwinistic Ideas and the Development of Women's Education in England, 1880–1920." *History of Education* 5, no.1 (1976): 41–58.

Evans, Robin. *The Fabrication of Virtue: English Prison Architecture 1750–1840.* Cambridge: Cambridge University Press, 1982.

———. "Figures, Doors and Passages." *Architectural Design*, no. 4 (1978): 267–78.

Faludi, Susan. *Backlash: The Undeclared War Against American Women.* New York: Anchor Books, Doubleday, 1991.

Fee, Elizabeth. "Psychology, Sexuality, and Social Control in Victorian England." *Social Science Quarterly* 58 (1978): 632–46.

Fellows, Richard A. *Sir Reginald Blomfield, An Edwardian Architect.* London: A. Zwemmer, 1985.

Firth, A. E. *Goldsmith's College: A Centenary Account.* London: Athlone Press, 1991.

Firth, C. B. *Constance Louisa Maynard: Mistress of Westfield College.* London: George Allen, 1949.

Fletcher, Shelia. *Feminists and Bureaucrats: A Study in the Development of Girls' Education in the Nineteenth Century.* Cambridge: Cambridge University Press, 1980.

Forty, Adrian. "The Modern Hospital in England and France: the Social and Medical Uses of Architecture." In *Buildings and Society*, edited by Anthony D. King. London: Routledge & Kegan Paul, 1980.

Foucault, Michel. *Discipline and Punish.* Translated by Alan Sheridan. London: Penguin Books, 1977.

Franklin, Jill. *The Gentleman's Country House and Its Plan 1835–1914.* London: Routledge & Kegan Paul, 1981.

Gardner, Alice. *A Short History of Newnham College Cambridge.* Cambridge: Bowes & Bowes, 1921.

Girouard, Mark. "Blackmoor House, Hampshire I & II, the property of the Earl of Selbourne." *Country Life* (29 August and 5 September 1974): 554–57, 614–17.

———. *Life in the English Country House.* New Haven: Yale University Press, 1978.

———. *The Return to Camelot: Chivalry and the English Gentleman.* New Haven & London: Yale University Press, 1981.

———. *Sweetness and Light.* New Haven: Yale University Press, 1977.

———. *The Victorian Country House.* New Haven: Yale University Press, 1979.

———. "Victorian Sweetness and Light." *Country Life* 150 (16 December 1971): 1704–06.

Glendinning, Victoria. *A Supressed Cry: Life and Death of a Quaker Daughter.* London: Routledge & Kegan Paul, 1969.

Gloucester, Richard and Hermione Hobhouse. *Oxford and Cambridge.* New York: Thames & Hudson, 1980.

Goodhart-Rendel, H. S. *English Architecture Since the Regency.* London: Century, 1953.

———. "North Oxford." *Architect and Building News* (28 February 1936): 284–86.

Gorsky, Susan R. "Old Maids and New Women: Alternatives to Marriage in Englishwomen's Novels, 1847–1915." *Journal of Popular Culture* 8 (1973): 68–86.

Grainer, Hilary Joyce. "The Architecture of Sir Ernest George and His Partners." Ph.D. dissertation, University of Leeds, 1985.

Grant, Julia M. *St. Leonard's School 1877–1927.* London: Humphrey Milford, 1927.

Gray, Arthur, and Frederick Brittain. *A History of Jesus College, Cambridge.* London: Heinemann, 1979.

Habron, Dudley. "Queen Anne Taste and Aestheticism." *Architectural Review* 94 (July 1943): 15–18.

Hamilton, Mary Agnes. *Newnham: An Informal Biography.* London: Faber & Faber, 1936.

Hammerton, A. James. "Feminism and Female Emigration 1861–1886." In *A Widening Sphere,* edited by Martha Vicnus. London: Methuen, 1980.

Harvie, Christopher. "Revolution and the Rule of Law." In *The Oxford History of Britain,* edited by Kenneth O. Morgan. Oxford & New York: Oxford University Press, 1988.

Harwood, Hilda. *The History of Milton Mount College.* London: Independent Press, 1959.

Hersey, G. L. *High Victorian Gothic: A Study in Associationism.* Baltimore & London: Johns Hopkins University Press, 1972.

Herstein, Shelia. *A Mid-Victorian Feminist, Barbara Leigh Smith Bodichon.* New Haven: Yale University Press, 1985.

Hibbert, Christopher. *The Illustrated London News: Social History of Victorian Britain.* London: Angus & Robertson, 1975.

Hinchcliffe, Tanis. *North Oxford.* New Haven & London: Yale University Press, 1992.

Hind, Marilyn. *Doves and Dons: A History of St. Mary's College, Durham.* Durham: Durham University Press, 1982.

Hirsch, Pam. *Barbara Leigh Smith Bodichon, 1827–1891, Feminist, Artist and Rebel* (London: Pimlico, 1999)

Hitchcock, Henry Russell. "G. E. Street in the 1850s." *Journal of the Society of Architectural Historians* xix, no. 4 (1960): 145–71.

Holcombe, Lee. "Victorian Wives & Property: Reform of the Married Women's Property Law 1857–1882." In *A Widening Sphere: Changing Roles of Victorian Women,* edited by Martha Vinicus. London: Methuen, 1980.

Horn, Pamela. *The Victorian and Edwardian Schoolchild.* Gloucester: Alan Sutton, 1989.

Horowitz, Helen Lefkowitz. *Alma Mater.* New York: Alfred A. Knopf, 1974.

Johnson, Bertha J. "The First Beginnings 1873–90." In *Lady Margaret Hall: A Short History,* edited by Gemma Bailey. London: Oxford University Press, 1923.

Kamm, Josephine. *How Different From Us: A Biography of Miss Buss and Miss Beale.* London: The Bodley Head, 1958.

Kemp, Betty. "The Early History of St. Hugh's College." In *St. Hugh's: One Hundred Years of Women's Education in Oxford,* edited by Penny Griffin. Basingstoke & London: Macmillan, 1986.

Lavedan, Pierre. *French Architecture.* London: Scolar Press, 1956.

Leonardi, Susan J. *Dangerous by Degrees: Women at Oxford and the Somerville College Novelists.* New Brunswick & London: Rutgers University Press, 1989.

Linna, Bentley. *Educating Women: A Pictorial History of Bedford College, University of London, 1849–1985.* Surrey: Alma Publishers, 1991.

Lowe, Roy. "Anglo-Americanism and the Planning of Universities in the United States." *History of Education* 15, no. 4 (1986): 247–59.

Macleod, Robert. *Style and Society.* London: RIBA Publications, 1971.

Maltby, Sally, MacDonald, and Colin Cunningham. "Alfred Waterhouse 1830–1905." Exhibition at Royal Institute of British Architects, Heinz Gallery, 1983.

Manthorpe, Catherine. "Science or Domestic Science? The Struggle to define and Appropriate Science Education for girls in early 20th century England." *History of Education* 15, no. 3 (1986): 195–213.

Matthews, Jaquie. "Barbara Bodichon: Integrity in Diversity." In *Feminist Theorists: Three Centuries of Women's Intellectual Traditions,* edited by Dale Spender. London: The Women's Press, 1983, 90–123.

McBride, Theresa M. *The Domestic Revolution: The Modernization of Household Service in England and France 1820–1920.* London: Croom Helm, 1976.

McConnell, James. *English Public Schools.* London: The Herbert Press, 1985.

McWilliams-Tulberg, Rita. "Women and Degrees at Cambridge University 1862–1897." In *A Widening Sphere,* edited by Martha Vicinus. London: Methuen, 1980.

———. *Women at Cambridge.* London: Victor Gollancz, 1975.

Megson, B., and J. Lindsay. *Girton College 1869–1959: An Informal History.* Cambridge: W. Heffer, 1959.

Meller, Helen. *Patrick Geddes: Social Evolutionist and City Planner.* London: Routledge, 1990.

Millet, Kate. "The Debate over Women; Ruskin vs. Mill." In *Suffer and Be Still,* edited by Martha Vicinus. London: Methuen, 1980.

Mintz, Steven. *A Prison of Expectations: The Family in Victorian Culture.* New York: New York University Press, 1983.

Muthesius, Stefan. *The High Victorian Movement in Architecture 1850–70.* London: Routledge & Kegan Paul, 1972.

Nead, Lynda. *Myths of Sexuality: Representations of Women in Victorian Britain.* Oxford: Basil Blackwell, 1988.

Newsome, David. *Godliness and Good Learning: Four Studies on a Victorian Ideal.* London: Cassell Publishers, 1961.

Orbach, Julian. *Blue Guide to Victorian Architecture in Britain,* London: A. & C. Black, 1987.

Pedersen, Joyce Senders. *The Reform of Girl's Secondary and Higher Education in Victorian England.* New York: Garland Publishing, 1987.

Peterson, M. Jeanne. "The Victorian Governess: Status Incongruence in Family and Society." In *Suffer and Be Still,* edited by Martha Vicinus. London: Methuen, 1980.

Pevsner, Nikolaus. *The Best Buildings of England.* Comp. by Bridget Cherry and John Newman. Harmondsworth: Viking Penguin, 1986.

———. *Cambridgeshire, Buildings of England.* 2nd. ed. Harmondsworth: Penguin Books, 1970.

———. *Oxfordshire, Buildings of England.* Harmondsworth: Penguin Books, 1970.

———. *South Lancashire, The Buildings of England.* Harmondsworth: Penguin Books, 1969.

Pinkerton, Roy M. *Patrick Geddes Hall: Scotland's First Hall of Residence,* 1978.

Poovey, Mary. *Uneven Developments: The Ideological Work of Gender in Mid-Victorian England.* London: Virago Press, 1989.

Reynolds, K. M. "The School and Its Place in Girls' Education." In *The North London Collegiate School 1850–1950: A Hundred Years of Girls' Education,* edited by R.M. Scrimgeour. London: Oxford University Press, 1950.

Rice-Oxley, L. *Oxford Renowned.* London: Methuen, 1925.

Rich, R. W. *The Training of Teachers in England and Wales During the Nineteenth Century.* Cambridge: Cambridge University Press, 1933.

Roach, John. "Boys and Girls at School, 1800–1870." *History of Education* 15, no. 3 (1986): 147–59.

Roberts, Helene E. "Marriage, Redundancy or Sin: The Painter's View of Women in the First Twenty-five Years of Victoria's Reign." In *Suffer and Be Still,* edited by Martha Vicinus. London: Methuen, 1980.

Rogers, Annie M. A. H. *Degrees by Degrees.* Oxford: Oxford University Press, 1938.

Saint, Andrew. *Richard Norman Shaw.* New Haven: Yale Univ. Press, 1976.

———. "Three Oxford Architects." *Oxoniesia* xxxv (1970): 53–102.

Scull, Andrew. "A Convenient Place To Get Rid of Inconvenient People: The Victorian Lunatic Asylum." In *Buildings and Society,* edited by Anthony D. King. London: Routledge & Kegan Paul, 1980.

Service, Alastair. *Edwardian Architecture and its Origins.* London: Architectural Press, 1975.

———. *Edwardian Architecture: A Handbook to Building Design in Britain 1890–1914.* New York & Toronto: Oxford University Press, 1977.

———. *Victorian and Edwardian Hampstead.* New Barnet, Hertfordshire: Historical Publications, 1989.

Sherborne, J. W. *University College, Bristol 1876–1909.* Bristol: Bristol Branch of the Historical Association, 1977.

Shimmin, A. N. *The University of Leeds: The First Half Century.* Cambridge: Cambridge University Press for the University of Leeds, 1954.

Showalter, Elaine. "Victorian Women and Insanity." In *Madhouses, Mad-Doctors and Madmen: the Social History of Psychology in the Victorian Era,* edited by Andrew Skull. London: Athlone Press, 1981.

Smith, A. H. *New College and Its Buildings.* Oxford: Oxford University Press, 1952.

Smith, F. Barry. "Sexuality in Britain 1800–1900." In *A Widening Sphere,* edited by Martha Vicinus. London: Methuen, 1980.

Sondheimer, Janet. *Castle Adamant in Hampstead: A History of Westfield College 1882–1982.* London: Westfield College, University of London, 1983.

Spurling, Hilary. *Ivy When Young: the Life of I. Compton-Burnett.* London: Allison & Busby, 1983.

Stamp, Gavin. "Architectural Notes." Paper presented at the Victorian Society Summer School, Glasgow 1992.

Steegman, John. *Victorian Taste.* Cambridge, Mass.: MIT Press, 1970.

Stephen, Barbara. *Emily Davies and Girton College.* London: Constable, 1927.

———. *Girton College.* Cambridge: Cambridge University Press, 1933.

Stevenson, Christine McKee. "The Design of Prisons and Mental Hospitals in the Neo-Classical Period, with Special Reference to the Work of C. F. Hansen (1756–1845)." Ph.D. dissertation, Courtauld Institute of Art, University of London, 1986.

Stewart, Charles H. *The Past One Hundred Years: The Buildings of the University of Edinburgh.* Edinburgh: Edinburgh University Press, 1973.

Strachey, Lytton. *Eminent Victorians.* 1918. Reprint, London: Chatto & Windus, 1928.

Sykes, Marjorie. "Pages of History: Manchester's Period Libraries." *Country Life* (20 January 1983).

Talbot, Rev. E. S. "The Foundation." In *Lady Margaret Hall: A Short History,* edited by Gemma Bailey. London: Oxford University Press, 1923.

Taylor, Jeremy. *Hospital and Asylum Architecture in England 1840–1914: Building for Health Care.* London: Mansell Publishing, 1991.

Thompson, F. L. M. *The Rise of Respectable Society: A Social History of Victorian Britain 1830–1900.* London: Fontana Press, 1988.

Thompson, John D., and Grace Goldin. *The Hospital: A Social and Architectural History.* New Haven: Yale University Press, 1975.

Thompson, Paul. *The Edwardians: The Remaking of British Society.* London: Weidenfeld & Nicolson, 1975.

———. *William Butterfield.* Cambridge, Mass.: MIT Press, 1971.

Tomlinson, Heather. "Design and Reform: the 'Separate System' in Nineteenth Century English Prisons." In *Buildings and Society,* edited by Anthony D. King. London: Routledge & Kegan Paul, 1980.

Tristram, Philippa. *Living Space in Fact and Fiction.* London: Routledge, 1989.

Truscot, Bruce. *Red Brick Universities.* Harmondsworth, England: Penguin Books, 1951.

Turner, Paul V. *Campus: An American Planning Tradition.* rev. ed. Cambridge, Mass.: MIT Press, 1990.

Vicinus, Martha. *Independent Women: Work and Community for Single Women 1850–1920.* London: Virago Press, 1985.

———. "'One Life to Stand Beside Me': Emotional Conflicts in First Generation College Women in England." *Feminist Studies* 8, no. 3 (Fall 1982): 603–28.

Waterhouse, Prudence. *A Victorian Monument: The Buildings of Girton College.* Cambridge: Prudence Waterhouse c/o Girton College, 1990.

Watkin, David. *The Architecture of Basil Champneys.* Cambridge: Newnham College Cambridge, 1989.

———. *Morality in Architecture.* Oxford: Clarendon Press, 1977.

Weiner, Deborah Elaine Blacker. "The Institution of Popular Education: Architectural Form and Social Policy in the London Board Schools, 1870–1904." Ph.D. dissertation, Princeton University, 1984.

Williams, Elizabeth. "An Architectural History of Royal Holloway College, Egham 1874–87." Reprinted from *Surrey Archaeological Collections,* 77.

Wood, A. C. *A History of The University College, Nottingham 1881–1948.* Oxford: B. H. Blackwell, 1953.

INDEX